How to use a law library

AUSTRALIA AND NEW ZEALAND
The Law Book Company Ltd.
Sydney : Melbourne : Perth

CANADA AND U.S.A
The Carswell Company Ltd.
Agincourt, Ontario

INDIA
N. M. Tripathi Private Ltd
Bombay
and
Eastern Law House
Calcutta and Delhi
M.P.P. House
Bangalore

ISRAEL
Steimatzky's Agency Ltd.
Jerusalem : Tel-Aviv : Haifa

MALAYSIA : SINGAPORE : BRUNEI
Malayan Law Journal (Pte.) Ltd.
Singapore and Kuala Lumpur

How to use a law library

SECOND EDITION

by

JEAN DANE
Law Librarian, University College, Cardiff

PHILIP A. THOMAS
Senior Lecturer in Law, University College, Cardiff

with contributions by:

Grainne Smith
Assistant Librarian, Law Library, Dublin

Elizabeth Madill
Sub Librarian (Law), Queens University, Belfast

G. H. Ballantyne
Librarian, Signet Library, Edinburgh

Ian Thomson
Official Publications Librarian, University College, Cardiff

Christine Miskin
Legal Information Resources Ltd.

LONDON
SWEET & MAXWELL
1987

First Edition 1979
Second Impression 1980
Second Edition 1987

Published in 1987 by
Sweet & Maxwell Limited
11, New Fetter Lane, London
Computerset by Promenade Graphics Limited, Cheltenham.

Printed in Great Britain by,
Richard Clay Ltd, Bungay, Suffolk

British Library Cataloguing in Publication Data
Dane, Jean
    How to use a law library.—2nd ed.
    1. Law libraries—England
    I. Title   II. Thomas, Philip A.
    026'.34   Z675.L2

ISBN 0–421–36030–5
ISBN 0–421–36040–2 Pbk

PREFACE

As a new law student you will quickly discover that you need to spend a great deal of time in the law library. You may be preparing for a tutorial, reading references given during a lecture, or researching for an essay. The study of law is essentially a library based subject. You therefore need to learn how to use the library effectively; otherwise you will waste a great deal of time, and your academic work may suffer. Acquiring an effective working knowledge of the library will pay dividends, not only during your formal education, but also when you become a practising member of the legal profession. Lawyers can carry only a limited amount of legal knowledge in their heads. A good lawyer is one who knows where to look for the relevant law, and is then able to understand and apply it successfully.

The purpose of this guide is to provide you with basic information about how a law collection is organised, and how it should be used. It will remain a useful reference source throughout your period of study. It is not intended that you should treat it as a textbook, but as a reference aid to be consulted whenever you have a problem. Consequently you might use the book selectively, referring to those parts which are useful at a particular point in your studies, or which are recommended by a lecturer. It is essentially a practical book, which tells you how to use the library materials properly. Consequently, the best place to read it is in the library, where you can see and handle the materials referred to in the book. The main sources of legal information relating to the law of England and

Wales, Scotland, Northern Ireland and the Republic of Ireland are included. In addition, chapters have been provided on the sources of European Community law and public international law. Should you require more detailed information, this can be found in:

E. M. Moys, ed., *Manual of Law Librarianship* (2nd ed.).

R. G. Logan, ed., *Information Sources in Law.*

J. Jeffries, *A Guide to the Official Publications of the European Communities* (2nd ed.).

Guides to legal materials in other common law jurisdictions, which are not covered in this book, may be found in:

M. A. Banks, *Using a law library* (3rd ed.) (Canadian materials).

E. Campbell, E. J. Glasson and A. Lahore, *Legal Research: Materials and Methods* (2nd ed.) (Australia).

M. O. Price, H. Bitner & S. R. Bysiewicz, *Effective Legal Research* (4th ed.) (American sources).

Your introductory library tour, valuable though it is, usually takes place during the first hectic weeks of your new life as a student. We hope that you will supplement this introduction by regular reference to this book. Some of the most important reference works can be difficult to use. To help you, we have provided summaries of the steps to be taken when consulting them and, in some cases, we have also provided algorithms (flow-charts). Both the summaries and the flow-charts are intended to be used in conjunction with the main text. Remember that the library staff are there to help you. If, after consulting this book, you are still unable to find what you want, do not hesitate to ask for assistance or information.

We would like to thank Phil Fennell for his most helpful comments: we are also grateful to Mr. Impey of Lawtel, and to the editors of several major reference works for their advice and assistance in ensuring the accuracy of the information. Any errors are, of course, our responsibility, and we would welcome comments and corrections from our readers.

August 25, 1987
Jean Dane
Philip A. Thomas
University College, Cardiff

ACKNOWLEDGEMENTS

The authors and publishers would like to thank the following for granting permission to reproduce material included in this book:

    Butterworth (Telepublishing) Ltd.
    Butterworths Law Publishers Ltd.
    Commission of the European Communities.
    Department of Justice, Dublin.
    Her Majesty's Stationery Offices.
    Incorporated Council of Law Reporting.
    Irish Law Reports Monthly at Irish Academic Press.
    Legal Information Resources Ltd.
    Oceana Publications Ltd.
    Professional Books.
    S.L.S. Publications, Belfast.
    Stationery Office, Dublin.
    Stevens & Sons Ltd.
    Sweet & Maxwell Ltd.

CONTENTS

6. HOW TO FIND INFORMATION ON A SUBJECT

11. EUROPEAN COMMUNITY LAW

12. PUBLIC INTERNATIONAL LAW

CHAPTER 1

Using a Library

INTRODUCTION

When you first visit a large library it can appear very confusing. **1–1**
However, most libraries are arranged on the same basic principles and once these have been mastered you should not
experience too much difficulty in finding your way around,
even in the largest library. A university, polytechnic or college
library will contain two main types of material: books and
periodicals (often called magazines or journals).

BOOKS   **1–2**

Arrangement of Books on the Shelves

Books are usually grouped on the shelves according to their **1–3**
subject. The subject dealt with in each book is indicated by
numbers, or letters and numbers, which are usually written on
the spine (or back) of the book. These symbols indicate the
exact subject matter of each volume. They are known as the classification number. The purpose of the classification number is
to bring together, in one area of the library, all books dealing
with the same subject. The classification number serves two
purposes. It indicates the subject of the book, and tells you
where the book is to be found on the shelves.

In some institutions, books on different subjects may be housed
in separate buildings on the campus. For instance, you may
find that the law books have been placed in a separate law

1

library. If this has not been done, the law books will be collected together (by means of the classification scheme) in one area of the general library.

There may be a number of separate sequences in the library. Some books, such as dictionaries and encyclopedias, are designed by their nature to be used as reference books, rather than as books to be read from cover to cover; these may be shelved in a separate reference collection. Very large books (folios) and very thin books (pamphlets) may be kept in a separate sequence. Thus, the size of the book may be important in helping you to find it on the shelves. There will normally be some indication on the catalogue entry (para. 1–4) if the book is shelved separately. Parliamentary papers and publications of international bodies such as the European Communities and the United Nations are often located in areas of the library set aside for this purpose. Most important, from your point of view, there may be a separate reserve, short-term loan or undergraduate collection of basic textbooks which are in great demand. These are normally available only for reference or short loan. Such a collection may include photocopies of articles from journals and extracts from books on your reading lists. The library may have some material (such as *The Times* newspaper) available only in the form of microfiche or microfilm, and there may be a collection of audio-visual material (cassettes, records, slides, etc.) press cuttings and other materials which do not form part of the normal book collection. Copies of examination papers set in previous years will often be available in the library.

Using the Library Catalogues to Find a Book

1–4 To find out what books are available in the library you need to consult the catalogues, which are generally in a prominent position. The catalogue may consist of a number of drawers containing cards, there being a card for every book in the library. Increasingly, you will find that the catalogue is held in a computer and the information is made available on microfiche. You read microfiche with a special machine. You may even be able to use a computer terminal to enquire directly of the computer whether a book is in the library.

Whatever the physical format of the catalogue, there are usually two main sequences: an author (or name) catalogue and a subject catalogue. The author catalogue contains records, arranged alphabetically by the authors' names, for all books in the library. In some libraries it may also include entries under the titles of books. The subject catalogue contains the same records, but rearranged in subject order (so that entries for books on the same subject are together).

If you know the author's name, look up the surname in the author (or name) catalogue. The entries are arranged in alphabetical order by the author's surname. If there are several authors with the same surname, *e.g.* Smith, the entries are then filed by the authors' forenames or initials, *e.g.*

SMITH, A.B.
SMITH, Alan Norman
SMITH, Barbara

We have said that the arrangement of the entries is alphabetical. Unfortunately, this is not as simple as it seems. There are two ways of arranging entries in alphabetical order. One system is to arrange them "letter by letter," that is, as if they all form part of one long word, ignoring any spaces between words. The other arrangement is "word by word." You should find out which arrangement is used in your library, otherwise you can miss entries. This is shown by the change in the order of the following examples, using the two different filing methods. Indexes to books, and lists of the names of cases, may use either method.

Letter by Letter	*Word by Word*
Law Commission	Law Commission
Lawler, J.	*Law Society*
Lawrence, R. J.	Lawler, J.
Law Society	Lawrence, R. J.
Lawson, F. H.	Lawson, F. H.

When you have located the author's name, you will find an entry for every book by that author which is available in the library. The entries are arranged alphabetically by the titles of the books (ignoring words such as "The" or "A" at the beginning of the title). If a book has run into several editions, they will be arranged in order, with the latest edition at the back or at the front of the sequence (libraries vary in their practice on this point).

Suppose that you are looking for a book which continues to be known by the name of the original author, even though that person is dead (and this is common practice in a law library). Let us take as an example, *Winfield and Jolowicz on Tort*. This is in its twelfth edition. Winfield has not been involved with the work for many years, but it is still referred to by his name. You would, therefore, find an entry in the author catalogue under Winfield, but, in addition, there would also be an entry under Rogers, W. V. H., who is the author of the present edition.

Many other well-known textbooks have been written jointly by two authors: Megarry and Wade (*The Law of Real Property*), Cross and Jones (*Introduction to Criminal Law*) Smith and Hogan (*Criminal Law*), Cheshire and Fifoot (*The Law of Contract*)— these are standard works with whose names you will soon become familiar. If you are looking for the book by Cheshire and Fifoot, you can look in the author catalogue under either Cheshire or Fifoot; you will find an entry in the catalogue under both names. Some authors have double barrelled names. Library practice varies on which part of the name the entry is filed under. For instance, a book by O. Hood Phillips may be under Phillips or Hood Phillips in the catalogue. Therefore, you may need to look under both forms of the name.

Sometimes a book does not appear to have an individual author. It has been published by an organisation or society and the organisation is, in effect, the author. In this case you will find an entry in the catalogue under the name of the body, *e.g.* Law Commission, Law Society, Legal Action Group, United Nations.

Finding a Book on the Shelves

1–5   The classification number (para. 1–3) will appear prominently on the catalogue entry. This number will enable you to trace the book on the shelves. If the library is a large one there is usually a guide near the catalogue showing you where books with that classification number are to be found.

If you have any difficulty in understanding how the books are arranged on the shelves, or in using the catalogue, ask a member of the library staff for help.

If the book is not on the shelves it may be (a) in use by another reader in the library; (b) on loan to another reader; (c) in a separate sequence of books which are larger or smaller than average, or which are in heavy demand (para. 1–3); (d) mis-shelved or missing; (e) removed by the library staff for some reason, *e.g.* rebinding. Ask the library staff at the issue desk (where you borrow books) if the book is on loan or if it is likely to have been removed from the shelves for any reason. If it is on loan, it may be possible for it to be recalled for you. If the book has been missing from the shelves for several days the library staff may institute a search for it or they may be able to suggest some other source from which you could obtain it.

Borrowing Books

Assuming that you have located the book you require, how do 1–6
you borrow it? It is not normally possible to borrow periodicals
and law reports. In some libraries books may not be available
for loan, or they may be borrowed for limited periods only, *e.g.*
overnight or at weekends. This is because the law library is
essentially a reference library and the material is in great
demand. The library staff will explain how many books you
may borrow, and how long you can keep them on loan. It is
usually necessary for you to join the library, *i.e.* to provide
details of your course, address, etc., before you borrow books.
You may be issued with a library ticket which you must produce every time you borrow a book. The date of return will be
stamped inside the book. Return it as soon as you have finished
with it, or if the library asks for it. It is antisocial to retain books
wanted by other readers and, as a result, you may be charged a
fine if the book is returned late.

LAW REPORTS AND PERIODICALS

In the course of your studies you will need to look at the reports 1–7
of cases which have been heard in courts both in this country
and abroad. These reports are published in a number of publications called law reports. Amongst the best known series of
law reports are the *All England Law Reports*, the *Weekly Law
Reports* and the *Law Reports*. We shall examine these series in
more detail in Chapter 2. The law reports are usually shelved in
a separate sequence in the law library and they will often be
grouped together by country, so that all the English law reports
are together. You may find that the international law reports are
shelved separately.

You will also find that you are referred to articles (essays) in
periodicals (journals or magazines). Your reading list should
give you the author and title of the article, the year, the volume
number, the title of the journal in which the article appeared,
and the first page number on which the article is printed, *e.g.*
East, "Jury Packing: a thing of the past" (1985) 48 M.L.R. 518.

The form in which this information is written varies but it is
important that you should learn to distinguish a reference to a
periodical article from a reference to a chapter or pages in a
book. If you are in any doubt as to the nature of the reference
(*i.e.* whether it is a book, a periodical article or a law report) ask
a member of the library staff for advice. Articles written in

periodicals are not entered in the library catalogue under the names of the authors.

Abbreviations

1–8 One of the major difficulties facing a new student is the tradition, adopted by lecturers and authors, of referring to periodicals and law reports only by an abbreviated form of their title. Instead of writing the name of the journal or law report in full they are invariably shortened to such cryptic abbreviations as: [1985] A.C.; [1984] 2 All E.R.; 136 N.L.J.; 4 L.M.C.L.Q. This may make it very difficult for you to know whether you are looking for a law report or a periodical article. Many of the references are confusingly similar, *e.g.* L.R. can be the abbreviation for both "law report" and "law review" (the law reports are shelved together, but separate from law reviews which are periodicals, or journals). Consequently, you could find yourself looking in the wrong sequence. A common mistake is to assume that a reference to a report of a case in "Crim.L.R." means that you must search amongst the law reports for a series entitled the Criminal Law Reports. There is no such series (although there is a series called the *Criminal Appeal Reports*). The reference "Crim.L.R." is to the *Criminal Law Review*, which is a journal, shelved with the periodicals. This contains both articles and reports of cases.

You will find a list of abbreviations which are in common use, together with the full title of the journal or law report, in:

> D. Raistrick, *Index to Legal Citations and Abbreviations;*
> *Sweet & Maxwell's Guide to Law Reports and Statutes;*
> The front pages of:
> > *Current Law Case Citators;*
> > *The Digest;*
> > *Index to Legal Periodicals;*
> > *Legal Journals Index;*
> > *Halsbury's Laws of England,* Vol. 1.
> *Manual of Legal Citations* (published by the University of London Institute of Advanced Legal Studies),
> Law dictionaries, *e.g. Osborn's Concise Law Dictionary.*

A list of the most commonly used abbreviations is in Appendix 1 of this work.

Tracing Periodicals and Law Reports

1–9 To find out if a periodical or law report is available look in the author catalogue, or in the separate periodicals catalogue, if there is one. The entry will indicate which volumes are available in the library and where they are shelved.

One point is especially worthy of note. Suppose that you are looking for a journal which includes the name of an organisation or body in its title, *e.g.* the *Journal of the Law Society of Scotland*, or the *American Bar Association Journal*. If the publication you require is the bulletin, transactions, proceedings, journal, yearbook or annual report of an organisation, you may find in some libraries that the title has been reversed, so that the entry appears under the name of the organisation. For instance, in some libraries, the *Journal of the Law Society of Scotland* would be entered under *Law Society of Scotland*, whilst in others it appears under *Journal*.

If the journal or report you need is not available in your own library, the staff may be able to help you to locate a copy in another library in the area, or it may be possible to obtain the journal, or a photocopy, on interlibrary loan.

WHICH LIBRARIES CAN I USE?

If you are studying at a university, polytechnic or college, the   **1–10** majority of the books you require should be available in your own institution's library. Remember that there may be more than one library available. For instance, in addition to the main library collection there may be a smaller collection of books and reports in your department or Faculty building. If you are living in a hall of residence, the hall's library may include some textbooks.

You may join the public library in the area in which you live, work or study. Most large towns will have some legal textbooks and law reports in their central library. If what you want is not available, the library staff may be able to borrow the material you require. This may take some time, so ask for the material well in advance of your actual need.

When you return home for the vacation, the university or polytechnic nearest your home may allow you to use their library for reference. Your own library staff can give you advice and provide you with the addresses and opening hours of libraries.

If you are studying for a professional examination, your professional body will have a library, from which you may be able to borrow books (by post, if necessary). The nearest large public library is another possible source of supply, and your employer may have a library to which you can have access.

Students studying for the Bar may use the library of their Inn. Local public libraries, the libraries attached to the courts, and the collections available in chambers are other possible sources. Those training to be solicitors can use the facilities of the Law Society's library, and the collections held by local law societies may be made available to students. If students are in difficulties they should approach the librarian of the nearest institution which has a law collection and explain their circumstances. Most libraries are willing to provide some assistance to students in genuine need.

The addresses of libraries can be found in the Library Association's *Libraries in the United Kingdom and the Republic of Ireland*, or the information can be obtained, by telephone or in person, from any public library. A more detailed guide is the *Directory of Law Libraries in the British Isles* (2nd ed.), edited by C. Miskin.

ASSISTANCE FROM LIBRARY STAFF

1–11   Remember that the library staff are there to help you. They will be pleased to explain how the books are arranged on the shelves, to decipher abbreviations, help with difficulties with reading lists and suggest possible sources of information. Do not hesitate to ask them for advice, no matter how busy they may appear to be. Never be afraid that your enquiry is too trivial or that you will appear foolish or ignorant by asking for advice. Most libraries produce handouts or library guides, which are usually available free. You should make a point of obtaining (and reading) those which are relevant. They will explain how the books are arranged on the shelves, how to use the catalogues, how to borrow books, etc. In academic libraries, tours of the library are often arranged at the beginning of the session. If such a tour is available you should certainly attend, as it will help you to familiarise yourself with the library.

DICTIONARIES

1–12   The newcomer to law rapidly discovers that lawyers have a language of their own, which is a mixture of Latin, French and English. There are several small pocket dictionaries of legal terms which are useful for students, *e.g.* P. G. Osborn, *Concise Law Dictionary* (7th ed.) and Mozley and Whiteley, *Law Dictionary* (9th ed.). Students should also consult standard English dictionaries, such as the multi-volumed *Oxford English Dictionary* or one of its smaller versions. W. A. Jowitt, *Dictionary of English Law* (2nd ed. with supplement) is a larger legal dictionary.

D. M. Walker, *Oxford Companion to Law* is another source of information on legal terms, institutions, doctrines and general legal matters. It includes lists of judges and law officers. Latin phrases and maxims may cause difficulties for students who have no classical languages. Latin phrases appear in most legal dictionaries. A collection of legal maxims will be found in H. Broom, *A Selection of Legal Maxims* (10th ed.), and see Appendix II, at the back of this book. If you are carrying out research in legal history you may need J. H. Baker, *Manual of Law French*.

TRACING PEOPLE AND ADDRESSES

If you want to trace the address of a solicitor or barrister, or to find the addresses of courts, legal firms, professional bodies, etc., there are a number of reference works available which provide this information. Waterlow's publish a *Solicitors' and Barristers' Directory and Diary* which gives alphabetical lists of solicitors and barristers, with their addresses. Lists of Q.C.'s, judges, Benchers of the Inns, Recorders, and members of the Institute of Legal Executives are also included. There are lists of barristers' chambers and solicitors' firms in each geographical area, with their membership. Similar information is to be found in *Butterworths Law Directory and Diary*, and in *Hazell's Guide to the Judiciary and the Courts* (which lists barristers, but not solicitors.) Law students looking for articles should consult the *Register of Solicitors Employing Trainees*, issued by the Law Society. The annual *Legal Aid Handbook* gives addresses of area legal aid offices, and details of eligibility for legal aid. Biographical details of prominent members of the legal profession can be found in *Who's Who*; whilst *Debrett's Correct Form* provides advice on the correct form of address when writing to, or addressing, members of the judiciary and other eminent people.

1–13

The addresses of many organisations and bodies are to be found in the *Directory of British Associations*, and in *Councils, Committees and Boards*. The humble telephone directory should not be overlooked as a source of information. The reference collection in your library will contain many other sources of this type of information: ask the reference librarian for advice if you need help.

CHAPTER 2

Law Reports

INTRODUCTION

2–1 A basic or primary source of English law is the information found in law reports. Traditionally the common law has developed through the practical reasoning of the judges. This is based on the particular facts of the case in question, social forces, and also upon previous judicial reasoning when it has a bearing on the case being heard. Legal principles stated in earlier decisions are given effect in later cases by the operation of the doctrine of precedent, which is described in detail in Glanville Williams, *Learning the Law*, Chap. 6. The successful development of the common law depends largely upon the production of reliable law reports which carry not only the facts, issues and decision but also, and most importantly, the legal principles upon which the judgment is made. Increasingly, the judiciary have also been called upon to consider the scope and application of particular Acts of Parliament.

It is not possible to report every case that is heard, nor is such a task necessary. A case is selected for reporting if it raises a point of legal significance. Because a case is widely reported in the media it does not follow that it will appear in law reports.

Judges, to a greater or lesser extent, follow or are influenced by their own previous decisions and those of colleagues and predecessors. Throughout your legal training and practice you will make constant use of law reports. Hence, a thorough working knowledge of them is essential. Glanville Williams (*Learning the Law* (11th ed.), p. 32) has offered the following advice to students of law:

> "The great disadvantage of confining oneself to textbooks and lecture notes is that it means taking all one's law at second hand. The law of England is contained in statutes and judicial decisions; what the textbook writer thinks is not, in itself, law. He may have misinterpreted the authorities, and the reader who goes to them goes to the fountainhead. Besides familiarising himself with the law reports and statute book, the lawyer-to-be should get to know his way about the library as a whole, together with its apparatus of catalogues and books of reference."

EARLY LAW REPORTS

Law reports have existed, in one form or another, since the reign of Edward I. These very early law reports are known as the *Year Books*. If you wish to see a copy, reprints of a number of these *Year Books* are available in the series of publications published by the Selden Society, in the Rolls Series (both of these will usually be found in the history section of a general library), and in facsimile reprints issued by Professional Books.   **2–2**

The *Year Books* were replaced by reports published privately by individuals, and these reports are normally referred to by the name of the author or compiler of the reports. For this reason they are collectively referred to as the *Nominate Reports*. They vary considerably in accuracy and reliability (Williams, *Learning the Law* (11th ed.), p. 35). Few libraries will have a complete collection of these old reports and, if you do obtain a copy, you may find that the antiquated print makes it difficult to read. Fortunately, the great majority of these Nominate Reports have been reprinted in a series called the *English Reports*, which we shall examine in detail later (para. 2–10).

MODERN LAW REPORTS

In 1865, a body called the Incorporated Council of Law Reporting commenced publication of a series entitled the *Law Reports*. These reports, which are semi-official, were rapidly accepted by the legal profession as the most authoritative version of law reports and, as a result, most of the privately published series ceased publication in 1865, or soon after that date. The *Law Reports* have maintained their superiority and today it is the   **2–3** report which appears in the *Law Reports* which is preferably cited (quoted) in courts. At the present time the *All England Law Reports* is the only general series of law reports which is still privately published. However, there are a number of specialist law reports, *e.g.* the *Criminal Appeal Reports* and the *Road Traffic Reports*, which are produced by commercial publishers.

A report of a case may appear in more than one series of reports. For instance, a report may appear in *The Times* newspaper, (under the heading "Law Report") the day after the case is heard. Several weeks later the case may be published in one or both of the two general series of law reports which appear weekly; the *All England Law Reports* and the *Weekly Law Reports*. A summary, or a full report, may be published in some of the weekly legal journals, such as the *New Law Journal* and the *Solicitors' Journal*, or in specialist law reports and journals (*e.g. Tax Cases*, the *Criminal Law Review*). Some time later a final, authoritative version (which has been personally checked by the judges concerned) will be published in the *Law Reports*. Thus you may be given, or you may find, references to more than one report of the same case.

Citation and Format of Law Reports

2–4 Law teachers, and writers of textbooks, often use abbreviations when referring to the sources where a report of a case can be found. These can appear very confusing at first, but constant use will rapidly make you familiar with the meaning of most of the abbreviations used. A reference to a case (which is called a *citation*) will normally look similar to the following example:

Holgate-Mohammed v. *Duke*[1] [1984][2] 2[3] W.L.R.[4] 660[5].

> [1] the names of the parties involved in the case;
> [2] the year in which the case is reported;
> [3] the volume number, *i.e.* the second volume published in 1984;
> [4] the abbreviation for the name of the law report;
> [5] the page number on which the case begins.

Thus, in this example, the case of *Holgate-Mohammed* v. *Duke* will be found in the 1984 volumes of the *Weekly Law Reports* (abbreviated to W.L.R.—for details of how to find the meaning of abbreviations see para 2–12.). There are three volumes of the *Weekly Law Reports* containing the cases reported in 1984. The case referred to will be found in the second volume, at page 660.

Let us now look at a typical example of a law report.

C.A.   CLEVELAND PETROLEUM *v.* DARTSTONE (Lord Denning, M.R.)   **201**

CLEVELAND PETROLEUM CO., LTD. *v.* DARTSTONE, LTD. AND ANOTHER.

[Court of Appeal, civil division (Lord Denning, M.R., Russell and Salmon, L.JJ.), November 26, 1968.]

Trade—Restraint of trade—Agreement—Petrol filling station—Solus agreement— Lease by garage owner to petrol supplier—Underlease to company to operate service station—Covenant in underlease for exclusive sale of supplier's products—Assignment of underlease by licence granted by supplier—Interim injunction to restrain breach of covenant.

S. the owner in fee simple of a garage, leased the premises to the plaintiffs for 25 years from 1st July 1960. The plaintiffs granted an underlease to C.O.S.S., Ltd., by which C.O.S.S., Ltd., covenanted, inter alia, to carry on the business of a petrol filling station at all times and not to sell or distribute motor fuels other than those supplied by the plaintiffs. After several assignments the underlease was assigned to the defendants who undertook to observe and perform the covenants. The defendants thereupon challenged the validity of the ties. The plaintiffs issued a writ claiming an injunction restraining the defendants from breaking this covenant. The plaintiffs obtained an interim injunction against which the defendants appealed.

Held: the appeal would be dismissed, the tie was valid and not an unreasonable restraint of trade because the defendants, not having been in possession previously, took possession of the premises under a lease and entered into a restrictive covenant knowing about such covenant, and thereby bound themselves to it (see p. 203, letters C, F and G, post).

Dicta in *Esso Petroleum Co., Ltd.* v. *Harper's Garage (Stourport), Ltd.* ([1967] 1 All E.R. at pp. 707, 714, and 724, 725) applied.

Appeal dismissed.

[As to agreements in restraint of trade, see 38 Halsbury's Laws (3rd Edn.) 20, para. 13; and for cases on the subject, see 45 Digest (Repl.) 443-449, *271-297*.]

Case referred to:

Esso Petroleum Co., Ltd. v. *Harper's Garage (Stourport), Ltd.*, [1967] 1 All E.R. 699; [1968] A.C. 269; [1967] 2 W.L.R. 871; Digest (Repl.) Supp.

Interlocutory Appeal.

This was an appeal by the defendants, Dartstone, Ltd., and James Arthur Gregory, from an order of Eveleigh, J., dated 1st November 1968, granting an interim injunction restraining the defendants from acting in breach of a covenant contained in an underlease made on 1st July 1960 between the plaintiffs, Cleveland Petroleum Co., Ltd., and County Oak Service Station, Ltd., and assigned to the defendants on 30th August 1968. The facts are set out in the judgment of Lord Denning, M.R.

Raymond Walton, Q.C., and *M. C. B. Buckley* for the defendants.
A. P. Leggatt for the plaintiffs.

LORD DENNING, M.R.: This case concerns a garage and petrol station called County Oak service station, at Crawley in Sussex. Mr. Sainsbury was the owner in fee simple. On 1st July 1960, there were three separate transactions: First, Mr. Sainsbury granted a lease of the entire premises to the plaintiffs, Cleveland Petroleum Co., Ltd., for 25 years, from 1st July 1960. The plaintiffs paid him £50,000 premium and agreed also to pay a nominal rent of £10 a year. Secondly, the plaintiffs granted an underlease of the premises to a company called County Oak Service Station, Ltd. That company was one in which Mr. Sainsbury had a predominant interest. The underlease was for 25 years, less three days from

The citation is *Cleveland Petroleum Co. Ltd* v. *Dartstone Ltd.* [1969] 1 All E.R. 201. Several key points in the illustration are numbered.

1. The names of the parties. In a civil case the name of the plaintiff (the person bringing the action) comes first, followed by the name of the defendant. A criminal case is usually cited as *R.* v. *Smith*. R. is the abbreviated form for the Latin words "Rex" (King) or "Regina" (Queen). The charge against Smith, the accused in a criminal offence, is brought on behalf of the Crown. The small letter "v." between the names of the parties to the action is an abbreviation of the Latin "versus" (against). When speaking of a case you say "against" in criminal cases, or "and" in civil cases, but never "v." or "versus." (Williams, *Learning the Law* (11th ed.), pp. 17 *et seq.*)

2. The name of the court in which the case was heard, the names of the judges (M.R.: Master of the Rolls; L.JJ.: Lords Justices) and the date on which the case was heard.

3. A summary (in italics) of the main legal issues of the case. You are advised not to rely upon this as it is neither necessarily complete nor accurate.

4. The headnote, which is a brief statement of the case, and the nature of the claim (in a civil case) or the charge (in a criminal case). Again, do not rely on the publisher's précis but instead read the case.

5. The court's ruling is stated, with a summary of reasons.

6. In certain reports, *e.g. All England Law Reports*, the major legal points are cross-referenced to *Halsbury's Laws* and *The Digest*.

7. A list of cases which were referred to during the hearing.

8. This is an appeal against the decision of a lower court to grant an interim or interlocutory injunction. An injunction is an order given by a judge telling a party to do something or refrain from doing it. It is interim or interlocutory in that it is temporary and meant to preserve the status quo before the legal rights are fully considered in court at a later date.

9. The names of counsel who appeared for the parties (Q.C.: Queen's Counsel).

10. The judgment of Lord Denning M.R.

FINDING VERY RECENT CASES

2–5   Because the law is constantly changing, with new cases being reported every week, you will often be asked to consult recent cases and these can present some difficulties. A reference to a report which appeared in *The Times* or "Financial Times" newspapers may be available in your library in one of several forms. The library may keep the daily copies (perhaps bound up into large volumes), or they may have replaced these by photographs of the pages which are on a reel of film, known as a microfilm. If they are available on microfilm the library staff will show you how to operate the machine which is needed to view the film. Depending upon the equipment available, they may be able to make a full-size photocopy of relevant items for you. Another possibility is that a law librarian may have cut all the law reports out of the newspaper and filed them in folders. Ask the library staff if the law reports from newspapers are available in your library and where they are kept.

If you are referred to a report of a case in the *All England Law Reports*, or the *Weekly Law Reports* (or, indeed, most other series of law reports) which has been published during the last few months, you will not find a bound volume on the shelves but a series of papercovered parts, or issues. However, your reference (citation) will make it appear that you are looking for a bound volume. So how do you find it? If you examine one of the weekly issues of the *All England Law Reports* you will find, at the top of the front cover, the date of that issue, the part (or issue) number, and the year, volume and page numbers covered by that issue.

For example:

21 November 1986   Part 8   [1986] 3 All E.R. 513–576.

This indicates that this issue (Part 8), will eventually form pages 513–576 of the third bound volume of the *All England Law Reports* for 1986. Also on the front cover appears a list of all the cases reported in that part, showing the page number on which each report begins.

Many other law reports are published in a number of parts during the current year. At the end of the year these are replaced by a bound volume or volumes. Every part will indicate on its cover the volume and pages in the bound volume where it will finally appear.

The *Weekly Law Reports* is a series (which commenced in 1953) that you will consult frequently. The arrangement of its weekly issues is rather confusing. Three bound volumes are produced each year, and each weekly issue contains some cases which will eventually appear in Volume 1 of the bound volumes for that year, and some cases which will subsequently appear in

All England Law Reports 21 November 1986   ISSN 0002-5569

21 November 1986   Part 8   [1986] 3 All ER 513–576

All ER 50 years
1936-1986

ALL ENGLAND LAW REPORTS

Editor
PETER HUTCHESSON Barrister New Zealand

Assistant Editor
BROOK WATSON of Lincoln's Inn Barrister

Consulting Editor
WENDY SHOCKETT of Gray's Inn Barrister

CASES REPORTED

BUTTERWORTHS London

Part 31

15 August 1986

[1986] 1 W.L.R. 1025–1095

[1986] 3 W.L.R. 365–398

Index

Cases in Volume 1 are those not intended to be included in the Law Reports

Annual subscription £82 (U.K.)
£89 (overseas)

ISSN 0019-3518

The Weekly Law Reports

Editor
CAROL ELLIS Q.C.

Assistant Editors
HILARY JELLIE
and
ROBERT WILLIAMS
Barristers-at-Law

THE
INCORPORATED COUNCIL
OF LAW REPORTING
FOR ENGLAND AND WALES

3 Stone Buildings
Lincoln's Inn,
London, WC2A 3XN

either Volume 2 or Volume 3. On the front cover of each issue
the contents of that part, and which volumes the pages in that
issue will eventually appear in, are shown. For example:

Part 31   15 August 1986
[1986] 1 WLR 1025–1095
[1986] 3 WLR 365–398.

Part 31 therefore contains pages 1025–1095 of what will eventually form the first volume of the *Weekly Law Reports* for 1986,
and pages 365–398 of the third volume. (A sheet of green paper
is inserted in the issue to mark the division between the pages
destined for Volume 1 and those forming part of Volume 3.) A
list of all the cases included in the part is printed on the front
cover, and the volume and page number for each case is shown.
You many wonder why the publishers (the Incorporated Council of Law Reporting, who also publish the *Law Reports*) have
chosen this method of publishing the issues. The reason is that
the cases in Volume 1 (which are less significant), will not
appear in the *Law Reports*, whilst those which appear in
Volumes 2 and 3 will be republished in the *Law Reports*.

You will probably find that the latest copy of law reports (and
journals) will be displayed in a separate area of the library. The
remainder of the issues for the current year may also be filed in
this area or they may be in a box on the shelves alongside the
bound volumes.

THE LAW REPORTS

2–6   The publication known as the *Law Reports* commenced in 1865.
It was originally published in 11 series, each covering different
courts. The rationalisation of the court structure since that time
has reduced this to four series. These are:

Appeal Cases (abbreviated to A.C.)
Chancery Division (Ch.)
Queen's Bench Division (Q.B.)
Family Division (Fam.)

You will normally find that the *Law Reports* are arranged on
the shelves in this order.

How the Law Reports are arranged on the shelves

2–7   The physical location of the various earlier series reflects their
relationship to the present four series. For example, the historical predecessors of the present Queen's Bench Division (called

the King's Bench Division when a King is on the throne) were the Court for Crown Cases Reserved, the Court of Common Pleas and the Court of Exchequer. These are therefore shelved before the Queen's Bench Division reports (because they are its predecessors) but after the Appeal Cases and Chancery Division reports. The same arrangement is applied with the other three current series (*e.g.* the predecessors of the present courts are filed at the beginning of each series).

The figure on page 20 shows the way in which the *Law Reports* are arranged on the shelves in most libraries. The abbreviations used to denote each series are shown, and also the dates during which each series appeared.

Citation of the Law Reports

You may notice that in some reported cases the date is printed in square brackets, whilst in other cases it is enclosed within round brackets. There are certain conventions concerning the way in which the citations (references) to cases in the *Law Reports* are written and these must be mastered.   **2–8**

Until 1890 it was the volume number and not the date which was the important part of the citation. Each volume in the various series had its own individual number and these numbers ran on from year to year. For example, the 10 volumes of the *Law Reports Exchequer Cases* published between 1865 and 1875 were individually numbered, 1 to 10, and it is this volume number, rather than the year, which is important in locating the correct volume. To show that the date is not essential, but is merely an aid, it is placed within *round* brackets, *e.g. Harrop* v. *Hirst* (1868–69) L.R. 5 Ex. 43. The abbreviation L.R. (for *Law Reports*) has been omitted from the citation for all series since 1875. The one exception to this was a series, published from 1957 to 1972, entitled *Reports of Restrictive Practices* cases. This was published by the Incorporated Council of Law Reporting and the citation took the form L.R. . . . R.P. In many libraries you will find that it is shelved separately from the *Law Reports*.

Since 1891, the individual numbering of volumes has been discontinued, except when there is more than one volume published in any particular year. When this happens the volumes within the year are numbered to distinguish them, as is done with the *Weekly Law Reports* and the *All England Law Reports*. The main arrangement within each series since 1891 has been by date. To indicate that the date is essential if you are to trace the report it is placed within *square* brackets, *e.g. Cowan* v. *Scargill* [1985] Ch. 270. This convention of using round and square

Law Reports

TABLE OF THE LAW REPORTS

The mode of citation is given in brackets. In the first, second and third columns, dots (. . .) are put where the number of the volume would appear in the citation. In the fourth column square brackets([ ]) are put where the year would appear in the citation.

1866–1875	1875–1880	1881–1890	1891–present
House of Lords. English and Irish Appeals (L.R. ... H.L.)			
House of Lords. Scotch and Divorce Appeals (L.R. ... H.L.Sc. or L.R. ... H.L.Sc. and Div.)	Appeal Cases (...App.Cas.)	Appeal Cases (...App.Cas.)	Appeal Cases ([ ]) A.C.)
Privy Council Appeals (L.R. ... P.C.)			
Chancery Appeal Cases (L.R. ... Ch. or Ch. App.)	Chancery Division (...Ch.D.)	Chancery Division (...Ch.D.)	Chancery Division ([ ]) Ch.)
Equity Cases (L.R. ... Eq.)			
Crown Cases Reserved (L.R. ... C.C., or, ... C.C.R.)	Queen's Bench Division (...Q.B.D.)		
Queen's Bench Cases* (L.R. ... Q.B.)		Queen's Bench Division (...Q.B.D.)	Queen's (or King's) Bench Division ([ ] Q.B. or K.B.)†
Common Pleas Cases (L.R. ... C.P.)	Common Pleas Division (...C.P.D.)		
Exchequer Cases‡ (L.R. ... Ex.)	Exchequer Division (...Ex.D.)		
Admiralty and Ecclesiastical Cases (L.R. ... A. & E.)	Probate Division (...P.D.)	Probate Division (...P.D.)	Probate Division ([ ]P.) Since 1972 Family Division ([ ]Fam.)
Probate and Divorce Cases (L.R. ... P. & D.)			

* Note that there is also a series called Queen's Bench Reports in the old reports (113–118 E.R.).
† After 1907 this includes cases in the Court of Criminal Appeal, later the Court of Appeal, in place of the previous Court for Crown Cases Reserved.
‡ Note that there is also a series called Exchequer Reports in the old reports (154–156 E.R.).

(Reproduced from G. Williams, *Learning the Law* (11th ed.), p.39.)

brackets is also used in other series such as the *All England Law Reports*. The use of brackets may be summarised as follows:

Date in round brackets: the date is not of major importance, but the volume number is: *e.g.* (1868) L.R. 6 Eq. 540.

Date in square brackets: the date is an essential part of the reference, *e.g.* [1895] A.C. 229; [1954] 3 W.L.R. 967; [1987] 2 All E.R. 608.

SUMMARY: CONVENTIONS GOVERNING THE CORRECT CITATION OF THE LAW REPORTS

1865–1875: (year) L.R. volume, abbreviation for series, page; *e.g. Rylands* v. *Fletcher* (1868) L.R. 3 H.L. 330.

1875–1890: (year) volume, abbreviation for series (L.R. is omitted), page; *e.g. Brogden* v. *Metropolitan Railway Co.* (1877) 2 App.Cas. 666.

1891 onwards [year] volume within year, abbreviation for series, page; *e.g. Carlill* v. *Carbolic Smoke Ball Co.* [1982] 2 Q.B. 484.

It is worth noting that the abbreviation H.L. (see the citation for *Rylands* v. *Fletcher,* above) does not stand for a series entitled Law Reports: House of Lords. It is the abbreviation for a series entitled *Law Reports: English and Irish Appeal Cases* which you will find shelved at the beginning of the Appeal Cases sequence.

OLDER LAW REPORTS

We have concentrated upon the modern series of law reports **2–9** because these are the reports which you will be using most frequently. However, from time to time you will need to look at older cases, that is, those reported in the first half of the nineteenth century, or even several centuries earlier. Reports of older cases can be found in several series: the *English Reports, Revised Reports, Law Journal Reports, Law Times Reports* and the *All England Law Reports Reprint* series. We shall now look at some of these series in more detail.

We have said that the reports published privately by individuals (and known as the *Nominate Reports*) ceased publication around 1865, when the *Law Reports* were first published. Thus the date 1865 is an important one for you to remember. If the date of the case you want is before 1865 you are most likely to find it in a series known as the *English Reports*. If this series is not available in your library, you may need to use the *Revised Reports*, which is similar but not identical in its coverage.

How to use the English Reports

2–10 If you know the name of the case, look it up in the alphabetical index of the names of cases, printed in Volumes 177–178 of the *English Reports*. Beside the name of the case is printed the abbreviation for the name of the original nominate reporter, and the volume and page in his reports where the case appeared. The number printed in **bold** type adjoining this is the volume number in the *English Reports* where the case will be found, and this is followed by the page number in that volume.

> *Daniel* v. *North*[a]   11 East, 372[b]   **103**[c] 1047;

[a] name of the case;
[b] volume, name of original reporter, page number in original report, *i.e.* original report appeared in Volume 11 of *East's Reports* at page 372;
[c] reprint of report appears in *English Reports*, Vol. 103, page 1047.

You will see that Volume 103 of the *English Reports* has the volumes and names of the *Nominate Reports* which are to be found in that volume printed on the spine. Page number 1047 appears in its normal position at the top outer corner of the

424 **DAN** (A) (B) Index of Cases		(C)
→ Daniel *v.* North, 11 East, 372	. . . . .	. **103** 1047
—— *v.* Phillips, 4 T. R. 499	. . . . .	. **100** 1141
—— *v.* Pit, Peake Add. Cas. 238	. . . .	. **170** 257
—— *v.* Pit, 6 Esp. 74	. . . .	. **170** 834
—— *v.* Purbeck, W. Kel. 97	. . . .	. **25** 510
—— *v.* Purkis, W. Kel. 97	. . . .	. **25** 510
—— *v.* Purkurst, 2 Barn. K. B. 214, 220	. . .	**94** 457, 461
—— *v.* Russell, 14 Ves. Jun. 393 ; 2 Ves. Jun. Supp. 376	.	. **33** 572 ; **34** 1139
—— *v.* Skipwith, 2 Bro. C. C. 155	. . .	. **29** 89
—— *v.* Sterlin, 1 Freeman, 50	. . .	. **89** 39
—— *v.* Thompson, 15 East, 78	. . .	. **104** 774
—— *v.* Trotman, 1 Moo. N. S. 123.	. . .	. **15** 649
—— *v.* Turpin, 1 Keble, 124	. . .	. **83** 852
—— *v.* Ubley, Jones, W. 137	. . .	. **82** 73
—— *v.* Uply, Latch, 9, 39, 134	. . .	**82** 248, 264, 312
—— *v.* Upton, Noy, 80	. . .	. **74** 1047
—— *v.* Waddington, Cro. Jac. 377.	. . .	. **79** 322
—— *v.* Waddington, 3 Bulstrode, 130	. . .	. **81** 111
—— *v.* Warren, 2 Y. & C. C. C. 290	. . .	. **63** 127
—— *v.* Wilkin, 7 Ex. 429	. . .	. **155** 1016
—— *v.* Wilkin, 8 Ex. 156	. . .	. **155** 1300
—— *v.* Wilson, 5 T. R. 1	. . .	. **101** 1
Daniel's Case, 2 Dy. 133 b	. . .	. **73** 291
—— Trust, *In re*, 18 Beav. 309	. . .	. **52** 122

before; but they could not agree on the person to be substituted, and therefore the original appointment stood as before.

Per Curiam. Rule absolute.

AMBROSE *against* REES. Wednesday, June 14th, 1809. Notice having been given for the trial of a cause at Monmouth, which arose in Glamorganshire, as being in fact the next English county since the st. 27 H. 8, c. 26, s. 4, though Hereford be the common place of trial; the Court refused to set aside the verdict as for a mis-trial, on motion; the question being open on the record.

Marryat opposed a rule for setting aside the verdict obtained in this cause, upon the ground of an irregularity in the trial. The venue was laid in Glamorganshire, and the cause was tried at Monmouth, as the next English county where the King's writ of venire runs (b); but it was objected that it ought to have been tried at Hereford, according to the general custom that all causes in which the venue is laid in any county in South Wales should be tried at Hereford. But the rule being that the cause should be tried in the next English county, and Monmouth being in fact the next English county to Glamorganshire, and more conveniently situated for the trial of the cause, there seems no solid ground for impeaching the validity of the trial; though the practice relied on is easily accounted for by the consideration that Monmouthshire was originally a Welch county, and till it became an English county in the 27th year of Hen. 8, Herefordshire was in fact the next English county to Glamorgan. And there is no reason for setting aside this verdict on the ground of surprize; for the defendant had not merely a notice of trial in the next English county, generally, which might have misled him by the notoriety of the [371] practice, but a specific notice of trial at Monmouth, to which he made no objection at the time.

Abbott, in support of the rule, relied on the known practice which had always prevailed, as well since as before the Statute 27 H. 8; and referred to *Morgan* v. *Morgan* (a), where the question arose in 1656, upon an ejectment for lands in Breknock-shire, which was tried at Monmouth; and afterwards judgment was arrested, on the ground of a mis-trial, as it ought to have been tried in Herefordshire; for that Monmouthshire was but made an English county by statute within time of memory; and that trials in the next English county of issues arising in Wales have been time out of mind and at the common law; so that a place newly made an English county cannot have such a trial. And he observed, that if this trial were good, all the judgments in causes out of Glamorganshire tried at Hereford have been erroneous.

Lord Ellenborough C.J. If the question appear on the record, then the defendant cannot apply in this summary manner. And as he did not object at the time, we shall not relieve him upon motion.

Per Curiam. Rule discharged.

→ [372] DANIEL *against* NORTH. Wednesday, June 14th, 1809. Where lights had been put out and enjoyed without interruption for above 20 years during the occupation of the opposite premises by a tenant; that will not conclude the landlord of such opposite premises, without evidence of his knowledge of the fact, which is the foundation of presuming a grant against him; and consequently will not conclude a succeeding tenant who was in possession under such landlord from building up against such encroaching lights.

[Considered and applied, *Wheaton* v. *Maple* [1893], 3 Ch. 57; *Roberts* v. *James*, 1903, 89 L. T. 286. For *Rugby Charity* v. *Merryweather*, 11 East, 375, n., see *Woodyer* v. *Hadden*, 1813, 5 Taunt. 138; *Wood* v. *Veal*, 1822, 5 B. & Ald. 457; *Vernon* v. *St. James's, Westminster* 1880, 16 Ch. D. 457; *Bourke* v. *Davis*, 1889, 44 Ch. D. 123.]

The plaintiff declared in case, upon his seisin in fee of a certain messuage or dwelling-house in Stockport, on one side of which there is and was and of right ought to be six windows; and stated that the defendant wrongfully erected a wall 60 feet high and 50 in length near the said house and windows, and obstructed the light and

(b) Vide 1 Term Rep. 313.   (a) Hard. 66.

page whilst the volume and page number of the original report are printed at the inner margin. This can sometimes cause confusion to students.

8	TABLE OF ENGLISH REPORTS				
Old Reports.	Volume in English Reports.	Abbreviation.	Period covered (approximate).	Series.	
Dow & Clark, 1 & 2	6	Dow & Cl.	1827–1832	H.L.	
Dowling & Ryland	171	Dowl. & Ry. N.P.	1822–1823	N.P.	
Drewry, 1–3	61	Drew.	1852–1859	V.C.	
„ 4	62				
Drewry & Smale, 1 & 2	62	Drew & Sm. or Dr. & Sm.	1860–1865	V.C.	
Dyer, 1–3	73	Dy.	1513–1582	K.B.	
East, 1–6	102	East.	1801–1812	K.B.	
„ 7–11	103				
„ 12–16	104				
Eden, 1 & 2	28	Eden.	1757–1766	Ch.	
Edwards	165	Edw.	1808–1812	Ecc. Adm. P. & D.	
Ellis & Blackburn, 1–3	118	El. & Bl.	1851–1858	K.B.	
„ „ 4–7	119				
„ „ 8	120				
Ellis, Blackburn & Ellis	120	El. Bl. & El.	1858	K.B.	
Ellis & Ellis, 1	120	El. & El.	1858–1861	K.B.	
„ „ 2 & 3	121				
Eq. Cases Abridged, 1	21	Eq. Ca. Abr.	1667–1744	Ch.	
„ „ 2	22				
Espinasse, 1–6	170	Esp.	1793–1807	N.P.	

Sometimes you may only have a citation (reference) to the original nominate report, *e.g.* 3 Car. & P. (*Carrington and Payne*), 2 Barn. & Ald. (*Barnewall and Alderson*). This reference is often printed in an abbreviated form. You do not know the name of the case, so you are unable to look it up in the index to the *English Reports*. Let us suppose, for example, that you have come across a reference to: (1809) 11 East 372. Because the date is before 1865, you know that it is likely to be found in the *English Reports*; but you do not know the name of the case. How do you find it? If the name of the report has been abbreviated, *e.g.* 3 Car. & P., you will need to look in Raistrick's *Index to legal citations and abbreviations* or one of the similar reference works (see para. 2–12) to find the meaning of the abbreviation. You then turn to the *Chart to the English Reports*. This may be displayed near the *English Reports*, or it may be a slim volume shelved with the *Reports* themselves. The *Chart* contains an alphabetical list of the names of all the reporters whose work has been reprinted in the *English Reports*, showing which volume their work appears in. The *Chart* indicates that Volumes 7 to 11 of East's Reports are reprinted in Volume 103 of the *English Reports*. If you open Volume 103 at random, you will see

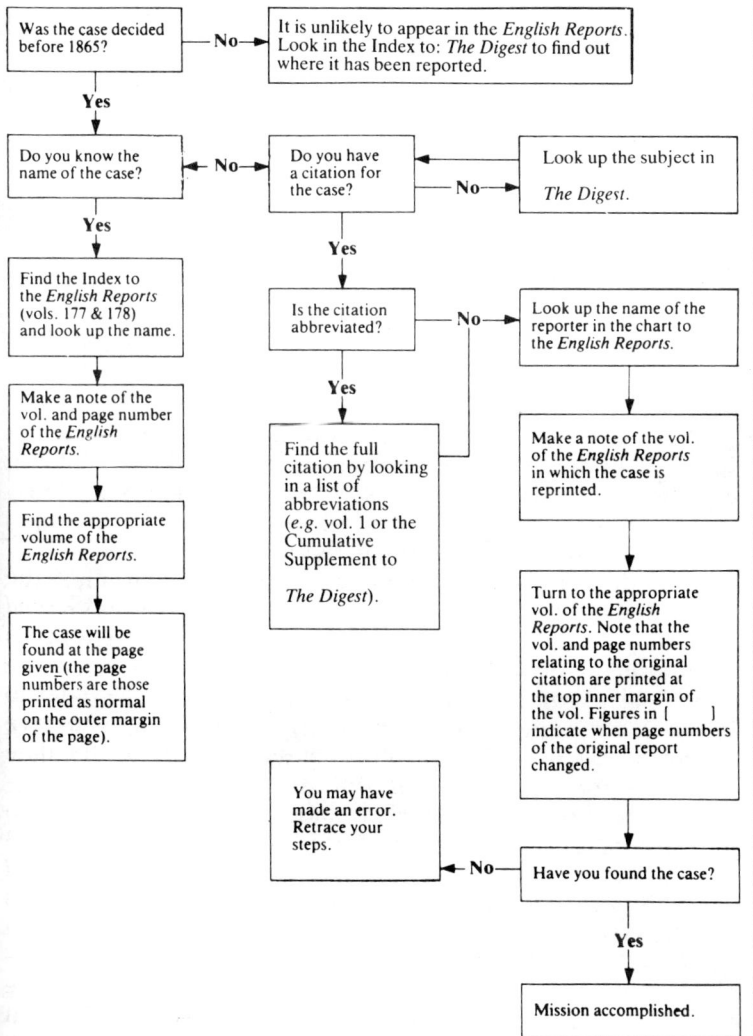

ALGORITHM DESIGNED TO SHOW HOW TO LOOK UP A CASE IN THE ENGLISH REPORTS

START

Was the case decided before 1865? —No→ It is unlikely to appear in the *English Reports*. Look in the Index to: *The Digest* to find out where it has been reported.

Yes

Do you know the name of the case? ←No— Do you have a citation for the case? —No→ Look up the subject in *The Digest*.

Yes

Find the Index to the *English Reports* (vols. 177 & 178) and look up the name.

Yes

Is the citation abbreviated? —No→ Look up the name of the reporter in the chart to the *English Reports*.

Make a note of the vol. and page number of the *English Reports*.

Yes

Find the appropriate volume of the *English Reports*.

Find the full citation by looking in a list of abbreviations (*e.g.* vol. 1 or the Cumulative Supplement to *The Digest*).

Make a note of the vol. of the *English Reports* in which the case is reprinted.

The case will be found at the page given (the page numbers are those printed as normal on the outer margin of the page).

Turn to the appropriate vol. of the *English Reports*. Note that the vol. and page numbers relating to the original citation are printed at the top inner margin of the vol. Figures in [   ] indicate when page numbers of the original report changed.

You may have made an error. Retrace your steps. ←No— Have you found the case?

Yes

Mission accomplished.

that, at the top of each page (at the *inner* margin) the volume
and page numbers of the original report are printed. Find the
volume and page reference which most nearly corresponds to
your reference. There is no entry at the top of the page for
Volume 11 of East's Reports, page 372, but there is an entry, at
the top inner margin, for page 371. If you look at the figure on
page 23, you will see the heading, 11 East 371, at the top of the
page. There are also numbers printed, in square brackets, in the
body of the text. These indicate when the page numbers in the
original report changed. For instance, in the original volume 11
of *East's Reports*, page 371 began with the words "practice, but a
specific notice of trial at Monmouth . . . ". Page 372 began with
the case of *Daniel* v. *North*.

Other Older Law Reports

2–11   The *All England Law Reports Reprint* is another useful source for
old cases between 1558 and 1935. The cases are reprinted from
the reports which originally appeared in the *Law Times Reports*,
which commenced in 1843, and from earlier reports. The *Reprint*
contains some 5,000 cases selected principally upon the criter-
ion that they have been referred to in the *All England Law
Reports* and in *Halsbury's Laws of England*. There is an Index
volume containing an alphabetical list of cases and a subject
index of the cases included in the reprint.

Two other series of nineteenth century cases are also referred
to regularly: the *Law Journal Reports* and the *Law Times Reports*.
The *Law Journal Reports* cover the period 1822–1949. They can be
complicated to use because usually two volumes were published each year, both bearing the same volume numbers. In
one volume were printed the cases heard in common law
courts, while the other printed equity cases. It is therefore
necessary to decide whether the case you want is likely to
appear in the common law or the equity volume for that year, or
you will need to check both volumes. To add to the difficulty,
the volume numbering and the method of citation changed during the course of its publication. The first nine volumes
(1822–1831) are known as the Old Series (L.J.O.S.). References to
the New Series (1832–1949) omit the letters N.S. Citations give
the abbreviation for the court in which the case was heard. It is
therefore necessary to decide if the court was a court of common
law or equity, so that you consult the correct volume. For
example, the reference 16 L.J.Q.B. 274 is a reference to the *Law
Journal (New Series)*, Volume 16 in the common law volumes
(since Queen's Bench was a court of common law) at page 274 of
the reports of Queen's Bench. Volume 16 contains law reports

from several different courts. Each court's reports have a separate sequence of page numbers. You are looking for page 274 in the sequence of Queen's Bench reports.

The *Law Times Reports* (L.T.) cover the period 1859–1947. Prior to this, the reports were published as part of the journal entitled *Law Times* and these are cited as the *Law Times, Old Series* (L.T.O.S.) which ran from 1843–1860. You may find this Old Series is shelved with the journals, not with the law reports.

HOW TO FIND THE MEANING OF ABBREVIATIONS

If you are faced with an abbreviation for a law report (or jour-   **2–12**
nal) which you do not recognise, you can find the full title of the
report by looking in any of the following works:

D. Raistrick, *Index to Legal Citations and Abbreviations*;
Sweet & Maxwell's Guide to Law Reports and Statutes;
Current Law;
The Digest (Vol. 1 and the Cumulative Supplement);
Halsbury's Laws of England (4th ed., Vol. 1, pp. 23–48);
Osborn's Concise Law Dictionary;
Manual of Legal Citations (Pts. I and II, published by the
    University of London Institute of Advanced Legal Studies).

The simplest source for the beginner is the list which is printed in the back of each issue of *Current Law*. If you do not find the answer here then move on to one of the alternative sources.

If you are unable to find the abbreviation in any of these books, ask a member of the library staff for help. Once you know the full title of the report, check in the library's catalogue or in its list of periodicals and reports (para. 1–9) to see if that series is available in the library, and where it is on the shelves. A list of some of the most commonly used abbreviations will be found in Appendix 1 of this book.

HOW TO FIND A CASE WHEN YOU ONLY KNOW ITS NAME

We will now turn to some of the problems frequently encoun-   **2–13**
tered by students and show how these are solved. Often you
know the name of a case but you have no idea where the case
was reported; or else the reference which you have been given
has proved to be inaccurate. How can you find out where a
report of the case appears?

The easiest way of tracing a case of any date is to look it up in the *Current Law Case Citators*. If you fail to find it there you should turn to other sources such as *The Digest* (para. 2–15) or the indexes to specific series of law reports, such as the *Law Reports*.

How to Use the Current Law Case Citators

2–14 The *Current Law Case Citator 1947–1976* contains an alphabetical
list of the names of cases (of any date) which have been published, or quoted in court, between 1947 and 1976. The *Citator*
includes many older cases, heard before 1947, which have been
referred to in court since 1947. Thus, if you are looking for the
1892 case of *Carlill* v. *Carbolic Smoke Ball Co.* you would find it in
the *Citator* because it has been referred to in court since 1947.

There are two versions of the *Citator;* one is entitled the *Scottish Current Law Case Citator* the other is simply called the *Current Law Case Citator.* If your library has the Scottish version, do
not think that is of no use to you because you are looking for an
English case. Despite the name, the *Scottish Current Law Case
Citator* does contain all the English cases, plus Scottish cases
(which are omitted from the other edition). The Scottish cases
form a separate alphabetical sequence at the back of the volume.

The information is kept up to date by the latest *Current Law
Case Citator* (which is republished annually). It contains details
of cases of any date which have been published or quoted in
court since 1977. The two volumes of *Current Law Case Citators*
should, therefore, be used together.

The cases are listed in alphabetical order. Cases beginning
simply with a letter of the alphabet, *e.g. S.* v. *C.* are at the beginning of that letter of the alphabet; criminal cases beginning *R* v.
— are at the beginning of the letter R. If the title of the case is *Re
Smith,* or *Ex p. Smith,* look under *Smith.* When you have traced
the case you require, you will find an entry similar to the
following:

CASE CITATOR 1947–76   **BIN**

Bigos *v.* Bousted [1951] 1 All E.R. 92; [95 S.J. 180; 211 L.T. 346; 67
    L.Q.R. 156] .... *Digested,* **1751**
—— *v.* J.R.S.S.T. Charitable Trust (Trustees of) (1965) 109 S.J. 273, C.A. *Digested,* 65/**2206**
Bilainkin *v.* Bilainkin [1959] 1 W.L.R. 139; 103 S.J. 90; [1959] 1 All
    E.R. 161, C.A. .... *Digested,* 59/**943**
Bilang *v.* Rigg [1972] N.Z.L.R. 954 .... *Digested,* 72/**1886**
Bilbee *v.* Hasse & Co. (1889) 5 T.L.R. 677 .... *Considered,* 30
Bilbow *v.* Bilbow and Zandos (October 25, 1957), unreported .... *Reported,* 57/**1019**
Bilcon *v.* Fegmay Investments [1966] 2 Q.B. 221; [1966] 3 W.L.R. 118;
    110 S.J. 618; [1966] 2 All E.R. 513 .... *Digested,* 66/**373**
Bildt *v.* Foy (1892) 9 T.L.R. 34 .... *Considered,* 67/**3093**
→ Biles *v.* Caesar [1957] 1 W.L.R. 156; 101 S.J. 108; [1957] 1 All E.R.
    151; [101 S.J. 141; 21 Conv. 169], C.A. ...... *Digested,* 57/**1943**: *Followed,* 59/**1834**:
                                            Applied, 68/**2181**; 69/**2037**
—— Bilham, *Re* [1901] 2 Ch. 169 .... *Distinguished,* 60/**3322**
Bill *v.* Short Brothers and Harland [1963] N.I. 1 .... *Digested,* 62/**2014**
Billage *v.* Southee (1852) 9 Hare 534 .... *Applied,* 52/**1485**: 70/**1145**
Billam *v.* Griffith (1941) 23 T.C. 757 .... *Applied,* 4758
Billericay U. D. C., Plot No. 9B, Pitsea Temporary Housing Site, *Re* (1950)
    1 P. & C.R. 239, Lands Tribunal .... *Noted,* **1498**

At first this mass of information may look confusing. However, it is well worth taking the trouble to find out what it means. You are provided with the complete "life history" of a case: where and when it was originally reported, where you can find periodical articles explaining the meaning of the case, and perhaps criticising the decision, and in which cases the decision in *Biles* v. *Caesar* has been quoted in court, and whether the court to which it was quoted agreed with the decision of the judges in *Biles* v. *Caesar*.

Let us look at each part of the entry in turn, to find out what it means.

(1) After the name of the case (*Biles* v. *Caesar*) you have a list of three places where you can find a full report of the case:

[1957] 1 W.L.R. 156, *i.e.* in the first of the three volumes of the *Weekly Law Reports* for 1957, at page 156.

101 S.J. 108—in Volume 101 of the *Solicitors' Journal* at page 108 (this, as its name suggests, is a periodical, which you will find shelved with the periodicals).

[1957] 1 All E.R. 151—in the first volume of the *All England Law Reports* for 1957, at page 151.

(2) The entries which are completely enclosed in square brackets—[101 S.J. 141; 21 Conv. 169]—are references to articles or comments in legal journals where the case is discussed in some detail. If you turn to Volume 101 of the *Solicitors' Journal*, or Volume 21 of the *Conveyancer*, you will find articles discussing the case of *Biles* v. *Caesar*.

(3) You will find that all the abbreviations which have been used—S.J., Conv., W.L.R., etc.—are listed at the front of the *Current Law Case Citator*, showing the full title of the journal or law report.

(4) The word *Digested* followed by the figures 57/1943 indicates that you will find a digest (a summary) of the case in the 1957 volume of the *Current Law Year Book* (see para. 6–10). Every item in the 1957 volume has its own individual number; you will find that item 1943 is a summary of the facts and decision in the case of *Biles* v. *Caesar*.

(5) You may sometimes wish to know whether the decision given in a particular case has been approved subsequently, *i.e.* whether the case has been quoted with approval by another judge in a later case. The case of *Biles* v. *Caesar* has been quoted in court three times since it was originally decided—in 1959, when the decision was

followed, and in 1968 and 1969 when the courts applied the decision in *Biles* case to two other cases, following the doctrine of precedent. You can find the names of the cases in which *Biles* was referred to by looking in the 1959 *Current Law Year Book*, at item 1834, and in the 1968 and 1969 *Year Books*, at the item numbers given.

The meaning of terms such as "applied" and "followed" is given in the front of the *Cumulative Supplement* to *The Digest* (para. 2–15) under the heading "Meaning of terms used in classifying annotating cases".

If you are unable to find the case you require in the *Current Law Case Citators*, it is likely to be (a) an old case, or (b) a very recent case, *i.e.* within the last year, or (c) not an English case. If you think that it is likely to be a very recent case, follow the procedure outlined in para. 2–17.

Tracing a case in The Digest

2–15   Older English cases, and cases heard in Scottish, Irish and Commonwealth courts, can most easily be traced using *The Digest* (formerly known as the *English and Empire Digest*). *The Digest* consists of the main work, several *Continuation Volumes* and a *Cumulative Supplement*.

To trace a particular case in *The Digest* go first to the *Consolidated Table of Cases*. This contains an alphabetical list of the names of cases reported from the earliest times to the present, showing where the cases are found in the various volumes of *The Digest*. Having found the case in the *Consolidated Table*, find the appropriate volume and look up the name of the case again, in the list of cases which appears at the front of the volume. This refers you to the *page* number (or to the *case* number—see the heading at the top of the column) where you can find the case. The *Consolidated Table of Cases* can never be completely up to date; you will need to consult the list of cases which appears at the front of the *Cumulative Supplement* for the latest cases.

There are two types of references in the Table of Cases in the *Cumulative Supplement*. The important thing is to ask yourself: Does the word "Reissue" appear after the volume number? For example:

Greene v *Broxtowe District Council* (1977): 20 (Reissue) Empt. 4477.

If the word "Reissue" *does* appear you are being referred to the appropriate volume of the *main work*. For instance, *Greene* v.

Broxtowe District Council is found in Volume 20 of the *Digest* under the subject heading of Employment (Empt.) at *case* number (*not* page number) 4477.

If the case number has an asterisk * in front of the number such as in this example

14 (1) (Reissue) Crim. *2203.

this means that the reference is to an Irish, Scottish or Commonwealth case. These cases form a separate, but parallel, sequence to the English cases (which do not carry an asterisk.) The asterisked cases are easily distinguished as they are printed in a smaller type face.

If the word "Reissue" does *not* appear after the volume number, for example

5 Bkpcy. 6934a

then you should turn to the *text* of the *Cumulative Supplement* itself and look for the entry for Volume 5, subject heading Bankruptcy (Bkpcy.), case number 6934a. There you will find a summary of the case, and a list of places where it can be found in the law reports.

Because the method of using *The Digest* may change as volumes are reissued, you should look at the instructions to users at the front of the *Cumulative Supplement* if you have any difficulty.

SUMMARY: TRACING A CASE IN THE DIGEST

1. Consult the *Consolidated Table of Cases*. This will tell you the volume and subject heading in *The Digest* where the case is to be found.
2. Locate the correct volume and look up the name of the case again in the *Table of Cases* at the front of the volume. This will tell you *either* the case number *or* the page number where the case is to be found in the volume. (Look at the heading at the top of the page.)
3. For more recent cases, look at the Table of Cases at the front of the *Cumulative Supplement*. Does the word "Reissue" appear after the volume number?
   Yes—Consult the appropriate volume of the main work under the volume, subject heading and case number. (Asterisked * cases are in a separate sequence and printed in smaller type.)

No—Look at the text of the *Cumulative Supplement* under the volume, subject heading and case number.

Tracing a Case in Indexes to Law Reports

2–16   In addition to the *Current Law Case Citators* and *The Digest*, there are a number of indexes to the cases in individual series of law reports. For instance, the *All England Law Reports* has published a volume containing a list of all the cases in the *All England Law Reports Reprint* (see para. 2–11), which covers selected cases between 1558 and 1935. In addition, there are three volumes containing the *Consolidated Tables and Index 1936–1981*. Volume 1 contains a list of all the cases included in the *All England Law Reports* between these dates. (The reference given is to the year, volume number and page number). More recent cases (since 1981) appear in the cumulative *Tables and Index* and the *Current Cumulative Tables and Index* (see para. 2–17).

If you know that the case you are looking for is old, you can turn to the index in Volumes 177 and 178 of the *English Reports*, and this will tell you if the case has been printed in the *English Reports* (see para. 2–10). Several other series of law reports also publish indexes and these can be useful if you know that a case is reported in a particular series but you have been given an incorrect reference.

The indexes to the *Law Reports* are very useful. From 1865 to 1949 a series of *Law Reports: Digests* were published. These contain summaries of the cases reported in the *Law Reports*, in subject order, and a list of cases is usually included. From 1950 this has been published as the *Law Reports Consolidated Index* (lettered on the spine *Law Reports Index*). Bound volumes have been published, covering 1951–1960, 1961–1970 and 1971–1980 cases. An annual paper-covered "red" index is published, containing cases from 1981 to the end of the last year, and this is supplemented by a "pink" index, issued at intervals during the year, which lists all the cases published during the current year. The main arrangement of all the indexes is by subject, but there are two alphabetical lists. The list of *Cases Reported*, at the front of each volume, covers recently reported cases, whilst the separate list of *Cases Judicially Considered*, at the back of the volume, gives information on older cases which have been mentioned in court during the period covered by the index. In addition to cases published in the *Law Reports*, the indexes also include cases published in the *All England Law Reports, Criminal Appeal Reports, Lloyd's Law Reports, Local Government Reports, Road Traffic Reports* and *Tax Cases*. If the *Current Law Case Citators* are

not available in your library, this index to the *Law Reports* will
fulfil a similar function.

HOW TO TRACE VERY RECENT CASES

If the case you want has been reported within the last year or so,   **2–17**
you will not find it in the *Current Law Case Citators*, nor in *The
Digest*. If, therefore, you think that a case is very recent, you
should adopt a different approach. Look in the *latest* issue of
Current Law, at the list of cases (the Case Citator) printed at the
back of each issue. If the name of your case appears, the reference given is to the monthly issue of *Current Law*, and to the
individual item number within that issue, where you will find a
summary of the case, and a note of where it has been reported.
For example, suppose the case gives a reference such as: Jan 129.
This means that if you look in the January issue of *Current Law*,
item 129 (not page 129) is a summary of the case, with a list of
places where the case is reported in full.

Other sources which can be used to trace a recent case are the
indexes to the *Law Reports* and the *All England Law Reports*. The
"pink index" to the *Law Reports* will cover cases reported in
several of the major series of law reports; the front cover
indicates the exact period covered by the index. If the case is too
recent to be included in here, look inside the latest copy of the
Weekly Law Reports. The front cover of the *Weekly Law Reports*
lists only the contents of that particular issue. The list inside
covers all cases reported in the series since the last "pink" index
was published.

Cases in the *All England Law Reports* are included in the
indexes to the *Law Reports*, but, in addition, a separate index to
the series is published. The *All England Law Reports Tables and
Index* covers cases reported in the series since 1981. The dark
blue covered main cumulative Tables are supplemented by a
pale blue publication entitled *Current Cumulative Tables and
Index*, which is replaced regularly and which contains the most
recent cases. Again, the list inside the latest *All England Law
Reports* brings the *Current Cumulative Tables* up to date.

A very recent case (*i.e.* within the last few weeks) can only be
traced by examining the summaries of cases which appear in
The Times, and in the various weekly journals, such as the *New
Law Journal* or the *Solicitors' Journal* (that is, assuming that you
cannot trace it in the index in the latest copy of the *Weekly Law
Reports* or the *All England Law Reports*).

SUMMARY: TRACING WHERE A CASE HAS BEEN REPORTED

1. If the date is unknown, look in the *Current Law Case Citators* (see para. 2–14). If not traced there, look in *The Digest (Consolidated Table of Cases)* and in the *Cumulative Supplement*) (see para. 2–15).
2. If the case is thought to be old, look in the index to the *English Reports*, or the Index to the *All England Law Reports Reprint*; if not there, then in *The Digest (Consolidated Table of Cases).*
3. If the case is thought to be very recent look in the latest issue of *Current Law* (see para. 2–17), or in the "pink" index to the *Law Reports* (see para. 2–17), and then in the latest issue of the *Weekly Law Reports* (see para. 2–17) or *All England Law Reports* (para. 2–17).
4. If the case is known to have been reported in one of the leading series but the reference you have is incorrect, look in the index to that series, if there is one, otherwise try *Current Law Case Citators* or *The Digest.*
5. For a Scottish case, look in the separate list of Scottish cases at the back of the *Scottish Current Law Case Citators*; if not available, or not traced here, look in *The Digest.*
6. For Irish cases check the *Irish Digest* or the *Index to Northern Ireland Cases*, (if available) or *The Digest.*
7. For Commonwealth cases check *The Digest.*

HOW TO TRACE PERIODICAL ARTICLES AND COMMENTARIES ON A CASE

2–18   You may want to find out if any periodical articles have been written about a case, or to trace comments on a recent court decision. Such articles and comments usually explain the significance of the case and relate it to other decisions on the same aspect of the law. Sometimes writers who disagree with a decision may even argue that the case provides a justification for a change in the law.

Periodical articles on a case can be traced by using the *Legal Journals Index* (para. 4–3), the *Current Law Case Citators* or the *Index to Legal Periodicals* (para. 4–5). If you look again at the specimen entry (*Biles* v. *Caesar*) from the *Current Law Case Citator* (para. 2–14) you will recall that the entries which were completely enclosed in square brackets were periodical articles on that case. Let us suppose that the case you are interested in is more recent, and is not included in the latest issue of the *Current Law Case Citator.* You should look at the latest monthly issue of

Current Law for more up to date information. In it you will find a case citator. If the name of your case appears here, is it printed in lower case type? If so, this may mean that there has been a periodical article on the case during the current year (or the case has been judicially considered during the present year). Turn to the monthly issue of *Current Law* indicated, and then to the item number. There you will either find another case in which your case has been cited, or a note of a periodical article which has been written about your case.

Legal Journals Index contains a "Case Index" which provides you with details of periodical articles and commentaries on a case. A particularly useful feature is that it contains entries in the index under the names of both parties to the case: so that, if you can only remember the name of the defendant, it is still possible to trace the case. *Legal Journals Index* covers periodical articles written from 1986 onwards, in all journals published in the U.K. which deal with law.

You can also trace articles on a case by looking in the back of the copies of the *Index to Legal Periodicals* (para. 4–5), under the heading "Table of Cases Commented Upon." Most of these will be American cases, but important British cases are included, if there has been a fairly lengthy article written about them.

If *Legal Journals Index* is not available, and you know roughly when the case was decided, you can look in weekly journals, such as the *New Law Journal*, and in the various relevant specialist periodicals (such as the *Criminal Law Review*) published at that time, to see if there were any shorter editorial comments or criticisms of the decision. Publications such as *Sweet & Maxwell's Students' Law Reporter* will highlight the significance of the decision. The *Law Quarterly Review*, *Modern Law Review* and more specialist journals such as *Public Law*, the *Criminal Law Review*, and *The Conveyancer* usually include notes and comments on recent cases. Because these are relatively short they often do not appear in the list of periodical articles printed in *Current Law*. So, if you are looking for comments on very recent cases, it is often easier to look through the pages and editorial columns of recent issues of the relevant specialist journals. Remember that general periodical articles may include a discussion of the case.

TRIBUNALS

The establishment of the Welfare State led to the creation of a   **2–19** large number of tribunals. They were set up to resolve disputes over entitlement to welfare benefits. Subsequently, other areas, such as problems between landlords and tenants, and between employer and employees because of unfair dismissal, have been subjected to resolution through tribunals. Tribunals can be extremely busy, hearing many thousands of cases each year, but only a comparatively small number of cases are eventually reported in the law reports. Some law reports, such as the *Industrial Cases Reports* and *Immigration Appeals*, carry reports of appeals from the tribunal to an appeal court but the majority of cases heard by tribunals are not reported.

Social Welfare Law

2–20   The most important decisions taken by the social security Commissioners are published individually by HMSO and are subsequently reissued in bound volumes. The form of *citation* for the Commissioners' decisions differs from that used in conventional law reports. All cases reported since 1950 bear the prefix R, followed, in brackets, by an abbreviation for the series. For example, the prefix R(U) indicates a commissioner's decision on unemployment benefit, and R(P) a decision on entitlement to pensions. Within each series, reports are cited by the report number and the year: R(U) 7/62 indicates a reported unemployment benefit decision, case number 7 of 1962.

The following abbreviations are used in the series which are available in the *Reported Decisions of the Social Security Commissioners* published by HMSO:

R(A)	Attendance allowance
R(F)	Child benefit
R(FIS)	Family income supplements
R(G)	General—miscellaneous (maternity benefit, widows benefit, death grant, etc)
R(I)	Industrial injuries benefit
R(M)	Mobility allowance
R(P)	Retirement pensions
R(S)	Sickness and invalidity benefit
R(SB)	Supplementary benefit
R(SSP)	Statutory sick pay
R(U)	Unemployment benefit

Some decisions are not published by HMSO, but they may be read at the Commissioners' offices. They are prefaced by C instead of R. For example, CP 3/81 is a reference to an unpublished 1981 commissioner's decision on pensions and CSB 15/82 is an unreported decision on supplementary benefits.

In 1982 a decision was taken to increase the number of reported cases (see, [1983] *Journal of Social Welfare Law* 46). Now Commissioners "star" decisions which they think should be published. They will be given preference over unreported cases. In exceptional circumstances unreported decisions may still be relied on in formulating appeals. The new system has resulted in some change in the form of the citation. "Starred" decisions are still retained in the Commissioners' files, but the year in "starred" cases *i.e.* those cases which are to be reported, is given in full, *e.g.* CS 161/1982, whilst unreported decisions have only the last two digits of the year, *e.g.* CS 10/81. The reported decision of the case, when it appears, is prefixed by R. as previously. Unreported cases are most common: for instance, there have been more than 75,000 decisions on aspects of social security benefit taken by the Commissioners since 1948, but less than 3,000 of these decisions have been printed by HMSO.

Reported cases from 1948–1950 had a different method of citation. They were prefixed by C, followed by a letter (*not* enclosed in brackets) representing the area of law covered. Thus, CI denotes an early decision on industrial injuries. Scottish or Welsh cases were prefixed with CS and CW respectively. The cases were numbered in sequence. However, only a minority were printed, which has resulted in gaps in the numerical sequences. For example, CWI 17/49 is followed by CWI 20/49. Cases numbered 18 and 19 of 1949 are unreported. The abbreviation (KL) after the citation is an indication that the case had been reported whilst the suffix (K) denotes a decision of limited value.

Earlier reported decisions of the Commissioners were pub-   **2–21**
lished in the *Reported Decisions of the Commissioner under the Social Security and National Insurance (Industrial Injuries) Acts.* The period from 1948–1976 was covered in seven volumes. They are known as the "blue books" because of their colour, and they contain decisions prefixed by R(I). Since 1976 these decisions appear in the bound volumes of *Reported Decisions of the Social Security Commissioner*, which cover all the different R series. The more recent decisions are available individually from HMSO; they are also summarised in the *Journal of Social Welfare Law* and in issues of the *Law Society Gazette*.

Decisions on a particular subject can be traced using   **2–22**
D. Neligan, *Social Security Case Law: Digest of Commissioners' Decisions*, issued by the DHSS and published by HMSO. This publication summarises the majority of the reported decisions, under appropriate subject headings. The appendix provides a

list of decision numbers, which will allow you to trace the summary of a particular case should the full report of the Commissioner's decision be unavailable.

Northern Ireland Commissioners' decisions are referred to in a similar fashion. For example, R 1/81 (I.I.) is a decision on Industrial Injuries benefit from Northern Ireland. Earlier reports were issued under the title *Reported Decisions of the Umpire*, published by HMSO, Belfast, and issued by the Northern Ireland Ministry of Labour and its successor bodies. The current decisions, issued by the Department of Health and Social Services for Northern Ireland, are available individually from HMSO, Belfast. The abbreviation for the series always follows the case number in Northern Ireland decisions; in more recent years the year has preceded the case number. R 1984/2 (SB) is thus a Northern Ireland decision on sickness benefit whilst R (SB) 2/84 is an English case on supplementary benefit. A list of Commissioners' decisions issued by both the Department of Health and Social Security and the Department of Health and Social Services for Northern Ireland is found in HMSO's *Annual Catalogues* under the name of the Department.

HMSO publish a number of guides to social welfare law. *The Law relating to Social Security and Child Benefit*, issued by the DHSS, contains the text of all relevant statutes and regulations. It is often referred to as the *"Brown Book."* The *"Yellow Book"* is a reference to another DHSS publication, *The Law relating to Supplementary Benefits and Family Income Supplements* which again reprints the relevant statutory material. Both publications are in a looseleaf format for easy updating.

Decisions of other Tribunals

2–23   The wide range of tribunals makes a complete guide impossible within the available space. What follows is selective. Immigration appeals are covered by *Immigration Appeals*, published by HMSO. Also available from HMSO are the *Value Added Tax Tribunals Reports*.

Many Lands Tribunal cases appear in *Property, Planning and Compensation Reports* and in *Estates Gazette* and the *Estates Gazette Law Reports*. The latter series also covers leasehold valuation tribunals. Barry Rose published a series of volumes entitled *Lands Tribunal Cases*.

A somewhat dated guide to sources of information on reports of tribunals can be found in (1971) 3 *Law Librarian* 10. Most reported cases, in subjects other than welfare law, appear in standard series of law reports and are conventionally cited. *Current Law* contains references to many tribunal decisions, under appropriate subject headings, and provides a summary for each one. Looseleaf encyclopaedias frequently refer to both published and unpublished decisions in the appropriate subject.

The *Industrial Tribunal Reports*, published until 1978, now form part of *Industrial Cases Reports*. These contain many cases heard by the Employment Appeal Tribunal and many E.A.T. decisions also appear in the *Industrial Relations Law Reports*.

CHAPTER 3

Legislation

INTRODUCTION

3–1 When a Bill (para. 5–9) has been approved by both Houses of Parliament and has received the Royal Assent it normally becomes law immediately, unless there is a statement to the contrary contained in the Act itself. The first printed version of an Act to become available is the copy produced by the Queen's Printer (published by Her Majesty's Stationery Office (HMSO)), which is issued within a few days of the Act receiving the Royal Assent.

A copy of an Act is reproduced below. This enables you to become familiar with its appearance and with the way in which Acts are cited.

PARTS OF AN ACT

3–2 The different parts of an Act (see illustration) are:

1 Short title
2 Official citation
3 Long title
4 Date of Royal Assent, *i.e.* March 17, 1977
5 Enacting formula
6 Section and subsection, *e.g.* section 2, subsection (1)
7 Marginal note
8 Date of commencement

If Schedules or Tables are included they are printed at the end of the Act.

---

c. **4** 1

$$\left[\begin{array}{c} \textbf{Royal Crest} \\ \textbf{omitted} \end{array} \right]$$

Roe Deer (Close Seasons) Act 1977 ①

1977 CHAPTER 4 ②

An Act to Amend the Deer Act 1963 with respect to close seasons for roe deer. ③   [17th March 1977] ④

B E IT ENACTED by the Queen's most Excellent Majesty, by and with the advice and consent of the Lords Spiritual and Temporal, and Commons, in this present Parliament assembled, and by the authority of the same, as follows:— ⑤

1. Schedule 1 to the Deer Act 1963 (which prescribes close Close seasons seasons for deer of the species and descriptions therein mentioned) for roe deer. shall be read and have effect as if under the heading " Roe Deer 1963 c. 36. (Capreolus capreolus) " in the said Schedule there were inserted the words—

" Buck........1st November to 31st March inclusive.". ⑥

2.—(1) This Act may be cited as the Roe Deer (Close Seasons) Short title, and Act 1977. commencement. ⑦

(2) This Act shall come into force on the 1st day of November 1977. ⑧

CITATION OF STATUTES

Statutes (or Acts) are commonly referred to by a shortened ver-   **3–3** sion of their title (the short title) and the year of publication, *e.g.* the Theft Act 1968. Every Act published in a year is given its own individual number and Acts may also be cited by the year in which they were passed and the Act (or chapter) number. Thus the Theft Act was the sixtieth Act passed in 1968 and is cited as 1968, c. 60. "Chapter" is abbreviated to "c." when written, but it is spoken in full.

The present system of citing statutes by their year and chapter number began in 1963. Before that date the system was more complicated. Prior to 1963 statutes were referred to by the year of the monarch's reign (the "regnal year") and the chapter number. For example, a citation 3 Edw. 7, c. 36 is a reference to the Motor Car Act 1903, which was the thirty sixth Act passed in the third year of the reign of Edward VII.

A session of Parliament normally commences in the autumn and continues through into the summer of the following year. A "regnal year" is reckoned from the date of the sovereign's accession to the throne and a session of Parliament may therefore cover more than one regnal year. In the case of Queen Elizabeth II, who came to the throne in February, the first part of a Parliamentary session, from the autumn until February, falls into one regnal year, whilst the latter part of the session of Parliament falls into a different regnal year. Statutes passed before February bear a different regnal year to those passed after the anniversary of her accession to the throne. Two examples make this clearer:

> The Children and Young Persons Act 1956 received the Royal Assent in March 1956, when the Queen had just entered the fifth year of her reign. It was the twenty-fourth Act to receive the Royal Assent during the Parliament which commenced sitting in the autumn of the fourth year of her reign, and which continued in session during the early part of the fifth year of her reign. The Act is therefore cited as 4 & 5 Eliz. 2, c. 24.

> By contrast, the Air Corporations Act 1956 was passed during the following session of Parliament and it received the Royal Assent in December 1956, when the Queen was still in the fifth year of her reign. Since, at that time, there could be no certainty that the Queen would still be on the throne in two months' time or that Parliament would still be in session in February, when she would be entering the sixth year of her reign, the statute was cited as 5 Eliz. 2, c. 3 (*i.e.* the third Act passed in the Parliament held in the fifth year of the reign). When the Queen subsequently survived to enter her sixth year, the statute would henceforth be referred to as 5 & 6 Eliz. 2, c. 3.

Both these Acts are to be found in the 1956 volumes of the statutes, which contain all the Acts passed during that year, regardless of the session of Parliament in which they were passed.

Until 1939, the volumes of the statutes contained all the Acts passed in a particular session of Parliament. After that date, the annual volumes contain all the statutes passed in a calendar year. This can give rise to some confusion. For instance, the volume for 1937 contains the statutes passed in the parliamentary session which extended from November 1936 to October 1937. Thus, some Acts which actually bear the date 1936 are included in the 1937 volume. The volume for 1938 includes some statutes passed in December 1937 (which one might normally expect to find in the 1937 volume.) The simple rule with older Acts is: if it is not the volume you expect to find it in, look in the two volumes on either side of it!

Citation of the Names of Monarchs and their Regnal Years

The names of the monarchs are abbreviated as follows: 3–4

Anne	Ann.
Charles	Car., Chas, *or* Cha.
Edward	Edw. *or* Ed.
Elizabeth	Eliz.
George	Geo.
Henry	Hen.
James	Ja., Jac. *or* Jas.
Mary	Mar. *or* M.
Philip and Mary	Ph. & M. *or* Phil. & Mar.
Richard	Ric. *or* Rich.
Victoria	Vict.
William	Will., Wm. *or* Gul.
William and Mary	Wm. & M., Will. & Mar. *or* Gul. & Mar.

A list of the regnal year of monarchs showing the equivalent calendar year, will be found in *Sweet & Maxwell's Guide to Law Reports and Statutes* (4th ed.), pp. 21–33; in J. E. Pemberton, *British Official Publications* (2nd ed.), pp. 120–125 and at the back of *Osborn's Concise Law Dictionary*.

EDITIONS OF THE STATUTES   3–5

MODERN STATUTES—OFFICIAL EDITIONS

Official copies of the Public General Acts are published   3–6
individually by HMSO as soon as they receive the Royal Assent. The publication of a new Act is recorded in the *Daily List of Government Publications* (see para. 5–18).

Public General Acts and Measures

3–7   At the end of the year, all Acts published during the year are bound together to form the official *Public General Acts and Measures of 19* . . . This series of red volumes has been published since 1831 (originally under the title *Public General Acts*). At the front of the annual volumes will be found a list of all the Acts passed during the year, in alphabetical order, showing where they are to be found in the bound volumes. There is also a chronological list (*i.e.* a list in chapter number order) giving the same information. The General Synod Measures of the Church of England are also printed in full at the back of the annual volumes of the *Public General Acts*. A list of Local and Personal Acts (see para. 3–27) published during the year is printed in the annual volumes, but the texts of Local and Personal Acts are published separately.

Statutes in Force

3–8   *Statutes in Force* is an official collection of all public general Acts of Parliament which are still law. The age of the Act is not important for so long as it is still law then it is covered in this series. The series is arranged by subject, under broad headings, *e.g.* criminal law, employment. These general headings are further sub-divided (*e.g.* criminal law has sub-divisions for offences against the person, sexual offences, piracy and the slave trade, etc.). Within each sub-division the Acts are arranged in date order.

The text of the Act is printed in the form in which it is currently in force: parts of an Act which have been repealed are omitted, and any amendments to an Act (made by subsequent Acts or delegated legislation) are incorporated into the Act as printed. Because it is in looseleaf form it is possible for it to be kept up to date by the issue of replacement copies of Acts which have been revised. The looseleaf format also allows the subscribers to arrange the publication in several different ways, to suit their own needs. Therefore, the exact location of the *Cumulative Supplements*, referred to below, may vary from library to library. You may find that the Cumulative Supplements for each subject are filed at the end of that subject heading; or they may be in a separate set of volumes, containing the supplements for all subjects.

Theoretically *Statutes in Force* should be the first place to turn to for up to date information on a particular Act, or to trace all the Acts dealing with a specific subject. Unfortunately, in practice, it is often badly out of date and lacks a proper index. Students may well find it easier to consult *Halsbury's Statutes* (see para. 3–14) in preference to *Statutes in Force*.

How to use Statutes in Force to find a particular Act of Parliament

1. Look at the volume containing the *Alphabetical lists of groups, Acts and Measures.* This is an alphabetical list of all Acts which are wholly or partly in force in the United Kingdom. The information gives the year of the Act, the chapter number, the group (or subject) number which has been assigned it in *Statutes in Force,* the subject heading, and, where there are several subdivisions of the subject, the appropriate sub-division. For example, if we are looking for the Sexual Offences Act 1956, the following entry appears in the *Alphabetical list of Acts*:

   Sexual Offences Act 1956 (c. 69) . . . 39 (Criminal Law)$_5$

   This entry tells you that the Sexual Offences Act 1956 is found in group 39 of *Statutes in Force,* under the heading "Criminal law." Criminal law is sub-divided into various sub-groups. This Act is printed in sub-group 5.

2. Go to the volumes of *Statutes in Force* and locate group 39, which is entitled "Criminal law." This is a large subject and there are several volumes containing information on criminal law. Find the volume which contains sub-group 5—"Sexual offences and obscenity." Within the sub-group the Acts are arranged in date order, from the earliest to the most recent. The text for the Sexual Offences Act 1956 is, at the time of writing of this book, that which was printed in 1978. Therefore, the Act incorporates all repeals and amendments made to the Act between 1956 and 1978. (See below.) Parts of the Act which have been repealed are shown by a row of dots.

3. We need to find out if there have been any changes to the Act since 1978 (which was when the Act was printed in this series). Turn to the *Cumulative Supplement* and find the entries for Group 39—Criminal law—sub-group 5 "Sexual offences and obscenity." Under the entries for the Sexual Offences Act 1956 we are informed, section by section, of any changes to the Act since 1978. It is important to see when the *Supplement* was published, as it may also be out of date. Look at the front cover for the publication date. If the information in the *Cumulative Supplement* is more than a few months old, we need to check for

An Act to consolidate (with corrections and improvements made under the Consolidation of Enactments (Procedure) Act 1949) the statute law of England and Wales relating to sexual crimes, to the abduction, procuration and prostitution of women and to kindred offences, and to make such adaptations of statutes extending beyond England and Wales as are needed in consequence of that consolidation.   [2nd August 1956]

PART I

OFFENCES, AND THE PROSECUTION AND PUNISHMENT OF OFFENCES

Intercourse by force, intimidation, etc.

1.– (1) It is felony for a man to rape a woman.   Rape.

(2) A man who induces a married woman to have sexual intercourse with him by impersonating her husband commits rape.

s. 1 amended by Sexual Offences (Amendment) Act 1976 (c. 82), s. 1 (1)

2.—(1) It is an offence for a person to procure a woman, by threats   Procurement of
or intimidation, to have unlawful sexual intercourse in any part of the   woman by
world.   threats.

(2) A person shall not be convicted of an offence under this section on the evidence of one witness only, unless the witness is corroborated in some material particular by evidence implicating the accused.

3.—(1) It is an offence for a person to procure a woman, by   Procurement of
false pretences or false representations to have unlawful sexual   woman by false
intercourse in any part of the world.   pretences.

(2) A person shall not be convicted of an offence under this section on the evidence of one witness only, unless the witness is corroborated in some material particular by evidence implicating the accused.

4.—(1) It is an offence for a person to apply or administer to, or   Administering
cause to be taken by, a woman any drug, matter or thing with intent to   drugs to obtain
stupefy or overpower her so as thereby to enable any man to have   or facilitate
unlawful sexual intercourse with her.   intercourse.

1

recent changes to the legislation, using another source. Consult *Is it in force?* (para. 6–23), the *Current Law Legislation Citator* (para. 6–25) or *Halsbury's Statutes* (para. 6–21) for more up to date information.

If you are trying to trace which Acts deal with a particular subject then turn to Chapter 6 (para. 6–16) where this is dealt with more fully.

MODERN STATUTES—UNOFFICIAL COLLECTIONS   3–9

Law Reports: Statutes

The Incorporated Council of Law Reporting publishes, as part   3–10
of the *Law Reports*, a series entitled *Law Reports: Statutes*. These are issued in several parts each year, each part containing the text of one or more Acts. At the end of the year the loose parts are replaced by an annual volume or volumes. Unfortunately, the loose parts are often not published until many months after the Act receives the Royal Assent, so you must look elsewhere for the text of recent Acts (*e.g.* in the individual copies published by HMSO or in annotated versions of the statutes (para. 3–11).

Annotated Editions of the Statutes

If your library does not receive all the statutes automatically, as   3–11
soon as they receive the Royal Assent, then the first copy of a new Act which appears in the library is likely to be an annotated version (*i.e.* the text of the Act is printed and notes are also included on the meaning of words and phrases used in the Act, the effect of the Act, etc.). Such annotated versions of the statutes can be very helpful but you should be aware that the notes have no official standing. Three annotated versions of the statutes are generally available: *Current Law Statutes Annotated*, *Halsbury's Statutes* and *Butterworth's Annotated Legislation Service*.

Current Law Statutes Annotated
Current Law Statutes Annotated publishes the full text of all   3–12
Public General Acts soon after they receive the Royal Assent. The more important Acts are annotated. This means they contain a detailed account of the background to the Act, a summary of the contents of the Act, and definitions and explanations of the meaning of individual sections of the Act. The annotations are in smaller print to avoid confusion with the Act itself.

Although the annotations have no official standing they are extremely useful and the author is often a leading authority on the subject matter. Some Acts are later reprinted as books by the publisher, Sweet & Maxwell.

The current year's Acts are originally issued in a booklet format for filing in the *Service File*. At the front of the Service File are alphabetical and chronological lists of all the Acts included. These lists tell you the chapter numbers (para. 3–3) of each Act. The Acts are arranged in the Service File by their chapter numbers. Not all the Acts are annotated. If the Act you want to look at is printed in *italic* type in the contents list, it means that it has not yet been published in this series. Acts printed on blue paper are not yet annotated, but an annotated replacement version will shortly appear.

The information in the Service File is re-issued during the year in bound volumes of *Current Law Statutes Annotated*, which contains all the Acts passed during the year. Annual volumes have appeared since 1948 when this series commenced publication. You may find that your library subscribes to *Scottish Current Law Statutes Annotated*. Despite the name, this contains information on all English legislation, and the arrangement is identical with *Current Law Statutes*.

Butterworth's Annotated Legislation Service

3–13 *Butterworth's Annotated Legislation Service* was formerly called *Butterworth's Emergency Legislation Service*. It reprints the text of selected Acts, with notes. Many of the volumes cover only one Act, with very detailed annotations. Every two years a cumulative index to the series is published, which lists all the Acts passed since 1939 and shows where they are to be found in the series. A number of the titles in this series have also been published individually as books, *e.g.* R. M. Goode, *Introduction to the Consumer Credit Act 1974*. The emphasis is on statutes which will be of use to the practitioner.

Halsbury's Statutes of England

3–14 *Halsbury's Statutes* is particularly useful for finding out what Acts of Parliament exist dealing with a particular subject. For this reason it is more fully dealt with in para. 6–19. In this chapter we explain how you can find the text of a particular Act in *Halsbury's Statutes*, and how to check whether the Act has been amended, or even repealed (*i.e.* what is its present content or whether it is still law).

The Fourth Edition

3–15 The fourth edition of *Halsbury's Statutes* is currently being published and will be completed in 1989. Thereafter an *Index* and alphabetical and chronological lists of statutes covering the 50 volumes will be issued. If these have been published consult them. If the edition is incomplete then look at the *Alphabetical List of Statutes* which is revised regularly. This contains a list of all Acts of Parliament which have been issued in the fourth edition. (If the Act you want is not included in this list it may be in the third edition as some volumes have yet to be replaced. (See para. 3–17.) The entry tells you the volume number (in heavy type) and the page number in *Halsbury's Statutes* (4th edition) where you will find the full text of the Act. If the volume number in the *List of Statutes* is followed by (S) you will find the Act printed in the looseleaf *Current Statutes Service* volume under the volume, title and page number given. Some Acts are not printed in full in one place, but are divided up, each portion of the Act being printed under the most appropriate title. If you want to look at the complete text of an Act which has been split up in this way, it may be easier to find the Act in the *Public General Acts* (para. 3–7) or *Law Reports: Statutes* (para. 3–10).

If you want to find the text of a very recent Act, look in the alphabetical List of statutes which appears in the first volume of the *Current Statutes Service,* under the heading "Contents." It is important to read the note at the beginning of the *List,* since different forms of type (italic type, brackets, etc.) are used to indicate where the entry is to be found. The majority of the entries give the volume, subject heading and page. This indicates that the text of the Act will be found in the looseleaf *Current Statutes Service* binder under that volume and title.

If the Act you want is not in the *Alphabetical List of Statutes* or in the "Contents" section of the *Current Statutes Service* then it may be available in those volumes of the previous (3rd) edition of the *Halsbury's Statutes* which have not yet been replaced (see below).

Once you have found your Act, either in the main volumes, or in the *Current Service* binders, you will find the official text of the Act printed in large type. Following each section there are notes, in smaller type, giving the meaning of words or phrases used, referring to cases on the interpretation of that section and providing details of any amendments which have been made to the text of the Act since it was first passed. You will also find references to statutory instruments which have been passed under the authority granted by that Act. At the beginning of each Act you are informed when it became law, and provided with a summary of the main provisions of the Act, together with an indication of whether the Act applies to Northern Ireland.

It is important to check that the information on the Act is still up to date (*i.e.* it has not been amended or repealed). To do this, make a note of the volume number, title and page number which contains the relevant Act. Turn to the *Cumulative Supplement.* This lists, volume by volume, and page by page, all changes which have taken place in the law since the main volumes were written. Turn to the entry in the *Supplement* for your volume and title, and see if there is an entry for your page number. If there is, then there has been a change in the law, and you must read the information in the *Cumulative Supplement* in conjunction with the entry in the main volume. If there is no entry, then the information in the main volume is unchanged, at least until a few months ago.

Very recent changes to the Act are found in the looseleaf *Noter-up Service* binder, under the appropriate volume, title and page number. This shows any amendment which have been made to your Act during the last few months. Your information is now up to date.

SUMMARY: TO FIND A PARTICULAR ACT IN HALSBURY'S STATUTES (4TH EDITION)

3–16
1. Look in the *Alphabetical List of Statutes,* or, for recent Acts, in the first volume of the *Current Statutes Service* binders (under "Contents"). If there is no entry in either, consult the index to the previous (3rd) edition.
2. Locate the Act, either in the main volumes, or the *Current Statutes Service,* as indicated in the *List of Statutes.* (If (S) follows the volume number, look in the looseleaf *Current Statutes Service.*)
3. To check if the law has changed since the Act was passed, consult, under the appropriate volume, title and page number:
   (i) The *Cumulative Supplement* and
   (ii) The *Noter-up Service* binder.
   Read the information found there in conjunction with that in the main volume. You are now up to date.

Halsbury's Statutes (3rd edition)
3–17 The third edition of Halsbury's Statutes is currently being replaced by a 4th edition. This will be completed in 1989. In the meantime it is still necessary to use the 3rd edition to trace the text of some Acts which have yet to appear in the 4th edition.

If you have checked the *Alphabetical List of Statutes* provided with the 4th edition, and the list in the front of the first *Current*

Statutes Service binder, and your Act does not appear in either, then it is still available only in the 3rd edition.

To locate the Act in the 3rd edition, turn to the *Table of Statutes and Index for Volumes 1–50*. This includes all Acts passed before 1981 (however old) which were printed in the 3rd edition, and tells you where to locate them in the 3rd edition volumes.

If the Act was passed between 1981 and 1984, consult the list of Acts at the front of the *Cumulative Supplement* to the 3rd edition. This refers you to the relevant volume and page number in the 3rd edition. Once you have located the Act in the main volumes of the 3rd edition you must find out if the law has changed subsequently. To do this look in:

(i) the *Cumulative Supplement* to the 3rd edition volumes; *and*

(ii) the *Noter-up Service* binder (to the 4th edition). Note that there are two sequences in the "Noter-up" section: make sure you consult the Noter-up for the *3rd* edition (unreplaced) volumes.

You must look in *both* the *Cumulative Supplement* and the *Noter-up* to see if there are any entries for your volume and page numbers. If there is an entry then the law has been changed since the main volumes of the 3rd edition were written. The *Cumulative Supplement* and the *Noter-up* provide details of these changes.

SUMMARY: USING THE 3RD EDITION

1. Only consult the 3rd edition if you have failed to locate   **3–18**
   the Act in the 4th edition (consult *Alphabetical List of Statutes* in the 4th edition and "Contents" in first *Current Statutes Service* binder).
2. To find the Act in the 3rd edition, consult the *Table of Statutes and Index for Volumes 1–50*. If there is no entry, consult the list of statutes at the front of the *Cumulative Supplement to the 3rd Edition* (for 1981–1984 Acts).
3. To bring the information up to date, consult:
   (i) the *Cumulative Supplement* to the 3rd edition under the appropriate volume and page number, *and*
   (ii) the looseleaf *Noter-up Service*—(entries for the 3rd edition)—under the appropriate volume and page numbers. You are now up to date.

OLDER STATUTES

3–19 So far we have been concerned with modern statutes. However, it will sometimes be necessary to look at an Act of Parliament which dates back several centuries. The earliest statute which is still part of the law of the land was passed in 1267. The first parliamentary statute dates from 1235 (the Statute of Merton) although some collections of the statutes commence in 1225. Collections of the legislation prior to 1225 do exist (*e.g.* A. J. Robertson, *The Laws of the Kings of England from Edmund to Henry I*) but they are not regarded as forming part of the Statutes of the Realm.

3–20 COLLECTIONS OF OLDER STATUTES

Statutes of the Realm

3–21 Produced by the Record Commission, *Statutes of the Realm* is generally regarded as the most authoritative collection of the early statutes. It covers statutes from 1235 to 1713, including those no longer in force, and prints the text of all Private Acts before 1539. There are alphabetical and chronological indexes of all the Acts and there is a subject index to each volume, as well as an index to the complete work.

Statutes at Large

3–22 The title of *Statutes at Large* was given to various editions of the statutes, most of which were published during the eighteenth century. They normally cover statutes published between the thirteenth and the eighteenth or nineteenth centuries.

Acts and Ordinances of the Interregnum

3–23 Acts passed during the Commonwealth are excluded from the collections of the statutes mentioned above. They can be found in C. H. Firth and R. S. Rait, *Acts and Ordinances of the Interregnum 1642–1660*.

Statutes in Force

3–24 A complete collection of all statutes, of whatever date, which are still in force is found in *Statutes in Force* (para. 3–8). Older statutes which are still part of the law of the land are also reprinted in *Halsbury's Statutes* (para. 3–14).

The various indexes to the statutes, which enable you to trace all the legislation on a particular subject which is still in force, are dealt with in Chapter 6.

SUMMARY OF THE COLLECTIONS OF STATUTES 3–25

TEXT OF OLDER STATUTES

Statutes of the Realm (1235–1713)
Statutes at Large (1225—approx. 1869) (depending on the editions available in your library)

MODERN STATUTES

Public General Acts and Measures (1831—date)
Law Reports: Statutes (1866—date)

ANNOTATED VERSIONS

Current Law Statutes (1948—date)
Halsbury's Statutes of England
Butterworth's Annotated Legislation Service (1939—date)

COLLECTIONS OF STATUTES IN FORCE

Statutes in Force
Halsbury's Statutes of England

HOW TO TRACE AN ACT IF YOU DO NOT KNOW ITS DATE

If you know the name of an Act but not the date when it was 3–26 passed, you can trace it in the Alphabetical Table of Statutes at the front of the *Current Law Legislation Citator* (para. 6–25) or in the *Alphabetical List of Statutes* contained in the 4th edition of *Halsbury's Statutes* (para. 3–15). (Because the 4th edition is currently incomplete you may also need to look at the *Table of Statutes and Index for Volumes 1–50* of the 3rd edition.) These sources will provide you with the year when the Act was passed. When you have the year you can easily look up your Act in the relevant volume of the *Public General Acts* or other editions of the statutes.

LOCAL AND PERSONAL ACTS

In addition to Public General Acts, which apply to the whole 3–27 population, or a substantial part of it, there are also published each year a few Local and Personal Acts. These Acts affect only a particular area of the country or a particular individual or body, *e.g.* Alexandra Park and Palace Act 1985: Valarie Mary Hill and Alan Monk (Marriage Enabling) Act 1985.

Citation of Local and Personal Acts

3–28   In the case of a Local Act, the chapter number is printed in roman numerals, to distinguish it from the Public General Act of the same number. Thus the Alexandra Park and Palace Act may be cited as 1985, c. ii (*i.e.* the 2nd Local Act passed in 1985), whilst 1985, c. 2 is the citation for a Public General Act, the Elections (Northern Ireland) Act.

Personal Acts are cited in the same way as Public General Acts, but with the chapter number printed in italics, *e.g. c. 3.* The citation of Local and Personal Acts was amended in 1963. Prior to that date they are cited by regnal years, in the same way as Public General Acts; *e.g.* 12 & 13 Geo. 5, c. xiv relates to a local Act, whilst 12 & 13 Geo. 5, c. 14 is a Public Act (para. 3–3).

Although most libraries will possess copies of the Public General Acts in some form, the Local and Personal Acts are not so widely available, as they are not printed in the volumes of *Public General Acts,* nor in any of the other major collections of statutes.

INDEXES TO STATUTES

3–29   Indexes to Local and Personal Acts are: the *Index to Local and Personal Acts 1801–1947;* the *Supplementary Index to the Local and Personal Acts 1948–1966,* and the *Local and Personal Acts 19—: Tables and Index* (published annually). A list (but not the text) of Local and Personal Acts passed during the year is included in the annual volumes of *Public General Acts.* More recent Acts can be traced in the daily and monthly lists of government publications (see para. 5–18). For public general Acts consult *Halsbury's Statutes of England* (para. 6–19) *Current Law Legislation Citator* (para. 6–25) or the *Index to the Statutes* (para. 6–18).

DELEGATED LEGISLATION

3–30   In an attempt to reduce the length and complexity of statutes, Parliament may grant to some other authority (usually a Minister of the Crown) power to make detailed rules and regulations on a topic which has been covered in more general terms by an Act of Parliament. For instance, the various Road Traffic Acts give the Secretary of State for Transport power, amongst other things, to impose speed limits on particular stretches of road, to vary these limits at any time, to create experimental traffic schemes, introduce new road signs, control the construction and use of vehicles, and impose regulations concerning parking, pedestrian crossings, vehicle licences, insurance and numerous other aspects of the law relating to motor vehicles. An advantage of this power is that the rules can be readily changed, without the necessity for Parliamentary debate and approval of every case. One disadvantage is that all the regulations (over 2,000 of them are issued every year) are part of the law of the land, and the citizen may be expected to be acquainted with each and every one of them—a task which is clearly impossible.

The Nature of Statutory Instruments

Delegated (or subordinate) legislation is a phrase which covers   **3–31** a number of different terms. Regulations, rules, orders and by-laws are different types of delegated legislation. The majority, but not all, delegated legislation, is published in the form of statutory instruments. Like statutes, statutory instruments may be of general or of purely local interest; local instruments (*e.g.* by-laws) are not always printed and published in the normal way. An Order in Council, made by the Queen and her Privy Council, is also a form of statutory instrument, and these are printed as an appendix to the annual volumes of statutory instruments, together with Royal Proclamations and Letters Patent.

Citation of Statutory Instruments

Several statutory instruments are published by HMSO on most   **3–32** most working days. Every instrument published during the year is given its own individual number. The official citation is: S.I. year/number. For example, The Road Vehicles (Construction and Use) Regulations 1986 was the one thousand and seventy eighth statutory instrument to be passed in 1986 and its citation is therefore S.I. 1986/1078.

Tracing Statutory Instruments

The statutory instruments published each day are listed in the   **3–33** *Daily List of Government Publications*. Every week a summary of the most important new instruments is printed in the coloured pages of the *New Law Journal*. The *Solicitor's Journal*, many specialist journals, and *Current Law*, all note recent changes in the law which have been brought about by statutory instruments. A *List of Statutory Instruments* is published monthly, showing the instruments published during a particular month; these monthly issues are replaced by an annual list.

In addition to containing alphabetical and numerical lists of all instruments issued during a particular period, the *List of Statutory Instruments* also prints the instruments under subject headings; a detailed Subject Index is provided, so that changes in the law relating to a particular topic can be easily traced.

The individual statutory instruments (which may not be available in all libraries) are replaced by a number of bound volumes, which cover the instruments published during a particular year. The instruments are now printed in these volumes in numerical order, although, until 1961, they were arranged by subject. The last volume of each yearly set of volumes now contains a subject index to all the instruments published during that year. The volumes for the year are in parts. The last volume of each part contains an interim index which is replaced by the complete index published in the last volume of Part III.

Statutory instruments on a subject can be traced by using the *Index to Government Orders* and its supplement, (see para. 6–28) together with the annual and monthly *Lists of Statutory Instruments*, which bring the information up to date. *Halsbury's Statutory Instruments* (see para. 6–27) can also be used to trace statutory instruments dealing with a particular subject.

All the statutory instruments which were still in force at the end of 1948 were reprinted in a series of volumes entitled *Statutory Rules and Orders and Statutory Instruments Revised.* This was arranged in subject order, showing all the instruments which were then in force. It is possible to check whether a particular instrument is still in force by using the *Table of Government Orders* (see para. 6–31) or by checking in *Halsbury's Statutory Instruments* (see para. 6–27).

If your library does not possess a complete set of statutory instruments (and many of the volumes are no longer available) then you may be able to trace the text of the instrument in *Halsbury's Statutory Instruments* or in one of the many specialist looseleaf encyclopedias which are now being published, *e.g.* the *Encyclopedia of Housing Law and Practice.* Failing this, a summary may often be found in *Current Law* or the *Current Law Year Book* under the appropriate subject heading (there is a list at the beginning of each Year Book showing where each instrument appears in the volume).

CHAPTER 4

Periodicals

TYPES OF PERIODICALS

Periodicals (or journals) are important to lawyers: they keep   **4–1**
you up to date with the latest developments in the law, and provide comments and criticisms of the law. In your preparations
for seminars, essays and moots, it is essential to show that you
are aware of what has been written in journals. You cannot rely
exclusively on textbooks which are always, to some degree, out
of date, and which may provide inadequate information on
some topics. You should develop the habit of glancing at the
title pages of recently published periodicals, which are normally kept on a separate display shelf. This will help to keep
you up to date with recent cases, statutes, official publications,
comments and scholarly articles.

For convenience, we can divide periodicals into four different
types, although there is some overlap between them. However,
they are treated similarly in libraries. There are a number of
weekly publications, such as the *New Law Journal, Justice of the
Peace, Solicitors' Journal* and *Law Society Gazette,* which aim to
keep practitioners and students up to date. They provide
reports and comments on recent cases, statutes, statutory
instruments, and the latest trends and developments in the law,
together with some longer articles, usually on topical or practical subjects. In contrast are the academic journals, published
less frequently, which contain lengthy articles on a variety of
topics, comments on recent cases, statutes and government
publications, and book reviews. Some examples are the *Law*

Quarterly Review, Modern Law Review (six a year) and the *Journal of Law and Society* (four a year). The third category is the specialist journal dealing with particular aspects of the law. This type of journal combines notes of recent developments with longer articles on aspects of that area of the law. Examples of such specialist journals are the *Criminal Law Review* (monthly), *Industrial Law Journal* (four a year), *Legal Action* (monthly) and *Family Law* (ten a year). The final group is foreign periodicals. English language publications, particularly from common law jurisdictions, are of assistance in providing a comparative view of similar United Kingdom issues. Examples of this group are the *Yale Law Journal* (eight a year), *Harvard Law Review* (eight a year), *Canadian Bar Review* (four a year) and the *Australian Law Journal* (monthly).

TRACING ARTICLES IN LEGAL JOURNALS

4–2   When you are collecting information on a subject you will be faced by two problems:

(1) Has there been anything written on this subject? Is there any commentary published on a particular case, statute, Law Commission report, or other document?
(2) Having found the details of apparently relevant material, how do I obtain a copy of the journal?

To answer the first question you need to use indexes to periodicals (including abstracts); to answer the second query you must consult the periodicals catalogue or, possibly, a *union list of periodicals*. A *Union List* covers the holdings of a number of libraries. Therefore, the periodicals listed may not be available in your local library.

There are a number of sources which can be used to trace periodical articles. You may not need, or wish, to consult all of them, but you should remember that the information given, and the journals covered, varies, and by using only one index you may miss helpful material.

Legal Journals Index

4–3   This began publication in 1986, and is the most useful source for tracing articles in British journals. It covers articles from *all* the legal journals published in the United Kingdom, and it is therefore more comprehensive than *Current Law*, the *Index to Legal Periodicals* and other titles mentioned later in this chapter.

SAMPLE ENTRY FROM *LEGAL JOURNALS INDEX*

Title of
article

Subject
Heading

Abstract or brief
description of the
article

INHERITANCE TAX. Exempt transfers. Protective trusts.
A determined failure. (Whether protective trusts had failed or
determined). Cholmondeley v Commissioners of Inland Revenue [1986]
S.T.C. 384. David Harris.
Tax.1986, 117(3062), 440-441

Case which is
main topic of
article

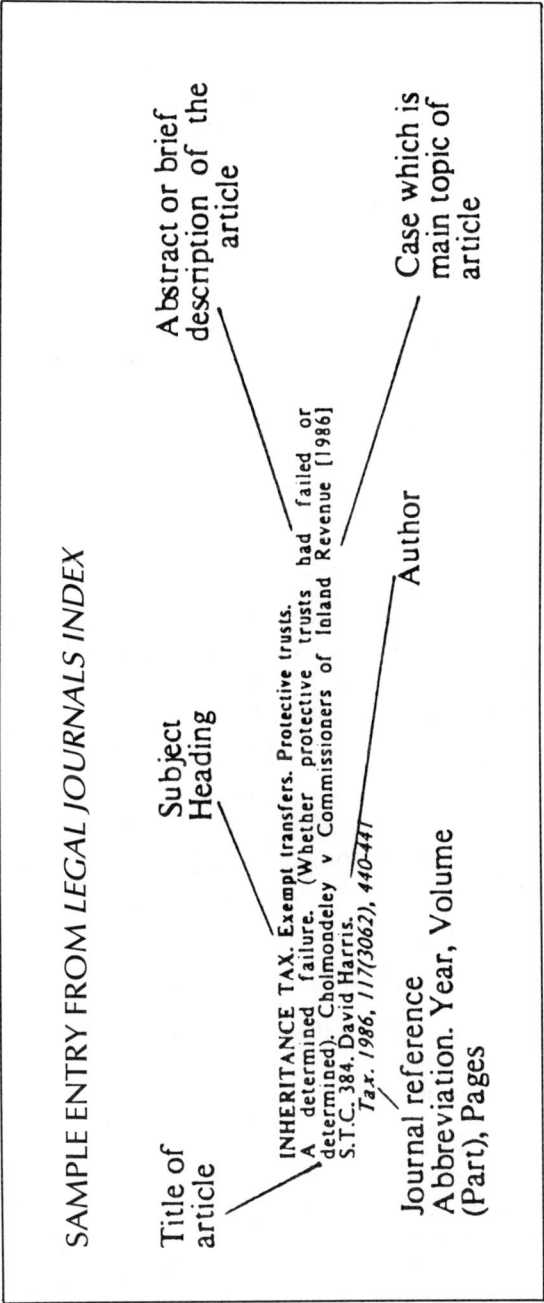

Author

Journal reference
Abbreviation. Year, Volume
(Part), Pages

The entries are arranged under subject headings; the same article may be indexed several times, under different subject headings. Where the title of the article does not clearly indicate the subject covered, a brief summary or description is added.

There are separate indexes under authors, under the names of cases, under books reviewed, and under the titles of Acts and other legislation which have been the subject of a periodical article or extended commentary. The case index is particularly useful, since it has entries under both the plaintiff and the defendant: so if you only know the name of the defendant, and are therefore unable to trace the case in the *Current Law Case Citators*, this index may enable you to locate it.

Legal Journals Index is issued monthly, with quarterly and annual cumulative volumes. The editors are able to undertake searches for information on a specific subject, for a fee, and to provide photocopies of the articles included in the index.

Current Law

4–4   *Current Law* commenced in 1947 and is arranged by subject (see para. 6–9). At the end of each subject heading, in each of the monthly issues, is a list of recent books and periodical articles which have been published on that subject. All the books listed separately under the relevant subject heading are also listed together on the back cover of each issue.

When the *Current Law Year Book* is published, the index to periodical articles is found at the back of the volume. (Before 1956, periodical articles were listed at the end of each subject heading.) The *Current Law Year Books* are useful for tracing older material. If you want a full list of recent periodical articles written in British journals then consult the *Legal Journals Index* (para. 4–3).

Index to Legal Periodicals

4–5   The *Index to Legal Periodicals* which commenced in 1908 is published in the USA. It also includes some journals from Britain, Canada, Ireland, Australia and New Zealand. If in doubt about the journals covered consult the list of periodicals indexed. This list appears in each issue.

Entries are arranged under author and also under the subject, in one single alphabetical sequence. There are separate indexes at the back of each issue which give cases and statutes which have been commented upon in periodical articles, and book reviews. The headings use American terminology and spelling and this may cause occasional difficulties. (For material relating to U.K. law students should consult *Legal Journals Index* as it is more comprehensive although it did not commence until 1986.) A typical subject entry from the *Index to Legal Periodicals* is printed below, with numbered explanations:

CONTRACTS[1]: consideration
Bankers' commercial credits among the High Trees.[2] M. Clarke.[3]
    Camb. L.J. 33: 260–92 N '74[4]
Contract restitution and total failure of consideration.[2] C.P.
    Seepersad.[3] New L.J. 123: 435–8 My 10 '73.[5]

[1] subject heading
[2] title of article
[3] author
[4] in Cambridge Law Journal, Vol. 33, pp. 260–292 (dated November, 1974)
[5] article in New Law Journal, Vol. 123, pp. 435–438 (dated May 10, 1973)

A typical author entry is printed below:

SEEPERSAD, C.P.[1]
Contracts: consideration[2] (C)[3]
Restitution[2] (C)[3]

[1] author entry for the second of the specimen subject entries (above)
[2] headings under which articles by Seepersad appear
[3] first letter of first word of the title (*i.e.* Contract . . .) of the article. The same article may appear under several subject headings. In this example it occurs under two headings: Contract and Restitution.

A list of the subject headings used in the *Index,* and of all the abbreviations used, is found at the beginning of the volume. The *Index* is published 11 times a year. There is a quarterly cumulative edition. These copies are later replaced by an annual volume containing all the periodical articles for that year. The annual volumes are replaced by volumes (called "cumulations") covering articles written during a three year period.

Index to Foreign Legal Periodicals

The *Index to Foreign Legal Periodicals* commenced in 1960. It **4–6** indexes articles on international and comparative law and the municipal law of all countries except the United States, United Kingdom and the common law of Commonwealth countries.

Many of the articles are not in English. The series contains sub-ject, geographical, book reviews and author indexes. Publi-cation is usually in a three-year cycle, at the end of which a cumulative volume is produced.

Halsbury's Laws

4–7   A selection of periodical articles written on a subject during a particular year can be found in the *Annual Abridgement* to *Hals-bury's Laws of England*. At the beginning of the entry for each subject there is a selective list of periodical articles written on that subject during the year.

A short cut for finding out what has been written on your subject is to examine the footnotes in a recent book or period-ical article on the topic. If well researched it will give you numerous citations to read. However, be warned, you may end up with an incomplete coverage and also possibly one which supports the view of the author!

HOW TO TRACE LAW-RELATED PERIODICAL ARTICLES

4–8   The effective study of law will of necessity take you into other disciplines. Articles on subjects such as housing, delinquency, sentencing, families, and town and country planning are found in a wide range of journals, many of which are not solely con-cerned with law and which as a consequence are not usually found in a law collection. You may wish to consult journals in other sections of the general library which carry articles by sociologists, economists, criminologists, social administrators or historians. To trace social science and arts material on law-related topics will require recourse to a different selection of indexes, most of which will be housed outside the law collec-tion.

Index to Periodical Articles Related to Law

4–9   This index commenced in 1958. It contains a selective coverage of articles published in English throughout the world and which are not included in either the *Index to Legal Periodicals* or the *Index to Foreign Legal Periodicals*. There is an index to articles by subject, a list of journals indexed and an author index. The first cumulative volume covered the period 1958–1968. The second cumulative volume takes you up to and includes 1973 and the third cumulative volume is to 1978. Thereafter, it appears quarterly, the last issue of a year being a cumulative issue.

The British Humanities Index

This covers a wide range of subjects and includes articles in   4–10
newspapers and popular weekly journals, as well as more
scholarly periodicals. Entries are under subjects and authors.

Social Sciences Index

This index, which replaces the *Social Sciences and Humanities*   4–11
Index, covers law, criminology, sociology, political science,
sociological aspects of medicine and other socio-legal topics.
Entries are under authors and subjects.

Criminology and Penology Abstracts

This is arranged by subject, each entry having its own individ-   4–12
ual number. There are detailed subject and author indexes
referring to individually numbered entries.

Psychological Abstracts

The scope of this is far wider than the title suggests, covering   4–13
abortion, drug use, alcoholics, etc. Entries are under subject and
there are detailed subject and author indexes.

Current Contents: Social and Behavioural Sciences

This covers the contents of recent issues of 1,160 journals in the   4–14
social and behavioural sciences (including law). The arrangement is by subject, with author and "key word" subject
indexes. It is published weekly.

The Philosopher's Index

This is a subject and author index with abstracts. Philosophy   4–15
and inter-disciplinary periodicals and books are indexed.

Sociological Abstracts

This abstracting service is indexed by subject and author. It   4–16
includes sections on sociology of law, police, penology and
correctional problems.

These are by no means the only subject indexes to the contents of periodicals. Indexes exist covering many different subjects. The library staff will help you find out which indexing or abstracting services are available to cover the subjects which interest you.

NEWSPAPER ARTICLES

4–17   In addition to factual reporting, newspapers often contain commentary, analysis and background information on recent legal developments and controversial topics. Some libraries operate a cutting service of the "quality" newspapers such as *The Times* and *The Guardian*, as well as cutting out the law reports. Many libraries keep back copies of *The Times* or have them on microfilm. An *Index to The Times* which includes "The Sunday Times" (but not the "Financial Times," which has a separate index) is published. This will help you identify and locate relevant material. *The Guardian Index* serves a similar function. Another source is *Keesing's Contemporary Archives*, established in 1931, which allows you to trace the date of a specific event. Thereafter you can turn to the newspapers and commentaries of that period.

LOCATING PERIODICALS IN THE LIBRARY

4–18   Having traced an article how do you locate the relevant copy of the journal? The first problem may be to decipher the abbreviation which has been used for the name of the journal. If you obtained your information from a periodical index or from the *Current Law Case Citators* a list of the abbreviations will be found at the front of the volume. If the information was obtained from elsewhere, *e.g.* from a footnote in a textbook, look up the abbreviation in *Legal Journals Index*, or D. Raistrick, *Index to Legal Citations and Abbreviations*, or in the *Index to Legal Periodicals*, in Sweet & Maxwell's *Guide to Law Reports and Statutes* or in Appendix 1 of this book.

Once the full title of the periodical is known, look up the name of the journal in the periodicals catalogue. The catalogue entry will guide you to the part of the library in which the journal is to be found, and will indicate which volumes of the journal are available in your library. If it is a law periodical they are usually arranged in alphabetical order. In a few cases the arrangement is less obvious (see para. 1–9).

LOCATING PERIODICALS FROM OTHER SOURCES

If the journal is not available in your library you may wish to try   **4–19**
to obtain it from elsewhere. Legal periodicals can be traced by
consulting the *Union List of Legal Periodicals* (published by the
University of London Institute of Advanced Legal Studies)
which gives the location of journals in libraries throughout the
U.K. Similar union lists are published covering more
specialised subjects, such as air law literature, West European
legal literature, Commonwealth and South African law, and
United States legal literature. If you wish to consult a large
number of journals or reports it may be more convenient to go
to another library and use the material there. (Before doing so
you should contact the librarian and ask for permission). If only
a few articles are required it may be easier to ask your library to
obtain them through the *interlibrary loan service*. Details of this
service may be obtained from the interlibrary loans staff in your
library. If you wish to use this service plan ahead and allow
time for your request to be processed and for the material to
arrive. This national facility may be available to students as well
as staff and is invaluable for materials not available in local law
libraries. The library staff may also be able to advise on which
periodicals are available in other libraries in the area.

CHAPTER 5

Government Publications

INTRODUCTION

5–1 Government publications are notoriously difficult to trace in a library. Some of them are issued by Her Majesty's Stationary Office (HMSO) and thus appear in official lists of government publications. Other publications are issued directly by government departments, such as the DHSS, and cannot readily be traced except through the series of microfiche of *British Official Publications not Published by HMSO*. This is issued by Chadwyck-Healey, with its accompanying *Catalogue of British Official Publications not published by HMSO*.

In this chapter we look at those government publications most likely to be encountered by law students, *e.g.*

Command Papers
House of Commons and House of Lords Papers
Bills
Official Reports of Parliamentary Debates (Hansard)

Further details of all the publications mentioned, together with specimen pages, are found in John E. Pemberton, *British Official Publications* (2nd ed.), which is now somewhat dated. A more recent guide to the literature is by D. Butcher, *Official Publications in Britain*. Acts of Parliament, which are, of course, government publications, were covered in Chapter 3.

This is a field in which you should not hesitate to seek the advice of library staff whenever you are in difficulty. Most libraries which have a collection of government publications have at least one person who is responsible for helping readers to use this material.

PARLIAMENTARY AND NON-PARLIAMENTARY PUBLICATIONS

HMSO publishes several thousand items each year. This represents only a small proportion of the vast number of official documents issued annually. HMSO divides publications into two groups: parliamentary publications and non-parliamentary publications. It is often difficult to know into which of these two categories an item falls, but the distinction is important for in many libraries the two categories are treated differently.   5–2

Parliamentary publications (or *parliamentary papers*) are those documents which are required by Parliament in the course of its work, *e.g.* Bills, records of the proceedings in the House, and information papers on a wide variety of topics. If your library has a complete collection of all parliamentary publications, these may be bound together in volumes containing all the material produced during a particular session of Parliament. These volumes are known as *sessional papers* or *sessional sets*. The conventional arrangement of the sessional papers until 1968/69 divided the parliamentary papers relating to the House of Commons into four main groups, *i.e.*

Group	Comprising	
1. Bills	House of Commons Bills	Drafts of public Bills arranged in alphabetical order by the titles of the Bills.
2. Reports from Committees	House of Commons Papers	Reports from House of Commons committees.
3. Reports from Commissioners	House of Commons Papers and Command Papers	Reports from other committees, Royal Commissions, etc.
4. Accounts and papers	House of Commons Papers and Command Papers	Accounts, "white papers," estimates. Treaty series, and other state papers.

From 1969/70 to 1978/79 two groupings were used: Bills (alphabetically) and reports, accounts and papers, arranged alphabetically by subject. Since the 1979/80 session there have been separate sequences of Bills, House of Commons Papers and Command Papers, each arranged in alphabetical order. A *Sessional Index* provides a subject approach to the material. The Sessional Papers are also available on microfiche. These are arranged by type of material (Bills, Command papers, etc.) and then in numerical order within each session.

If the library has a large collection of government publications it does not usually enter parliamentary publications in the library catalogues. Instead it relies on the indexes produced by HMSO (para. 5–18) to trace relevant material in the collection. If your library has only a small collection of parliamentary publications these may be catalogued individually (usually under the heading "Great Britain"). There may also be an entry in the catalogue under the title of the report but library practice on this does vary.

More recent parliamentary publications (*i.e.* those published within the last two to three years) will usually be gathered together in boxes. Every parliamentary paper has its own individual number and the papers will usually be arranged by these numbers in boxes comprising:

House of Commons Papers
House of Commons Bills
House of Lords Papers and Bills
Command Papers

These recent publications can also be traced through the various indexes to government publications (para. 5–18). You will probably find that all the parliamentary publications have been housed in an official publications collection, in a separate area of the library (which may not form part of the law library). In some libraries government publications' collections may be held on microfiche or microfilm. Therefore, you should ask the librarians whether there is a collection of government publications available and get them to show you where they are located and how they are arranged.

Non-parliamentary publications may be scattered throughout the library, according to the subjects with which they deal. Unlike parliamentary publications, they are normally entered in the library catalogues, usually under the heading "Great Britain" followed by the name of the government department which produced the publication, *e.g.* Great Britain. *Home Office.* A very large number of works issued by government bodies are not published by HMSO but directly by the relevant body. Many of these publications can be traced in the *Catalogue of British Official Publications Not Published by HMSO.* Much of the listed material is made available on microfiche by Chadwyck-Healey.

AVAILABILITY OF PARLIAMENTARY PAPERS

5–3   Older parliamentary papers may only be available in your library on microfiche or microfilm (para. 5–22) or in the form of reprints published by bodies such as the Irish University Press. (These reprints are arranged in subject order). If your library does not have a complete collection of older material, it may be possible to trace a summary of a report in the *Breviates of Parliamentary Papers,* produced by P. & G. Ford. Material which is still in print may be purchased from any branch of HMSO (addresses appear on the *Daily List* and in the monthly and annual catalogues) or through any bookseller. Photocopies of out of print publications can be purchased from HMSO. The current cost of new publications is given in the catalogue *HMSO in Print* (on microfiche). Publications may also be available on loan through the inter-library loan service.

PARLIAMENTARY PUBLICATIONS

We shall now look in more detail at some of the most important   5–4
types of parliamentary publications and how they are arranged in the library.

Command Papers

This is a very important category of parliamentary papers and   5–5
one to which you may frequently be referred. It includes many major government reports, *e.g. The Scarman Report on the Brixton Disorders* (1981), some, but not all, of the reports of the Law Commission, and the reports of all Royal Commissions. A Command Paper is, as it states on the front cover, presented to Parliament "By Command of Her Majesty." In practice, this means that it is presented to Parliament by a Minister of the Crown on his own initiative; its preparation has not been requested by Parliament. Command Papers are often statements of government policy, which are likely to be the subject of future legislation, or they are presented for the information of the Members of Parliament. Command Papers include:

  statements of government policy (often referred to as "white papers");
  some annual statistics and annual reports (many more are issued as non-parliamentary publications);
  reports of Royal Commissions;
  reports of some committees (other committee reports may be issued as non-parliamentary publications);
  reports of tribunals of enquiry, *e.g.* Report of the tribunal appointed to inquire into the Vassall Case (Cmnd. 2009);
  state papers (including the Treaty series (para. 12–7).

Citation and Location of Command Papers

5-6   Command Papers are each given an individual number, prefaced by an abbreviation for the word "command." This abbreviation, and the number, are printed at the bottom left hand corner of the cover of the report. The numbers used run on continuously from one session of Parliament to another. The present abbreviation, "Cm." has been used for publications issued since 1986. Prior to 1986 different abbreviations of the word "command" were used. They are:

1st series 1833–1869	[1]–[4222] (the abbreviation for "Command" was omitted in the first series)
2nd series 1870–1899	[C. 1]–[C. 9550]
3rd series 1900–1918	[Cd. 1]–[Cd. 9239]
4th series 1919–1956	[Cmd. 1]–Cmd. 9889
5th series 1956–1986	Cmnd. 1–Cmnd. 9927
6th series 1986–	Cm. 1–

(The use of square brackets was abandoned in 1922). It is important to note exactly the form of the abbreviation so that you have some idea of the date of the report. For instance, Cmd. 6404 which relates to social insurance and allied services (the Beveridge Report) is a different item from Cmnd. 6404 which is an international agreement relating to pensions. One was published in 1942 and the other in 1976.

If your library keeps all the Command Papers together in boxes, arranged by command numbers, you will have no difficulty in tracing the report you want. However, if the publications are arranged by sessions or are bound into sessional sets, (see para. 5–2) it will be necessary to have some idea of the date of the Command Paper. You may find the *Concordance of Command Papers 1833–1972*, which is in *Pemberton*, (para. 5–1), pp. 65–66, of help. Occasionally, a report is published later than the Command Papers with adjoining numbers, with the result that it appears in a different session of Parliament (and is therefore in a different sessional set). If you know the command number of a publication issued before 1979/80 and wish to locate it in the bound sessional sets, first ascertain the correct session, by consulting Pemberton's list (para. 5–1) or the annual catalogues of government publications (see para. 5–18). Then go to the *sessional index*, which is in the last volume for each session. There you will find a list of command numbers indicating, for each one, the volume and page within the sessional set where it can be found. Command Papers bound in the sessional sets issued from 1979/80 onwards can be readily traced under the Command Paper number.

Some Command Papers also form part of another series. For instance, some of the reports of the Law Commission (but not all) are Command Papers: but each Law Commission report also bears its own running number. For convenience, law libraries may keep all Law Commission reports together, regardless of whether they are issued as Command Papers, House of Commons papers, or non-parliamentary papers (and some of the series have been issued in all these categories). Another major series, within the Command Papers, are the State Papers known as the *Treaty Series* (para. 12–7). These are Command Papers, and each has a command number, but, in addition, each has its own Treaty Series number. If they are not bound into the sessional sets, the library may keep all the Treaty Series together. There are separate annual and three or four-yearly consolidated indexes to the series; in addition, they also appear in HMSO's catalogues of government publications. Both the Treaty Series number and the Command Paper numbers are given. In 1970, HMSO published an *Index of British Treaties 1101–1968* (compiled by Clive Parry and Charity Hopkins), (see para. 12–15). There are entries under subjects (Vol. 1) and by the date of the treaties (Vols. 2 and 3).

How to Trace a Command Paper

If the number is known, note the spelling of the abbreviation **5–7**
for the word "Command" (see para. 5–6) as this will give you some idea of the date of the report. Cm. means that it was published in or after 1986: Cmnd. means that the paper was published between 1956 and 1986. If the library binds its parliamentary publications into sessional sets (para. 5–2) and you are looking for any Command Paper issued prior to 1979 consult the list in Pemberton (para. 5–1), pp. 65–66 to discover the session in which the report was published. You can then trace the appropriate volume in the sessional set by consulting the sessional index (para. 5–2). In and after the 1979/80 session the Command Papers in the sessional sets can be readily traced by the Command Paper numbers. Full details of the title, etc. can also be found in the annual catalogue of government publications for the appropriate year (para. 5–18).

Bills

Bills (House of Lords and House of Commons) are draft ver- **5–8**
sions of Acts of Parliament, which are laid before Parliament for

their consideration and approval. If your library has a complete
collection of parliamentary papers, the Bills will be shelved with
this collection; if not, they may be available in the law library. If
the library's parliamentary papers are bound up into sessional
sets, the Bills will form the first volumes of each set. The most
recent Bills are likely to be shelved separately in boxes.

A Bill may be introduced into Parliament by a Member of
Parliament (or by a peer) as an independent action (called a Private
Member's Bill), or it may be introduced by a Minister as a
government Bill. Ultimately, however, it becomes a Public
General Act whoever introduces it. (Private Members' Bills are
not always published by HMSO: if not otherwise available they
can usually be obtained by writing directly to the M.P. concerned.)

Stages in the Passage of a Bill

5–9   Before a Bill can become law it passes through a number of
stages. The exact stage which any Bill has reached on its passage
through Parliament can be discovered by consulting the *House
of Commons Weekly Information Bulletin* (para. 5–10) A Bill may
be introduced into the House of Lords or into the Commons.
The following stages show the progress of a Bill which commenced
in the House of Commons:

(i)   *First Reading*—a purely formal reading of the Bill's title by
the Clerk of the House; after this the Bill is printed, a day
is fixed for its Second Reading and it becomes available
to the public.

(ii) *Second Reading*—the principles of the Bill are debated. If
the Bill fails to gain the approval of the House at this
stage it cannot proceed. The debate is reported in *Hansard* (see para. 5–15).

(iii) *Committee stage*—the whole House may sit in committee
to examine the clauses of a Bill. More usually, the Bill is
committed to a Standing Committee for discussion. The
*Parliamentary Debates: House of Commons: Official Reports
of Standing Committees* debates are published separately
from *Hansard*. They are issued daily, and each issue
covers the discussions on one Bill. The daily copies are
later replaced by bound volumes. There are various
Standing Committees, and when using the unbound
copies it is necessary to find out which committee discussed
the particular Bill you are interested in. This may
be done by looking in the *House of Commons Weekly
Information Bulletin* (para. 5–10) or in the monthly and
annual catalogues of government publications (see

para. 5–18) under the heading "House of Commons: Minutes of Proceedings" (until 1975) or "Standing Committee . . ." (1976 onwards).

(iv) *Report stage*—if the Bill has been amended by the Standing Committee, this stage gives the House an opportunity to consider the changes. If necessary, the Bill may be referred back to the committee. (If the Bill was debated and approved without amendment in a Committee of the whole House, then this stage is formal).

(v) *Third Reading*—a general discussion of the Bill as amended, after which it is passed to the House of Lords for its concurrence.

(vi) *Lords' stages*—The Bill is reprinted when it is passed to the Lords for their consideration and approval. If the Lords make any amendments, these are referred back to the Commons for their approval. Normally both Houses must be in agreement on the text before the Bill can receive the Royal Assent. The Parliament Acts 1911 and 1949 provide for certain exceptions to this rule. Money Bills are the standard exception.

Bills fail if they do not pass through all these stages before the end of the parliamentary session. Therefore, a new Bill must be introduced in the next session if the legislation is to ensue. In order to see what stage a Bill has reached on its passage through Parliament consult the latest copy of the *House of Commons Weekly Information Bulletin* (para. 5–10).

Citation of Bills

Most Bills submitted to Parliament are printed and placed on sale to the public by HMSO as soon as they are given their first reading. The *Weekly Information Bulletin* states if the Bill has been printed. The Bill is given a number, which appears in the bottom left hand corner of the first page. If the number is printed enclosed in *square* brackets, this indicates that the Bill is a House of Commons Bill, *i.e.* it is at present being considered by the House of Commons. If the number is enclosed in *round* brackets, this indicates a Bill which is at present under consideration by the House of Lords. It is important to notice whether round or square brackets are used, as this will enable you to trace the correct Bill. The initials H.C. or H.L. are used to indicate the two different Houses of Parliament and the parliamentary session is also given. Without this information it is difficult to trace the Bill. A citation to a Bill therefore gives: the initials of the House; the session of Parliament; the Bill number in round (Lords) or square [Commons] brackets, *e.g.* H.L. Bill

5–10

1986–87 (9) Ministry of Defence Police Bill; H.C. Bill 1985–86 [129] Public Order Bill. When Parliament discusses the Bill some amendments may be incorporated. If these are only minor amendments, this is done by issuing a sheet of paper stating the amended version of the text. This bears the same number as the original Bill but with the addition of a lower case letter, *e.g.* (38a). If a major alteration is made, the complete text of the Bill is reprinted and this reprinted version is given a completely new number. If there have been a number of amendments, a marshalled list of amendments may be published which bears the same number as the original Bill but with the addition of a roman number, *e.g.* [123 II].

Most Bills require the approval of both Houses of Parliament. The Bill is again reprinted, with a new number, when it is passed to the other House for approval. Thus, there may be several versions of the same Bill in the library, and it is often important that you should consult the latest copy, which incorporates all the amendments. The *House of Commons Weekly Information Bulletin* will indicate which is the latest copy of the Bill.

For instance, the entry opposite from the *Weekly Information Bulletin* relates to a government Bill, the *Financial Services Bill*, which was introduced into the House of Commons by Mr. Channon. The Bill was printed three times during its passage through the Commons—House of Commons Bills numbers [51], [122] and [222] in parliamentary session 1985/86. The version of the Bill which was considered by the House of Lords was H.L. Bill (196); there was a later printing, H.L. Bill (246), incorporating subsequent amendments. The Bill received its first reading in the House of Commons (1R) on December 18, 1985; after the second reading (2R), it was referred to *Standing Committee E* (Comm. (SC E)) which discussed it during January, February and March 1986. The report stage (Rep.) followed. The third reading (3R) took place on June 12, 1986. The Bill was then passed to the House of Lords where it went through a similar procedure. After the Commons had considered the Lords amendments (LA) at the end of October, the Bill received the Royal Assent on November 7, 1986, and became law as the Financial Services Act 1986, c. 60. (A full list of the abbreviations used will be found in the *Weekly Information Bulletin*). The debates on the Bill will be found in *Hansard* (para. 5–15, 5–21) on the appropriate dates. The reports of the debates in Standing Committees are issued separately (para. 5–9).

At the end of each session a House of Commons paper entitled *Public Bills: Return of the Number of Public Bills* is

FINANCIAL SERVICES   Mr P Channon/Lord Lucas of Chilworth   *(Government)*
  A)   Commons: (51,122,222)   1R: *18.12*   2R: *14.1*   Comm (SC E): *28.1-25.3*
                Rep: *11 & 12.6*   3R: *12.6*   LA: *30 & 31.10*
     Lords: (196,246)   1R: *23.6*   2R: *11.7*   Comm: *21, 23, 28, 29.7*   Rep: *14, 16, 20.10*
               3R: *27.10*   Royal Assent (cap 60, 1986): *7.11*

FIRE PRECAUTIONS (AMENDMENT)   Mr T Lloyd
  Y)   Commons: (50)   1R: *17.12*

FOOTBALL BETTING LEVY BOARD   Mr T Pendry
  Y)   Commons: (172)   1R: *10.6*

FORESTRY   Sir J Stradling Thomas/Lord Gisborough
  X)   Commons: (112,157)   1R: *19.3*   2R: **2.5*   Comm (SC C): *14.5*   Rep & 3R: **16.5*
     Lords: (164)   1R: *19.5*   2R: *3.6*   Comm: *17.6*   3R: **1.7*
           Royal Assent (cap 30, 1986): *8.7*

FREEDOM OF SPEECH (UNIVERSITIES AND INSTITUTIONS OF HIGHER EDUCATION)   Mr F Silvester
  Y)   Commons: (80)   1R: *11.2*

GAMING (AMENDMENT) [HL]   Lord Harris of Greenwich/Mr M Carlisle
  Z)   Lords: (26,73)   1R: *4.12*   2R: *23.1*   Comm: *6.2*   Rep: **18.2*   3R: *27.2*
     Commons: (108)   1R: *13.3*   2R: **11.4*   Remaining stages: *18.4*
          Royal Assent (cap 11, 1986): *2.5*

GAS   Mr P Walker/Lord Belstead   *(Government)*
  A)   Commons: (13,102,109,210)   1R: *28.11*   2R: *10.12*   GM: *17.2*   Comm (SC F): *17.2-6.3*
                 Rep: *17.3*   3R: *25.3*   LA: *21.7*
     Lords: (111,187,222)   1R: *25.3*   2R: *10.4*   Comm: *24 & 29.4, 8 & 19.5, 3, 5 & 11.6*
            Rep: *1, 7 & 9.7*   3R: *17.7*   Royal Assent (cap 44, 1986): *25.7*

GREATER LONDON COUNTY HALL   Mr Simon Hughes
  Y)   Commons: (86)   1R: *18.2*

HEALTH SERVICE JOINT CONSULTATIVE COMMITTEES (ACCESS TO INFORMATION)
(Title changed from Local Government (Access to Information) Act 1985 (Extension))
           Mr R Squire/Baroness Carnegy of Lour
  W)   Commons: (36,130)   1R: *4.12*   2R: *31.1*   Comm (SC C): *9.4*   Rep & 3R: *2.5*
     Lords: (151)   1R: *7.5*   2R: *5.6*   OCD: **17.6*   3R: **24.6*
          Royal Assent (cap 24, 1986): *26.6*

HEARING AID COUNCIL ACT 1968 (AMENDMENT)   Mr L Pavitt
  X)   Commons: (74)   1R: *31.1*

HIGHWAYS (AMENDMENT)   Mr M Cocks/Lord Dean of Beswick
  X)   Commons: (89)   1R: *19.2*   2R: **21.2*   Remaining stages: **28.2*
     Lords: (95)   1R: *3.3*   2R: *18.3*   OCD: **8.4*   3R: *28.4*
          Royal Assent (cap 13, 1986): *2.5*

HORTICULTURAL PRODUCE   Sir J Wells/Lord Stanley of Alderley
  W)   Commons: (35,134)   1R: *4.12*   2R: **31.1*   Comm (SC C): *16.4*   Rep & 3R: *18.4*
     Lords: (134)   1R: *21.4*   2R: *20.5*   OCD: **12.6*   3R: **16.6*
          Royal Assent (cap 20, 1986): *26.6*

HOUSING (MULTIPLE OCCUPATION) [HL]   Baroness Vickers
  Z)   Lords: (92,168)   1R: *26.2*   2R: *25.4*   Comm: *21.5*   Rep: **16.6*   3R: **30.6*

HOUSING (SCOTLAND)   Mr M Rifkind/Lord Gray of Contin   *(Government)*
  A)   Commons: (10,81,178,227)   1R: *14.11*   2R: *28.11*   Comm (1st Scot SC): *10.12-11.2*
                 Rep: *27.2 & 4.3*   3R: *4.3*   LA: *2.7, 4.11*
     Lords: (98,142,159,178)   1R: *5.3*   2R: *18.3*   Comm: *28.4*   Rep: *13.5*   3R: *11.6*
               CA: *29.10*   Royal Assent (cap 65, 1986): *7.11*

HOUSING AND PLANNING   Mr N Ridley/Lord Elton   *(Government)*
  A)   Commons: (63,131,224,231)   1R: *23.1*   2R: *4.2*   Comm (SC H): *13.2-10.4*   Rep & 3R: *24.4*
                 LA: *3 & 5.11*
     Lords: (145,245,250,257)   1R: *1.5*   2R: *30.7*   Comm: *7, 9, 13.10*   Rep: *22.10*
               3R: *28.10*   CA: *4.11*
           Royal Assent (cap 63, 1986): *7.11*

HOUSING CONDITION SURVEY (SCOTLAND)   Mr A Kirkwood
  Y)   Commons: (208)   1R: *15.7*   *(not printed)*

HUMAN RIGHTS AND FUNDAMENTAL FREEDOMS [HL]   Lord Broxbourne/Sir E Gardner
  Z)   Lords: (21,119)   1R: *21.11*   2R: *10.12*   Comm: *20.3*   Rep: *9.4*   3R: *30.4*
     Commons: (175)   1R: *10.6*

IMMIGRATION ACT 1971 (AMENDMENT)   Mr M Madden
  Y)   Commons: (121)   1R: *25.3*

INCEST AND RELATED OFFENCES (SCOTLAND) [HL]   Lord Wilson of Langside/Mr J Wallace
  Z)   Lords: (20,64,213)   1R: *21.11*   2R: *9.12*   Comm: *28.1*   Rep: **24.2*
               3R: **11.3*   CA: *14.7*
     Commons: (150)   1R: *29.4*   2R: **16.5*   Comm (2nd Scot SC): *11.6*
          Rep & 3R: *4.7*   Royal Assent (cap 36, 1986): *18.7*

INDECENT DISPLAYS (NEWSPAPERS)   Ms C Short
  Y)   Commons: (104)   1R: *12.3*

published, showing which Bills considered during the session received the royal assent and which were dropped, postponed or rejected. The same information is more readily available in the last issue of the House of Commons *Weekly Information Bulletin* published during that parliamentary session, or in the *Sessional Information Digest* produced by the Public Information Office of the House of Commons Library.

5–11   Tracing Bills

Recent Bills

5–12   The number(s) assigned to a recent Bill, and any amendments, can be found by using the latest copy of the House of Commons *Weekly Information Bulletin* (para. 5–10) or by looking through the *Daily List of Government Publications* (para. 5–18). The progress of the Bill can be checked in the latest *Weekly Information Bulletin*. If this is unavailable the coloured pages printed weekly in the *New Law Journal* provide similar information, as does *Current Law* (under the heading "Progress of Bills"). Bills published a few months ago can be traced in the monthly and annual catalogues of government publications (para. 5–18) which replace the *Daily List*, or in the latest copy of the *Weekly Information Bulletin* published during the appropriate session of Parliament.

The House of Commons Bills will be shelved together. In the case of House of Lords Bills, these may be interfiled with the House of Lords papers, for both the papers and the Bills shared the same numerical sequence until session 1987/88, after which they are separately numbered.

Debates on the Bill which take place at the committee stage may be found in the *Official Reports of Standing Committees* (para. 5–9). Debates in the House are reported in *Hansard* (paras. 5–15 and 5–21). When a Bill receives the Royal Assent this will be noted in publications such as the *Weekly Information Bulletin*, the *New Law Journal* and *Current Law*. When the Royal Assent is given, a copy of the Act is printed, and an entry for the Act appears in the *Daily List*.

Tracing Older Bills

5–13   It is seldom necessary to refer to Bills from earlier sessions, for they will either have become law (in which case you should consult the resultant Act) or they will have lapsed. However, if you do need to consult older Bills, and your library has the bound sessional sets available, the text of all the versions of the Bill together with all amendments will be found, in alphabetical order, in the volumes entitled "Bills" at the beginning of the sessional set. If the bound volumes are not available, details of

all the published versions of the Bill will be found at the beginning of the annual catalogues of *Government Publications* or the
copy of the *Weekly Information Bulletin* for the appropriate
period may be consulted.

Papers of the House of Lords and House of Commons

The *House of Lords Papers and Bills* are issued in a common   **5–14**
numerical sequence, so that Papers and Bills are integrated.
(From 1988 onwards these are in two separate sequences.) The
number of each item is printed in round brackets at the foot of
the front cover. The citation is: H.L. session (paper number),
e.g. H.L. 1985–86 (21) Human Rights and Fundamental Freedoms Bill.

The *House of Commons Papers* are issued in a separate numerical sequence from the Commons Bills. The citation includes the
initials H.C., the session, and the paper number. The Papers of
the House of Commons include reports of some committees,
together with accounts, statistics and some annual reports
which are required by Parliament for its work.

Parliamentary Debates

The first semi-official reports of Parliament's debates were pub-   **5–15**
lished in 1803 by William Cobbett. The man whose name is so
closely linked with the publication, *Hansard,* was a subsequent
printer of the reports. There have been six series of *Parliamentary Debates, i.e.* first series, 1803–20; second series, 1820–30;
third series, 1830–91; fourth series, 1892–1908; fifth series,
1909–1981; sixth series, 1981–date. Since 1909 the *Official
Reports of Parliamentary Debates* have been published by the
House of Commons itself. The House of Lords Debates have
been published separately since 1909. Previously, both Lords
and Commons Debates were published together.

The *Official Report of Debates (Hansard)* is published daily and
the daily issues are later replaced by volumes containing
reports of the debates during a parliamentary session, with a
sessional index. There are also indexes at the back of each
individual bound volume. A *Weekly Hansard* (containing all the
daily reports, in one issue) is also published, and a fortnightly
Index to the debates is also available.

Citations to debates usually give the volume number/House/
series/date/column number. Each column (rather than each
page) is numbered, and references in the index are to column
numbers, not page numbers. If the column number is printed in

and incisiveness; and, therefore, request me to respond to the committee's concern and that of the city council and others by establishing a public inquiry into the policing of civil disorder in the light of the events of the summer of 1981, with terms of reference including the use of CS and other measures, to provide a basis for future policy. I understand that a letter explaining the context of the recommendation will be sent to me shortly. At present, I am considering what reply it would be appropriate to give to the recommendation.

Prison Rules

Mr. Greenway asked the Secretary of State for the Home Department when prison rules were last revised; if he has any proposals to update the rules; and if he will make a statement.

Mr. Mayhew: Prison rules were laid before Parliament in their entirety on 11 March 1964 and came into operation on 25 March 1964.

There has been no general revision since, although individual rules have from time to time been amended. The last occasion was on 29 March 1982, upon the introduction of partly-suspended sentences, amending prison rule 5.

Rules will be needed to enable the implementation of the youth custody provisions of the Criminal Justice Act, and we shall consider in due course what implications that may have for the prison rules.

Young Offenders

Mr. Greenway asked the Secretary of State for the Home Department how many young offenders are detained in adult prisons; and in which prisons.

Mr. Mayhew: The latest readily available information is given in the following table:

Population ' aged 21 in adult prisons† in England and Wales on 30 September 1982

Prison	Number
Askham Grange	7
Bedford	49
Birmingham	122
Bristol	35
Brixton	7
Canterbury	69
Cookham Wood	11
Drake Hall	19
Durham	37
Exeter‡	80
Gloucester	15
Grendon‡	57
Holloway	72
Leeds	197
Leicester	35
Lewes	180
Lincoln	103
Liverpool‡	266
Manchester‡	388
Moor Court	6
Norwich	6
Oxford	37
Reading	53
Shrewsbury	33
Styal	24
Winchester	5
TOTAL	1,913

* Includes remand prisoners.
† Excludes remand centres.
‡ Adult prisons with young prisoner wings.

Prisons (Evening Classes)

Mr. Greenway asked the Secretary of State for the Home Department which evening classes exist in each prison; and how these compare with the provision during the past 10 years.

Mr. Mayhew: The information requested is not readily available, but my noble Friend will write to my hon. Friend as soon as possible.

Racial Incidents (Lambeth)

Mr. Proctor asked the Secretary of State for the Home Department if he will publish in the *Official Report* the first figures from the new police system sponsored by his Department for monitoring racial attacks and incidents in the Lambeth police district of London between May and September; and if he will make a statement.

Mr. Mayhew: I understand that in response to a request the police informed the Lambeth community-police consultative group of 37 incidents in the Lambeth police district, believed to be racially motivated, which were reported to them between 1 May 1982 and 30 September 1982.

Brixton (Incidents)

Mr. Proctor asked the Secretary of State for the Home Department if he will call for a report from the Commissioner of Police of the Metropolis concerning incidents involving black youths and the police which took place in Brixton on Thursday 21 October; and if he will make a statement on the substance of this report.

Mr. Whitelaw: I understand from the Commissioner that there were two incidents in Railton Road on the afternoon of 21 October. In the first, two officers chased and caught a man suspected of having robbed a passer-by. A crowd of about 50 people gathered and attacked the officers in an attempt to release the suspect; the officers, however, drew their truncheons and were able to keep the man in their custody. In the second incident, when two constables stopped a car the passengers in it prevented them from arresting their companion for driving while disqualified and enabled him to escape. The driver was apprehended after a chase, but called on passers-by for help and again escaped in the struggle which followed. When other officers arrived, a bottle of soft drink was thrown at a police vehicle, causing slight damage. The passengers in the car which had been stopped by the police, and one member of the crowd, were arrested, as on the following day was a man understood to have been the driver.

The persistence of the officers who arrested the suspected robber, and held him under intimidating circumstances, was particularly praiseworthy. I am encouraged to learn from the Commissioner that responsible members of the community in Brixton continue to support the actions of the police in their efforts to prevent and detect crime.

italic type, this is a reference to the written answers which are in a separate sequence at the back of the volume, and not to the column in the Debates which bears that number (See figures on pages 78 & 79.) In the current (sixth) series the practice of placing a "w" after the column numbers, not page numbers. If the column number is printed in number in the index serves the same purpose. Entries in the index are under the names of speakers, as well as subjects. The first issue of *Hansard* for each session contains a list of all members of the House of Commons. Members of the Government are listed in each volume of *Hansard*.

NON-PARLIAMENTARY PUBLICATIONS

5–16   These are publications which are not presented to Parliament. They include statutory instruments (para. 3–31). In many libraries these publications are entered in the library catalogues, normally under the heading "Great Britain," followed by the name of the government department which produced the publication, *e.g.* Great Britain, *Lord Chancellor's Department*. A large number, but by no means all, of these government reports are published by HMSO. They are usually scattered around the library according to the subject matter of the report, rather than being kept together as a separate collection. A microfiche collection of reports not published by HMSO is found in *British Official Publications not published by HMSO*, issued by Chadwyck-Healey, who produce a bi-monthly and annual *Catalogue* to this material, the majority of which is available in the microfiche collection. The *Catalogue of British Official Publications not published by HMSO* covers the publications issued by over 400 bodies, financed or controlled partly or wholly by the government, whose publications are not issued by HMSO. Examples are the Child Poverty Action Group, Commission for Racial Equality, Civil Service Department, Common Agricultural Policy, Director of Public Prosecutions, Equal Opportunities Commission and the National Consumer Council. A *Keyword Index* to the same collection is also available on microfiche, containing entries under all the key words in the title of the publications.

5–17   **TRACING GOVERNMENT PUBLICATIONS**

Indexes

5–18   A *Daily List of Government Publications* is produced, and this is most useful for tracing very recent copies of Acts and other government publications. It is divided into parliamentary

DAILY LIST

HMSO BOOKS

HMSO AND INTERNATIONAL ORGANISATIONS PUBLICATIONS

HMSO Publications Centre
(Mail and telephone orders only)
PO Box 276, London SW8 5DT   Telex 297138
Telephone order (01) 622 3316 ⎫ queuing system
General enquiries (01) 211 5656 ⎭ in operation

HMSO Bookshops
49 High Holborn, London, WC1V 6HB (01) 211 5656 (Counter service only)
258 Broad Street, Birmingham, B1 2HE (021) 643 3740
Southey House, 33 Wine Street, Bristol, BS1 2BQ (0272) 264306
9-21 Princess Street, Manchester, M60 8AS (061) 834 7201
80 Chichester Street, Belfast, BT1 4JY (0232) 238451
13a Castle Street, Edinburgh, EH2 3AR (031) 225 6333

Publications may also be ordered through HMSO's accredited agents (see Yellow Pages) or any good bookseller.

This list is normally issued daily (Monday to Friday)
by Her Majesty's Stationery Office
Price 5p

Annual Subscription: posted daily £57.50 posted weekly £32.50

Subscriptions to the Daily List and other journals should be sent to the Subscriptions department, PO Box 276, London SW8 5DT or nearest HMSO Bookshop.

Please note: Northern Ireland publications with ISBNs beginning 0 337 are available only from HMSO Bookshop, Belfast.

HMSO Prestel lead frame 50040 (orders accepted)

All prices are net

Please quote full title, price and ISBN when ordering.

Holborn Bookshop — Saturday opening
Holborn Bookshop will be opening on Saturdays from 6.6.87 to 26.9.87 inclusive. The shop will be open between the hours of 9.00 a.m. and 1 p.m.

List Number 112   Monday 15th June 1987

PARLIAMENTARY PUBLICATIONS
(Issued on 12th June 1987)

House of Commons Papers (Session 1986-87)
143-xii   Trade and Industry Committee. The motor components industry: minutes of evidence, Wednesday 6 May 1987: Department of Trade and Industry. pp. 290—305. (30cm). (0 10 292987 4)   £3.00

208-iii   Select Committee on House of Commons (Services). Minutes of proceedings, Tuesday 12 May 1987. iii. pp. (30cm). (0 10 293187 9)   £0.85

230-viii Committee on Welsh Affairs. The condition and repair of privately-owned housing: appendices to the minutes of evidence. iii. pp. pp. 280—452. (30cm). (0 10 291687 X)   £10.20

(063142)   1   SEE OTHER SIDE

publications (House of Lords and Commons Papers and Bills, Command Papers, Acts and Debates), and non-parliamentary publications (arranged by the government department produ cing the report) including statutory instruments. There is also a list of publications by bodies such as the EEC, UN, and WHO, whose publications are sold, but not published, by HMSO.

The *Daily List* is replaced (several months later) by *HMSO Monthly Catalogue*. This monthly catalogue contains lists of House of Lords and House of Commons Papers and Bills, arranged in number order, a list of Command Papers in numerical order (which can be used to trace the title of publications, if you only have the Command number); and a list of Acts published during that month. The second part of the catalogue consists of a list of both parliamentary and non-parliamentary publications (excluding Bills, Acts and Debates, which appear only in the first part of the catalogue). This list is arranged by government departments and includes all items published by each department during that month, with details of their prices, and the command numbers, or Lords or Commons Paper numbers (in the case of parliamentary papers). (See figure on page 83.) Where the name of the Ministry began with the word "Ministry" or "Department," the entry was formerly inverted, *e.g.* Environment, Department of. Entries now appear under the normal form of the name, *e.g.* Department of the Environment. An index gives entries under the key word of the titles. Statutory instruments are excluded—a separate monthly index is published (para. 3–33). The monthly issues are replaced by an annual catalogue formerly entitled *Government Publications 19. . . .* It is now referred to as the *HMSO Annual Catalogue 19. . . .* Every five years a consolidated index was published, *e.g.* 1961–65, 1966–70, 1971–75, 1976–80. In many libraries the catalogues for these years are bound together. To allow for this, the pagination of the catalogues was continuous over the five-year period.

The annual and five-yearly catalogues contain:

(1) Lists of parliamentary publications, arranged by parliamentary session and then in numerical order (by Bill numbers, Paper numbers and Command Paper numbers).

(2) A classified list of both parliamentary and non-parliamentary publications (excluding Bills, Acts and Debates, which appear only in the first list). The list is arranged by the name of the government department which produced the publication, and full details of prices, command numbers, etc., are given.

Criminal law: codification of the criminal law: a report to the Law Commission – *Mr Justice Ralph Gibson (Chairman)* – vi, 246p.; 25 cm [H.C. 270] Contents: Introduction by the Law Commission p. 1-12. Report of team, chaired by J.C. Smith, to Law Commission p. 13-245, including draft codification bill [0 10 227085 6] £9.90

Criminal law: offences against religion and public worship – *Mr Justice Ralph Gibson (Chairman)* – v, 51p.; 25 cm [H.C. 442] [Law Com. no. 145] [0 10 244285 1] £4.90

Criminal law: report on criminal libel – *Mr Justice Ralph Gibson (Chairman)* – iv, 80p.; 25 cm [Cmnd 9618] [Law Com. no. 149] [0 10 196180 4] £5.80

Criminal law: report on poison-pen letters – *Mr Justice Ralph Gibson (Chairman)* – v, 39p.; 25 cm [H.C. 519] [Law Com. No. 147] [0 10 251985 4] £4.40

Family law: custody of children: jurisdiction and enforcement within the United Kingdom: report on a reference under s. 3 (1) (e) of the Law Commissions Act 1965 – *Mr Justice Ralph Gibson (Chairman);* Scottish Law Commission; *Peter Maxwell, Lord Maxwell (Chairman)* – x, 277p.; 25 cm [Cmnd 9419] [Law Com. no. 138]; [Scot. Law Com. no. 91] [0 10 194190 0] £10.65

Private international law: polygamous marriages: capacity to contract a polygamous marriage and related issues – *Mr Justice Ralph Gibson (Chairman);* Scottish Law Commission; *Peter Maxwell, Lord Maxwell (Chairman)* – v, 65p.; 25 cm [Cmnd 9595] [Law Com. no. 146]; [Scot. Law Com. no. 96] [0 10 195950 8] £3.40

Property law: 2nd report on land registration: inspection of the Register – *Mr Justice Ralph Gibson (Chairman)* – iii, 43p.; 25 cm [H.C. 551] [Law Com. no. 148] [0 10 255185 5] £4.40

Property law: liability for chancel repairs – *Mr Justice Roy Beldam (Chairman)* – v, 47p.; 25 cm [H.C. 391] [Law Com. no. 152] [0 10 203986 0] £4.90

Report on the consolidation of the Housing Acts: Housing Bill, Housing Associations Bill, Landlord and Tenant Bill – *Mr Justice Ralph Gibson (Chairman);* Scottish Law Commission; *Peter Maxwell, Lord Maxwell (Chairman)* – 49p.; 25 cm; [Law Com. no. 144]; [Scot. Law Com. no. 94]; [Cmnd 9515] [0 10 195150 7] £4.90

Statute law revision: 12th report: Draft Statute Law (Repeals) Bill – *Mr Justice Roy Beldam (Chairman);* Scottish Law Commission; *Peter Maxwell, Lord Maxwell (Chairman)* – 11p.; 25 cm; [Law Com. no. 150]; [Scot. Law Com. no. 99]; [Cmnd 9648] [0 10 196480 3] £6.70

Working papers

88 Private international law: the law of domicile – *Mr Justice Ralph Gibson (Chairman);* Scottish Law Commission; *Peter Maxwell, Lord Maxwell (Chairman)* – vi, 92p.; 21 cm; [Consultative memoranda: 63 Scottish Law Com.] [0 11 730169 8] £2.25

89 Private international law: choice of law rules in marriage – *Mr Justice Ralph Gibson (Chairman);* Scottish Law Commission; *Peter Maxwell, Lord Maxwell (Chairman)* – ix, 171p.; 21 cm; [Consultative memoranda: 64 Scottish Law Com.] [0 11 730170 1] £3.50

90 Family law: transfer of money between spouses: the Married Women's Property Act 1964 – *Mr Justice Ralph Gibson (Chairman)* – iii, 29p.; 21 cm [0 11 730171 X] £1.75

91 Family law: review of child law: guardianship – *Mr Justice Ralph Gibson (Chairman)* – viii, 205p.; 21 cm [0 11 730172 8] £5.00

92 Transfer of land: formalities for contracts for sale etc. of land – *Mr Justice Ralph Gibson (Chairman)* – iv, 79p.; 21 cm [0 11 730173 6] £2.25

93 Transfer of land: formalities for deeds and escrows – *Mr Justice Ralph Gibson (Chairman)* – iv, 44p.; 21 cm [0 11 730174 4] £1.75

94 Trusts of land – *Mr Justice Roy Beldam (Chairman)* – 76, [37]p.; 21 cm [0 11 730175 2] £3.65

Law Society

Accounts

Legal Aid Fund account 1983-84: account prepared pursuant to s. 18 (1) of the Legal Aid Act 1974 of the receipts and expenses of the Law Society paid into and out of the... Fund in the year ended Mar. 31, 1984, together with the report of the Comptroller and Auditor General thereon; 11p.; 25 cm [H.C. 165] In continuation of HCP 288 of 1983-84 [0 10 216585 8] £2.00

Legal aid: 34th annual reports of the Law Society and the Lord Chancellor's Advisory Committee [1983-84] – Lord Chancellor's Advisory Committee on Legal Aid; Lord Chancellor's Department (*Passive Author*) – v, 382p.; 25 cm [H.C. 151] [0 10 215185 7] £14.00

Law Society of Northern Ireland

Accounts

Legal Aid Fund (Northern Ireland) account 1983-84: account prepared pursuant to art. 20 (1) of the Legal Aid, Advice and Assistance (Northern Ireland) Order 1981 of the receipts and expenses of the Law Society of Northern Ireland paid in to and out of the Legal Aid Fund (Northern Ireland). in the year ended Mar. 31, 1984: together with the report of the Comptroller and Auditor General thereon; 7p.; 25 cm [H.C. 349] In continuation of HCP 406, 1983-84 [0 10 234985 1] £1.35

Legal aid: annual reports of the Law Society and of the Lord Chancellor's Advisory Committee 1983-84 – Lord Chancellor's Department (*Passive Author*) – iii, 62p.; 25 cm [H.C. 422] With correction slip [0 10 242285 0] £6.20

Law Society of Scotland

34th annual report of the Law Society of Scotland on the Scottish legal aid scheme from Apr. 1, 1983 to Mar. 31, 1984 – Scottish Home and Health Department (*Passive Author*) – 42p.; ill., tables; 25 cm [0 11 492447 3] £3.80

Accounts

Legal Aid (Scotland) Fund: account prepared pursuant to s. 11 (1) of the Legal Aid (Scotland) Act 1967 of the receipts and expenses of the Law Society of Scotland paid into and out of the Legal Aid Fund in the year ended Mar. 31, 1984, together with the report of the Comptroller and Auditor General thereon – Scottish Office (*Passive Author*) – 8p.; 25 cm [H.C. 222] [0 10 222285 1] £1.90

Law, statutes, etc. *see also Public general acts in Parliamentary section*

Liaison Committee (House of Commons, Parliament)

Minutes of proceedings

Minutes of proceedings: Nov. 15, 1984-June 27, 1985 – *Terence L. Higgins (Chairman)* – ix p.; 25 cm [H.C. 609] [0 10 260985 3] £1.85

Reports [1984-85]

1st report from the Liaison Committee: the Select Committee system: report, appendix and proceedings of the Committee relating to the report – *Terence L. Higgins (Chairman)* – lxix p.; 25 cm [H.C. 363] [0 10 236385 4] £5.40

London Electricity Board

Report and accounts 1984-1985; 51p.; ill., tables; 30 cm [0 903999 12 9] £1.50, sold by HMSO

London School of Hygiene and Tropical Medicine. Infectious diseases during pregnancy... – *see* Office of Population Censuses and Surveys. Studies on medical and population subjects. no. 49

(3) A list of periodicals published by HMSO with prices.
(4) An alphabetical index, with entries under the key words of titles and under the names of authors and chairmen of committees. Statutory instruments are not included but a separate annual catalogue of statutory instruments is published. A quarterly microfiche lists *HMSO in Print on Microfiche*. It provides a complete list all HMSO publications of whatever date which are currently available in print.

Indexes covering longer periods are also available. There is a *General Alphabetical Index to the Bills, Reports and Papers printed by Order of the House of Commons and to the Reports and Papers presented by Command,* covering a ten-year period, *e.g.* 1950–59, (session 1962–63, H.C. 96) and a *General Index* 1900–1949. Indexes and breviates (summaries) of nineteenth century papers also exist.

Tracing Lords and Commons Papers

5–19   If you have the paper number, the citation (para. 5–14) should include the session, the paper number, and whether it relates to the Lords or the Commons. If the library has bound the papers into sessional sets, the appropriate volume and page can be traced from the index to the session. In more recent sessions, the papers have been arranged in the sessional sets in numerical order.

Tracing Reports if You Know the Chairman

5–20   If you know only the name of the chairman of the report but lack further details (except possibly some idea of the subject matter) you should consult:

S. Richard, *British Government Publications: an index to chairmen of committees and commissions of enquiry. Vol. I. 1800–1899*

S. Richard, *British Government Publications: an index to chairmen and authors, 1900–1940, [Vol. II]*

S. Richard, *British Publications: an Index to Chairmen and Authors, Vol. III, 1941–1978, Vol. IV, 1979–1982.*

More recent reports can be traced in the *Index to Chairmen of Committees,* now renamed *Committee Reports published by HMSO, Indexed by Chairman.* The annual catalogues of government publications also include entries under chairmen in their indexes.

Tracing Parliamentary Debates

The last bound volume of the *Parliamentary Debates* for each   **5–21**
session contains a *Sessional Index*. Discussions on a Bill are
entered under the name of the Bill. The abbreviations 1R, 2R, 3R
indicate the first, second and third readings. There are entries
under subject and under the names of Members. For earlier
series, entries give the volume number in square brackets, and
the column number (not the page number). Column numbers in
italic type refer to the written answers which are printed separately at the back of each volume. From 1984 onwards (6th series)
entries give the volume, the column number (prefaced by "c")
and, where it is a written answer, "w" appears after the column
number. Thus a reference 59 c174–5w refers to Volume 59 of the
Sixth series, columns 174–5 in the written answers (which are
found in the back of the volume.)

Indexes to the House of Commons and House of Lords
debates are also published fortnightly as part of (but issued
separately from) the daily and *Weekly Hansard*. The arrangement is the same as the indexes to the sessional volumes.

The House of Commons *Weekly Information Bulletin*
(para. 5–10) will refer you to the relevant dates when debates on
a Bill took place. These can then be traced easily in *Hansard*.
Remember that debates of Standing Committees are bound
separately from *Hansard* (see para. 5–9).

Tracing Publications on a Subject

Parliamentary and some non-parliamentary publications on a   **5–22**
subject can be traced in the daily, monthly, annual and five-
yearly catalogues of government publications (see para. 5–18)
and in the *General Indexes 1900–1949, 1950–1959* (see para. 5–18).
If bound sessional sets are available, the sessional indexes may
be used as an alternative to consulting the annual catalogues. A
series of *Sectional Lists* cover the publications which have been
produced by a particular government department, *e.g.* the
Home Office, and which are still in print (*i.e.* still available for
purchase from HMSO). These may serve as a form of subject
index. If your library shelves its non-parliamentary publications by subject, the library's subject catalogue will enable
you to trace relevant publications.

For research on nineteenth century material Chadwyck-
Healey have produced a microfiche edition of the *House of
Commons Parliamentary Papers 1801–1900* together with a *Subject
Catalogue of the House of Commons Parliamentary Papers*

1801–1900. This publisher provides, for recent twentieth century publications, a *Keyword Index to British Official Publications
not published by HMSO* (on microfiche) and annual *Catalogues of
British Official Publications not published by HMSO* with a subject
index.

Tracing Statutes, Statutory Instruments, Treaties

5–23   The *Chronological Table of the Statutes* (para. 6–24) and *Index to
the Statutes* (para. 6–18) can be used to trace Acts, and a separate
annual list of statutes is also published. Statutory instruments
are traced through the *Daily List* and through monthly and
annual *Lists of Statutory Instruments* (para. 3–33). Treaties are
listed in the daily, monthly and annual government catalogues.
In addition there are separate Indexes to Treaty series
(para. 12–8) and the *Index of British Treaties 1101–1968*
(para. 12–15). There is also a *sectional list* (list giving all Treaty
series from 1919–date).

Law Commission Reports and Working Papers

5–24   Some of the *Law Commission Reports* are published as Command
Papers, others are House of Commons papers, whilst many
more are non-parliamentary papers. As a result, they may be
widely scattered in the library. In many law libraries they will
be kept together and may be available only from a member of
the library staff. Every report and working paper has its own
individual number within the series. A complete list of all the
reports and working papers which have been published is
given in the latest copy of the Law Commission's Annual
Report (issued as a House of Commons paper). The list gives
the Command number or paper numbers, where relevant, and
indicates, for each report, whether the Commission's proposals
for reform have been implemented.

Statistics

5–25   The Government produces a wide range of official statistics. A
useful short guide, *Government Statistics: a brief guide to sources,*
is produced annually by the Government Statistical Service.
Under the heading "Justice and Law" it lists such publications
as *Criminal Statistics, England and Wales,* issued annually in the
Command Papers series; *Prison Statistics; Offences of Drunken-
ness; Offences relating to motor vehicles; Statistics on the misuse of
drugs; Statistics on the operation of section 62 Criminal Law Act*

1977, etc. The Central Statistical Office issues a more comprehensive *Guide to Official Statistics*. Both are published by
HMSO.

CHAPTER 6

How to Find Information on a Subject

INTRODUCTION

6–1 One of the most difficult tasks facing you will be to discover the law relating to a particular topic. Your essays, moots and seminar preparation will require you to know not simply the present state of the law but also its development and such criticisms and suggestions for reform as have been made.

To find information on a subject you will need to consult some or all of the following sources:

Acts of Parliament
Delegated legislation
European Communities legislation, and international Treaties and Conventions
Cases
Textbooks
Periodical articles
Relevant government publications, including Law Commission Reports (especially those which have made suggestions for reform of the law)
Reports and comments in newspapers
Bills and Parliamentary Debates

In order to tackle a legal problem you may need to ask yourself the following questions:

QUESTION: Where can I find a general statement of the law on this subject?

ANSWER: In encyclopedias, such as *Halsbury's Laws of England* (para. 6–3) and in textbooks (para. 6–34).

QUESTION: What books are there on this subject?

ANSWER: Consult the library catalogues (para. 1–4) and bibliographies (para. 6–33).

QUESTION: What periodical articles have been written on this subject?

ANSWER: Consult indexes to periodicals (para. 4–2).

QUESTION: What cases have there been on this topic?

ANSWER: Use digests and indexes to case law (para. 6–8).

QUESTION: What judicial interpretation has been placed on particular words?

ANSWER: Look in *Words and Phrases Legally Defined* (para. 6–15) and similar works (para. 6–15).

QUESTION: What Acts of Parliament are in force dealing with this subject?

ANSWER: Use *Statutes in Force,* (para. 6–17) *Is it in force?* (para. 6–23), *Halsbury's Statutes* (para. 6–19), or the *Index to the Statutes* (para. 6–18).

QUESTION: Are there any relevant statutory instruments?

ANSWER: Use *Index to Government Orders* (para. 6–28), *Lists of Statutory Instruments* (para. 6–29), or *Halsbury's Statutory Instruments* (para. 6–27).

QUESTION: Have there been any government reports or Law Commission reports on this topic?

ANSWER: Use indexes to government publications (para. 5–18) and the annual reports of the Law Commission (para. 5–24).

QUESTION: Are there any Bills before Parliament which would change the law on this subject? Has the issue been discussed in Parliament?

ANSWER: Consult the House of Commons *Weekly Information Bulletin* (para. 5–10) and Parliamentary Debates (paras. 5–15, 5–21).

Having mapped out the ground, you can now proceed to tackle these questions. In attempting to carry out a search on a legal subject you may have some difficulty. Never be afraid to ask the library staff or your lecturer for help. Remember that other students may also be working on the same subject—start work well within the time limits set, otherwise you may discover that the material is unavailable because of high demand.

LEGAL ENCYCLOPEDIAS

These contain a detailed up-to-date statement of the law on a particular subject. The major general legal encyclopedia is   **6–2**

Halsbury's Laws of England, which is now in its fourth edition. It is a most useful source of information on a wide variety of topics. In addition, there are a number of more specialised encyclopedias, many of them issued in looseleaf form, so that the information can be kept continuously up to date.

Halsbury's Laws of England

6–3   This is the major legal encyclopedia covering all areas of English law. It is a very useful starting point for research on any subject. Because it is kept up to date it has the advantage over textbooks of including recent information.

The current edition is the 4th edition, which was completed in 1986. Earlier editions have been superseded and should be ignored.

How to use Halsbury's Laws, 4th Edition

6–4   Start by looking up the subject that interests you in the *Index.* The entry refers you to the appropriate volume number, (in heavy type) and *paragraph* number (not page number). The presence of "n" followed by a small number indicates that you are being referred to one of the footnotes at the end of the appropriate paragraph number. Thus the entry for "Arrestable Offence—meaning," reproduced on page 91, refers you to Volume 11, paragraph 109, footnote 1 for information on the meaning of an arrestable offence. Information on concealing an arrestable offence is contained in Volume 11, paragraph 961. If you turn to paragraph 961 (see figure on page 92) you will find there a statement of the law relating to concealment of offences, together with footnotes which refer you to relevant statutes and, where appropriate, to cases and other sources of information. *Halsbury's Laws* provides a straightforward statement of the law relating to a particular subject, together with footnote references to relevant statutes and cases.

Remember that it is possible that the information in the volumes is out of date. New legislation, or other changes in the law, could have made the information incomplete or inaccurate. The encylopedia provides for this possibility. To find out if there have been any changes in the law, since the volumes were published, make a note of the relevant volume and paragraph numbers, and turn to the *Cumulative Supplement.* For example, the information on concealing offences was contained in Volume 11, paragraph 961. If you turn to the latest *Cumulative Supplement* (only the latest Supplement should be used) and look up the entry for Volume 11, paragraph 961, you will find

Paras. 958-961   Vol. 11: *Criminal Law, Evidence and Procedure*   958

958. Unlawful disposal of a dead body. It is an indictable offence at common law to prevent or conspire to prevent the burial of a dead body or to dispose of a dead body in order to prevent an inquest being held upon it[1].

1 See CORONERS, vol. 9, para. 1048; CREMATION AND BURIAL, vol. 10, para. 1018.

959. Acknowledging recognizance etc. in name of another. Every person who, without lawful authority or excuse[1], acknowledges in the name of any other person any recognizance[2] or bail or any cognovit actionem[3] or judgment or any deed or other instrument before any court, judge or other person lawfully authorised in that behalf[4] commits an offence and on conviction on indictment is liable to imprisonment for a term not exceeding seven years[5].

1 Proof of lawful authority or excuse lies on the defendant: Forgery Act 1861, s. 34. See also para. 356, ante.
2 "Recognizance" refers to a valid recognizance into which a person may lawfully be required to enter and a recognizance imposing an obligation for which there is no authority is not within ibid., s. 34: R v McKenzie [1971] 1 All ER 729.
3 I.e. a written instrument by which the plaintiff acknowledges the justness of the defendant's claim. It has been superseded by orders of the court made by consent and is now obsolete.
4 This includes a commissioner for oaths: see the Commissioners for Oaths Act 1889, s. 1 (3), and evidence.
5 Forgery Act 1861, s. 34; Criminal Justice Act 1948, s. 1 (i); Criminal Law Act 1967, s. 12 (5) (a).

(iv) Offences in respect of Witnesses at Public Inquiries

960. Threatening etc. witnesses at public inquiries. A person who threatens or in any way punishes or injures or attempts to punish or injure any person for having given evidence upon any inquiry[1], or on account of the evidence which he has given upon any such inquiry, unless such evidence was given in bad faith, commits an offence and is liable on conviction to a penalty of not more than £100 or to imprisonment for not more than three months[2]. The offender may also be ordered to pay compensation to the person injured[3].

1 "Inquiry" means any inquiry held under the authority of any royal commission or by any committee of either House of Parliament, or pursuant to any statutory authority, whether the evidence of which inquiry is or is not given on oath, but does not include any inquiry by any court of justice: Witnesses (Public Inquiries) Protection Act 1892, s. 1.
2 Ibid., s. 2; Criminal Law Act 1967, s. 1. The offence must be dealt with summarily unless the prosecutor or the defendant wishes it to be sent for trial: Witnesses (Public Inquiries) Protection Act 1892, s. 3; Courts Act 1971, s. 56, Sch. 8, Part II, para. 16.
3 See the Witnesses (Public Inquiries) Protection Act 1892, s. 4, 5.

(7) OFFENCES RELATING TO THE EXECUTION OF CIVIL OR CRIMINAL PROCESS

(i) Concealing Offences

961. Concealing offences. Where a person has committed an arrestable offence[1], any other person who, knowing or believing that the offence or some other arrestable offence has been committed, and that he has information which might be of material assistance in securing the prosecution or conviction of an offender for it, accepts or agrees to accept for not disclosing that information any consideration other than the

---

959   *Offences against the Government and the Public*   Paras. 961, 962

making good of loss or injury caused by the offence, or the making of reasonable compensation for that loss or injury, is liable on conviction on indictment to imprisonment for not more than two years[1].

Proceedings for this offence may not be instituted except by or with the consent of the Director of Public Prosecutions[2].

1 For the meaning of "arrestable offence" see para. 1109, note 1, ante.
2 Criminal Law Act 1967, s. 5 (5). Offences under s. 5 (1), and indictment to commit them, may be tried summarily with the consent of the defendant where the arrestable offence to which they relate or, by any enactment is to be treated as, triable with the consent of the defendant under the Magistrates' Courts Act 1952, s. 19, Sch. 1 (see MAGISTRATES): Criminal Law Act 1967, s. 5 (4).
The compounding of an offence other than treason is not now an offence otherwise than under s. 5, s. 5 (5). Nor is misprision now an offence except in the case of treason (see para. 818, ante), the common law offence of misprision of felony having ceased to exist with the abolition (see para. 41, ante) of the distinctions between felony and misdemeanour. But as to advertising rewards on certain terms for the return of lost or stolen goods, see para. 1294, post.
3 Ibid., s. 5 (3). As to the effect of this limitation, see para. 971, ante.

(ii) Offences in relation to Constables

962. Assaulting or obstructing a constable. Any person who assaults a constable[1] in the execution of his duty or a person assisting a constable in the execution of his duty commits an offence and is liable [2] on summary conviction to imprisonment for a term not exceeding six, or the issue of a second or subsequent offence, nine months, or to a fine not exceeding £100, or both[3]; (2) on conviction on indictment to imprisonment for a term not exceeding two years or to a fine or both[4]. A person assaulting a constable does not commit an offence unless the constable was acting strictly within the limits of his powers and legal duty[5]. The justification of self-defence is available to a defendant charged with assaulting a constable where the assault occurred in resisting an act on the constable's part which was technically an assault[6].

Any person who resists or wilfully obstructs[7] a constable in the execution of his duty, or a person assisting a constable in the execution of his duty commits an offence and is liable on summary conviction to imprisonment for a term not exceeding one month or to a fine not exceeding £20, or to both[8].

1 As to the office of constable, see POLICE. The constable's appointment need not be proved: Berryman v Wise (1791) 4 Term Rep 366. Prison officers while acting as such have by virtue of their appointment all the powers, authorities and protection and privileges of a constable: Prison Act 1952, s. 8; see also Notting v Clifton [1937] 1 KB 382. Knowledge that the person assaulted was a police officer is not necessary; the offence consists in assaulting a constable being in the execution of his duty, not in knowing him to be in the execution of his duty: R v Forbes and Webb (1865) 10 Cox 362; R v Maxwell and Clanchy (1909) 2 Cr App Rep 26, CCA; see also McBride v Turnock [1964] Crim LR 456, DC. But as to an assault where the defendant genuinely and reasonably believed the person assaulted was not a constable, see Kenlin v Gardiner [1967] 2 QB 510, [1966] 3 All ER 931, DC; R v Mark, Brown and Mark [1961] Crim LR 173.
2 There is no right to claim trial on indictment (i.e. under the Magistrates' Courts Act 1952, s. 25: see MAGISTRATES): R v Woolwich JJ, ex parte Tooley [1967] 2 A.C.1, [1966] 2 All ER 429, HL.
3 Police Act 1964, s. 51 (1). As to the offence committed by a person who at the time of committing or being arrested for an offence under s. 51 (1) has in his possession a firearm or imitation firearm, see para. 891, ante. As to assault with intent to resist arrest, see para. 965, post.
4 The cardinal principle is that which is done in accordance with the law: ... done must be done in accordance with the law: Arthur Yates & Co (Property) Ltd v Vegetable Seeds Committee (1945) 72 C.L.R 37 at 66 (Aust. HC), per Sir John Latham CJ. As to the duties of a constable, see Rice v Connolly [1966] 2 QB 414 at 419, [1966] 2 All ER 649 at 651, DC, per Lord Parker CJ (... it is part of the obligations and duties of a police constable to take all steps which appear to him necessary for keeping the peace, for preventing crime and for protecting property from criminal injury. There is no exhaustive

that there have been some changes in the law since volume 11 was written. (See figure on page 94.) It is therefore important to read the information in the *Cumulative Supplement* in conjunction with that found in the main volume.

The information in these two volumes brings you up to date to the end of last year. But have there been changes in the law since then? To find out, turn to the looseleaf *Current Service* volume, and consult the part at the front called the *"Key."* The *key* is a list of volume numbers and paragraph numbers which have had some change made to them in the last few months. (See the figure on page 95.) Does your volume and paragraph number—Volume 11, paragraph 961—appear in this list? At the time of writing there is no entry in the *Key* for that volume and paragraph number. If there had been an entry, the note at the foot of the page would have informed you whether you needed to look in the *Reviews* or in the *Noter-up* section of the *Current Service* volume (under the number given in the Key) in order to find details of a recent change in the law.

SUMMARY: HOW TO USE HALSBURY'S LAWS, 4th ed.

6–5

1. Look up the subject in the *Index*. This tells you the *volume* and *paragraph* number which contains the information.
2. Find the relevant volume and paragraph number in the main work.
3. To make sure the information is up to date consult:
    (a) the *Cumulative Supplement* under the relevant volume and paragraph numbers and
    (b) the *Key* in the *Current Service* volume, under the relevant volume and paragraph numbers. The *Key* refers you to the *Reviews* or *Noter-up* section of the *Current Service* for the latest changes in the law.

Remember there are four steps in using *Halsbury's Laws*:

INDEX
MAIN WORK
CUMULATIVE SUPPLEMENT
CURRENT SERVICE

If you are looking for a relatively new subject, which is too recent to be included in the *Index*, consult the index which is printed at the back of the *Cumulative Supplement*, and the index in the back of the *Current Service* volume. These will direct you to the appropriate part of the work for the latest information.

953   Embracery
   TEXT and NOTE 2—This offence is obsolescent, conduct covered by it being more appropriately dealt with as conspiracy to pervert the course of justice or contempt of court: *R v Owen* [1976] 3 All ER 239, [1975] 1 WLR 840, CA.
   NOTE 6—A sentence of immediate imprisonment is appropriate unless the circumstances are wholly exceptional: *R v Owen* supra.

955   Perversion of the course of justice
   NOTES 1–7—The offence is restricted to acts which interfere with pending or imminent proceedings or with investigations which might end with criminal proceedings being brought: *R v Salvage* [1982] QB 372, [1982] 1 All ER 96, CA.
   NOTE 2—See also *R v Rowell* [1978] 1 All ER 665, [1978] 1 WLR 132, HL; *R v Machin* [1980] 3 All ER 151, [1980] 1 WLR 763, CA.
   NOTE 8—See also *R v Murray* [1982] 2 All ER 225, [1982] 1 WLR 475, CA (attempt to pervert course of justice by motorist who tampered with blood sample sent by him for analysis).
   TEXT and NOTE 3—See *Tsang Ping-Nam v R* [1981]1 WLR 1462, PC.
   NOTE 9—See also *R v Thomas, R v Ferguson* [1979] QB 326, [1978] 1 All ER 577, CA (assisting police suspect to avoid arrest); *Tsang Ping-Nam v R* [1981] 1 WLR 1462, PC.

960   Threatening etc witnesses at public inquiries
   NOTE 2—The offence is now triable only summarily: Criminal Law Act 1977, s 15 and the maximum fine is now level 3 on the standard scale: Criminal Justice Act 1982, ss 38, 46. As to the standard scale, see ibid, s 37, para 520A ante.

961   Concealing offences
   NOTE 1—"Arrestable offence" has the meaning assigned to it by Police and Criminal Evidence Act 1984, s 24 (see para 109A ante): Criminal Law Act 1967, s 4(1A); 1984 Act, Sch 6, para 17.
   NOTE 2—Criminal Law Act 1967, s 5(4) repealed: Criminal Law Act 1977, Sch 13. The offences are now triable either way by virtue of Magistrates' Courts Act 1980, s 17, Sch 1.

962   Assaulting or obstructing a constable
   NOTE 1—In circumstances which would entitle a private citizen to take steps to prevent an offence being committed, it is no defence that the accused was unaware of the police officer's status: *Albert v Lavin* [1982] AC 546, [1981] 3 All ER 878, HL.
   NOTE 2—1952 Act, s 25 repealed: Criminal Law Act 1977, s 65(5), Sch 13.
   TEXT and NOTE 3—This offence is no longer triable on indictment; the maximum penalty on summary conviction, whether of a first or subsequent offence, is a fine at level 5 on the standard scale or imprisonment for six months or both: Criminal Law Act 1977, ss 15, 30, Sch 1; Criminal Justice Act 1982, s 46. As to the standard scale, see ibid, s 37, para 520A ante.
   TEXT and NOTE 4—As to the limits of a constable's authority to search and remove clothing of an arrested person for his own safety, see *Lindley v Rutter* [1981] QB 128, DC. See also *R v Thornley* (1980) 72 Cr App Rep 302, CA (police constable on premises at invitation of occupier entitled to remain on premises for reasonable time to investigate complaint; still acting in execution of duty despite request by co-occupier to leave).
   NOTE 4—*Ludlow v Burgess,* cited, applied in *Pedro v Diss* [1981] 2 All ER 59, DC (metropolitan police constable detaining person under Metropolitan Police Act 1839, s 66, must inform him of grounds). See also *Bentley v Brudzinski* (1982) 75 Cr App Rep 217; *Collins v Wilcock* [1984] 3 All ER 374, DC.
   NOTE 6—This requires a criminal intention to obstruct the constable: *Willmott v Atack* [1977] QB 498, [1976] 3 All ER 794. See also *Ricketts v Cox* (1981) 74 Cr App Rep 298, DC. A warning to postpone commission of a crime until the danger of detection has passed amounts to obstruction: *Green v Moore* [1982] 1 All ER 428, [1982] 2 WLR 671, DC; *Moore v Green* [1983] 1 All ER 663, DC. An act intended to interfere with an arrest by a constable amounts to obstruction: *Hills v Ellis* [1983] QB 680, [1983] 1 All ER 667, DC. The motive is irrelevant: ibid. Dictum of Lord Goddard CJ in *Hinchcliffe v Sheldon*, cited, applied in *Lewis v Cox* [1985] QB 509, DC, not following *Hills v Ellis*, supra.
   TEXT and NOTE 7—Maximum fine now level 3 on the standard scale (see supra): Criminal Law Act 1977, s 31, Sch 6; Criminal Justice Act 1982, s 46.

967   Escape
   NOTE 4—Lawfulness must be proved by appropriate evidence: *Dillon v R* [1982] AC 484, [1982] 1 All ER 1017, PC.
   TEXT and NOTE 6—The offence of escape from lawful custody is an offence complete in itself, and the outcome of a trial of a principal charge in favour of a prisoner cannot be a defence to the charge of escape: *R v Frascati* (1981) 73 Cr App Rep 28, CA.

VOLUME 10—*cont.*		Key				VOLUME 11	
PARA.	NO.	PARA.	NO.	PARA.	NO.	PARA.	NO.

VOLUME 10—cont.

PARA.	NO.
578	MM548
580	MM549
588–590	MM281
612	MM1365
623	MM1366
625	MM1367
626	MM1368
627	MM1369
631	MM1370
636	MM1371
652	L578
653	MM550
Courts	
705	MM1201
706	MM1201
715	L907
745	L907
745	MM551
761	MM552
849	MM553
850	MM553
850	MM554
853	MM164
857	MM555
869	MM1119
879	MM21
888	MM1120
900	MM556
916	MM1121
936	MM282
936	MM1122
946	MM283
949	MM557
Cremation and Burial	
1187	MM22
VOLUME 11	
Criminal Law	
24	L349
24	L742
24	L1129
43	L511
44	MM99
46	L511
49	MM1123
50	L588
58	L753
63–65.2	L174
7?	L28
92	L587
97	MM881
98	L915
98	MM558
98	MM882
98c	MM1202
101	L356
108	L356

PARA.	NO.
120	L587
120A7	L1021
120B5	MM346
123A1	MM883
125	MM424
125B	L29
125B	L1020
126–135	L365
136	L462
145	L361
154	MM1124
155	L31
155	L357
155	L359
156	MM1125
158	L361
165A	L31
165A1	MM1126
165A2	MM1127
165A4	MM1128
165A5	L914
173	L357
174	L914
175	L914
210	MM559
212	L1196a
213	L180
214	L753
263	MM51
290	L354
294	L918
297	L181
299	L1132
305	L179
306	L179
309	L755
309	L921
310	MM884
311	L756
312	MM23
323	L922
323	L924
357	L360
359	L592
360	L592
363	L363
364	L590
366	L919
368	L589
369	L1195
377	L33
381	L33
386	MM165
387	L180
387	L182
410	L751
410A1	L1136
410A1	MM1372
412	L751
418	L591

PARA.	NO.
431	MM560
438	L32
442	L752
446	MM1203
453	L1138
454	L1137
457	L1137
455	L917
457	L917
464	MM166
481	L1052
481	L1232
482	L516
483	L265
483	L268
483	L516
483	L849
483	L1052
483	L1053
483	L1232
495	L269
495	L848
504	L1233
520	L349
554	L517
554	MM1204
556A	L517
568	MM1205
586	MM425
590	L593
591	L593
624	MM561
649	L749
652	L749
652	L755
652	L913
652	L924
664	L266
668	L749
695	MM24
711	L367
754	L1195
754A	L985
754B	L983
760	L750
760	L808
768	L986
770	L72a
770A	L72a
770A	L984
776	MM763
788	L915
796	L588a
796	MM685
798	MM686
803	L264
804	L263
804	L847
805	L175
805	L740

PARA.	NO.
805	L910
843–847A	L911
843	L744
846	MM885
848	L176
848	MM886
849	MM886
850	L356
850	MM887
850	MM1029
852	L583
852	MM168
852	MM888
855	MM889
856–858	MM890
860–862	MM891
875	L783
969–973	MM1373
999	L741
1025	MM892
1058	L585
1068	1352
1092	L360
1092	L1130
1093	L742a
1099A	MM1206
1099A2–5	MM1206
1118	MM893
1122–1150	MM894
1157	L743a
1160	L33
1163	MM1207
1164	MM284
1165	L27
1166	L27
1172	L743
1176	L738b
1185–1190	MM1129
1194	MM950
1198	MM169
1200	L26
1214	L416
1229	L351
1230	L351
1241	L25
1261	MM170
1263	L1131
1269	L586
1274	L24
1274	L756
1277	L739
1278	L350
1278	L1133
1279	L28
1281	L747
1291	L1132
1292	L1131
1305	MM171

The prefix L indicates the Reviews, and MM the Noter-up

Each volume of the main work also contains, at the back, detailed subject indexes to *each* of the subjects dealt with in that volume.

The last two volumes of *Halsbury's Laws* (volumes 51–52) are devoted to the law of the European Communities, and its effect upon United Kingdom law. A similar but more sophisticated system of paragraph numbers is used in these two volumes and footnote references refer you to the relevant Directives, Decisions and Regulations of the European Communities. Volume 52 contains a useful glossary of technical terms as well as a detailed index to both volumes. The information is kept up to date by the information in the *Cumulative Supplement* and *Current Service* volume.

The *monthly reviews* (filed in the *Current Service* volume) can be used as a general means of keeping up with new developments in subjects you are studying since they give, under subject headings, recent changes in the law of each subject. These monthly reviews are replaced by an *Annual Abridgement*, also arranged by subject, which summarises all the changes in the law during a particular year (commencing in 1974 when the first abridgment appeared). At the beginning of the volume a section headed "In brief" summarises the major development in the law of each subject during the year. At the beginning of each subject there is a reference to the main volume of *Halsbury's Laws* which deals with that subject and there is a highly selective list of periodical articles written on the subject during the year.

Specialised Encyclopedias

6–6   There are a number of specialised encyclopedias which can provide you with an up-to-date statement of the law in particular subject areas. Many of these are issued in looseleaf format, so that the information can be up-dated by the insertion of replacement pages whenever there is a change in the law. One important series, *The Local Government Library*, published by Sweet & Maxwell, covers such topics as Housing, Planning, Environmental Health, Compulsory Purchase and Compensation. A number of other publishers have issued similar works covering, for example, Social Welfare Law (Oyez), Landlord and Tenant (Butterworths), and Consumer Credit (Longmans). Looseleaf encyclopedias are particularly useful in subjects such as taxation, where the law changes very rapidly. Before using a looseleaf encyclopedia you should check the pages near the beginning of the volume which tell you how recent the infor-

mation is. This will enable you to be certain that the latest supplementary pages have all been inserted. Looseleaf
encyclopedias usually contain an explanation of the law,
together with the up-to-date versions of the relevant statutes,
statutory instruments and government circulars, and notes of all
relevant cases. Publishers are now issuing some practitioners'
books, such as *Buckley on the Companies Acts*, in conjunction
with a looseleaf volume, so that the book can be kept completely
up to date. This is a development of the long-established practice of issuing cumulative supplements in between editions, to
modernise the last edition.

Precedent Books and Rule Books

These are principally intended for the practitioner. The basic   6–7
object of precedent books is to provide specimens of wills, conveyances, tenancy agreements and other forms of legal documents which solicitors are called upon to draw up. In addition,
there are some precedent books which provide specimens of
the types of forms which will be required whenever a case is
taken to court. Rule books contain the rules which govern procedure in court, and specimen copies of the various orders and
forms used by the courts, and by the parties to litigation.

The *Encyclopaedia of Forms and Precedents* aims to provide a
form for every transaction likely to be encountered by practitioners, except for court forms. The entries are arranged by
subject, *e.g.* Animals, Mortgages. Some idea of the wide scope
of the work can be obtained by glancing through the subject
headings. For instance, the section on animals covers such
diverse topics as the sale and leasing of animals, applications
for a licence to keep mink, or to keep an animals' boarding
establishment, a veterinary surgeon's certificate for the destruction of an animal, and the relevant documents prohibiting
movement of animals during an outbreak of disease. The looseleaf service volume keeps the information up to date. The
Cumulative Index refers you to the volume (in bold type) and
paragraph number which you require. Each individual volume
also has its own index. References in the index to paragraph
numbers in square brackets refer to precedents: paragraph
numbers not enclosed in brackets refer to the preliminary notes.
Checklists on procedures to be followed are provided under
some subject headings.

Atkins' Encyclopaedia of Court Forms in Civil Proceedings is a
complementary publication, covering the procedure in civil
courts and tribunals. The volume on divorce, for instance, con-

tains all the necessary documents needed during the court action, together with a detailed list of the steps to be taken and the forms required at each stage. The volumes are re-issued from time to time to incorporate new material. An annual supplement and a half-yearly service booklet keep the information up to date, and an annual *Consolidated Index* is published.

Precedents for the Conveyancer (issued as a supplement to the journal *The Conveyancer*) is an example of a more specialised precedent book.

The rules and procedures governing various courts are set out in a number of places. The *County Court Practice*, and the *Supreme Court Practice* (often referred to as the "*White Book*") set out the documents required for those appearing in those courts. *Archbold's Criminal Pleading, Evidence and Practice* is used by those engaged in criminal work. Some practitioners' textbooks will include precedents; these can be traced through the library's subject catalogue.

The coloured pages in each issue of the *New Law Journal* are of particular interest to practitioners. These often include specimen forms and precedents, and details of Home Office circulars and practice directions. Practice directions are also published in the major series of law reports, *e.g. All England Law Reports, Weekly Law Reports*.

TRACING CASES ON A SUBJECT

6–8   Cases on a particular subject can be traced by consulting:

> *Current Law;*
> *Current Law Year Books;*
> *The Digest;*
> *Halsbury's Laws of England;*
> Indexes and digests to individual series of law reports, *e.g.*
>   *Law Reports Indexes, Consolidated Tables and Index to the All*
>   *England Law Reports;*
> Relevant textbooks and periodical articles.

How to use Current Law

6–9   *Current Law* is published monthly. It is an important publication and it is essential that you should learn how to use it.

The main part of each monthly issue is arranged by subject and under each subject heading is given a summary of: recent cases on the subject; new statutes and statutory instruments; government reports; and recent books and periodical articles or

[1934] 1 K.B. 448; *Church of Scientology of California* v. *North News*, May 17, 1973, C.A. (Unrep.) considered).
BARNET v. CROZIER, *The Times*, December 30, 1986, C.A.

LIMITATION OF ACTIONS

182a. Accrual of cause of action—surveyor's report—whether statute-barred

The duties of a surveyor are not analogous to those of an engineer or architect, but are confined to exercising reasonable skill and care in reporting reasonably discoverable faults existing at the time of survey. Thus any cause of action accrues at the time of reliance upon the surveyor's report.

In February 1975 a firm of surveyors prepared a report on a new building of which the Secretary of State was considering acquiring a lease. The Secretary of State, relying on the report, had committed himself to acquiring the lease by July 1975. Defects allegedly based on faulty design, first appeared in February 1982. In January 1982 the Secretary of State issued a writ against the surveyors claiming damages in tort for alleged negligence in failing to report the faulty design. The preliminary issue was whether the claim was statute-barred.

Held, dismissing the action, that any action accrued at the time of reliance upon the report (*Philips* v. *Ward* [1956] C.L.Y. 936 applied. *Pirelli General Cable Works* v. *Faber Oscar & Partners* [1983] C.L.Y. 2216 distinguished).

SECRETARY OF STATE FOR THE ENVIRONMENT v. ESSEX, GOODMAN AND SUGGITT [1986] 1 W.L.R. 1432, Judge Lewis Hawser Q.C. sitting as Official Referee.

182b. Personal injuries—power to override time-limit—discretion

[Limitation Act 1980 (c.58), ss.14, 33.]

P claimed as widower and administrator of his wife's estate. P's wife worked for D for 12 months in 1954. In June 1978 she began to get short of breath and was admitted to hospital. A pleural biopsy was performed which revealed a tumour consistent with mesothelioma. P and his wife were told she had cancer, probably caused by exposure to asbestos dust. She died at 44, in 1979. P took no steps to issue proceedings as he was upset and depressed. He had to look after four children and work as a long-distance lorry driver. He consulted a solicitor in 1982. A letter before action was sent to D in August 1982. Legal aid were granted in January 1983 but discharged as P failed to maintain contributions. There were further delays on P's part. Legal aid was finally granted in August 1983. A writ was issued on October 4, 1983.

Held, that (1) P had knowledge within s.14(1) at the date of death but not before May 1978 when his wife first became ill; (2) the 18-month delay between the date of expiry of the three-year limitation period following the deceased's death and the issue of proceedings was insignificant when considering the cogency of the evidence likely to be adduced by the parties upon liability; (3) P did not act promptly but this was understandable; (4) D had not been prejudiced by the delay; (5) a letter before action had been sent to D 14 months before the issue of the writ. It was therefore equitable to allow the case to proceed.

RULE v. ATLAS STONE CO., December 11, 1984; Simon Brown J. [*Ex rel Field Fisher & Martineau, Solicitors.*]

LITERARY AND SCIENTIFIC INSTITUTIONS

183. Imperial War Museum

IMPERIAL WAR MUSEUM (BOARD OF TRUSTEES) ORDER 1986 (No. 2239) [45p], made under the Imperial War Museum Act 1955 (c.14), s.1(2); operative forthwith; makes provision regarding the membership of the Imperial War Museum's board of trustees.

LOCAL GOVERNMENT

184. Communities

DINEFWR (COMMUNITIES) ORDER 1986 (No. 2077) [£2·40], made under the Local Government Act 1972 (c.70), s.67(4) and (5), Sched. 10, para. 7; operative on April 1, 1987, except art. 2(1) which comes into force on January 1, 1987; continues 17 communities, abolishes seven and constitutes six new ones in Dinefwr.

that subject. Full details are given to enable you to trace the cases and other materials mentioned in your own library.

At the back of each issue is a *Cumulative Case Citator*, which contains a list of all the cases which which have been reported during the current year. It is therefore only necessary to look at the citator in the *latest* issue of *Current Law* to trace a case reported at any time during the year. (This list of cases brings the information in the *Current Law Case Citators* up to date (para. 2–14).

The monthly issues of *Current Law* also contain a *subject index*. Again, it is cumulative, so it is only necessary to consult the index in the latest month's issue. This enables you to trace any development in the law during the current year. The reference given, *e.g.* Contract, Jan 24 is to the appropriate monthly issue of *Current Law* (in this example, the January issue). Every item in each issue has its own individual number; the item you require in the January issue is number 24, and there you will find a recent case, or some other development in the law of contract summarised.

If your library possesses *Scottish Current Law* (which has a green cover), the pages printed on green paper (and which have a higher series of item numbers than the remainder of the issue) relate to changes in Scottish law. Despite the name, *Scottish Current Law* covers changes in both English and Scottish law. The green pages give the Scottish information: the white pages are identical with those in the English *Current Law*.

A list of new books and periodical articles is printed under each subject heading.

As we have already seen (para. 2–14) the *Current Law Case Citators* provide you with a list of reports for a case. This information can be brought up to date for the current year by looking at the list of cases in the latest issue of *Current Law*. Suppose, however, that you know that there has been a recent case on the subject but you do not know the name of the parties. In this instance you can trace the cases on that subject during the current year by looking in the cumulative subject index in the latest issue of *Current Law*. If you have spelt the name of the parties incorrectly, or have an incomplete reference, you can trace the case by the subject approach, using the subject index to *Current Law*.

How to Use the Current Law Year Books

6–10   The monthly issues of *Current Law* are replaced by an annual volume, the *Current Law Year Book*. (Your library may possess the Scottish version, the *Scottish Current Law Year Book*. Despite the name, this includes all the English materials, plus a separate section at the back of the volume containing Scottish developments during the year. There are separate indexes to the English and Scottish sections.)

The *Year Book* is arranged by subject, in the same way as the monthly issues, and contains a summary of all the cases, legislation and other developments in that subject during the year. (As noted above, developments in Scottish law are printed in a separate sequence at the back of the *Scottish Current Law Year Book*). Lists of periodical articles and books written on a subject during the year are printed at the back of the volume. (The 1956 *Year Book* contains a list of periodical articles published between 1947 and 1956).

The 1976 *Year Book* contains, at the back, *a subject index to all the entries in all the Year Books from 1947–1976*. Entries give the last two digits of the year, and a reference to the individual item number within that year's volume, *e.g.* 69/3260 is a reference to item 3260 in the 1969 *Year Book*. Entries which have no year in front of them will be found in the *Current Law Consolidation 1947–1951*. A new subject index for all entries in all the *Year Books* published after 1971 began in 1977. The entry in the *latest Year Book* should therefore be consulted, together with the entry in the 1976 *Year Book*, and the index in the *latest* monthly issue of *Current Law*. These three sources will provide complete coverage of any developments in the law of that subject since 1947.

Master volumes were published in the 1956, 1961, 1966 and 1971 *Year Books*. These volumes contain, under the usual subject headings, detailed entries for all developments during the year in which they were published, together with a summary of the developments during the previous four years. References are given to enable you to trace the full details in the appropriate *Current Law Year Book*. Thus, it is possible, by using the *Master Volumes* and the *Current Law Consolidation 1947–1951*, to see at a glance every entry which has appeared in *Current Law* on a particular subject over a five year period. For instance, the 1971 *Year Book* prints in full details of all cases, legislation, etc. which took place during 1971, together with summaries of all developments in that subject during 1967–1970. The location of the full details of each case, etc., in the 1967, 1968, 1969 and 1970 *Year Books* is given. The *Master Volumes* therefore enabled you to survey the developments in the law of a particular subject over a five year period, in more detail than was possible in the subject index.

SUMMARY: HOW TO USE CURRENT LAW

(1) If you know the name of a case, and want to find out where it has been reported, and whether the case has subsequently been judicially considered, consult:
   Current Law Case Citator 1947–1976 and the latest *Current Law Case Citator and*
   List of cases in the *latest* monthly issue of *Current Law.*

(2) To trace any developments (cases, statutes, etc.) on a particular subject, consult:
   the index (covering 1947–1976) at the back of the 1976 *Current Law Year Book and*
   the index at the back of the *latest Year Book and*
   the subject index in the *latest* monthly issue of *Current Law.*

(3) To obtain a general view of developments in a topic over a number of years, consult:
   Current Law Consolidation 1947–1951 *and* the *Master Volumes* (1956, 1961, 1966 and 1971 *Year Books*) and
   all the *Year Books* published since the last Master Volume was issued *and*
   all the monthly issues of *Current Law* for this year.

(4) To trace books and periodical articles on a subject look in the back of the 1956 *Year Book and each* subsequent *Year Book,* and in the monthly issues of *Current Law* under the appropriate subject heading. (N.B. There are other sources for tracing periodical articles: para. 4–2, and books: para. 6–32 *et seq.*).

Remember that *Current Law* only contains information on cases reported or mentioned in court since 1947 and other developments in the law since 1947. To trace earlier cases use *The Digest* and to trace other developments in the law prior to 1947 use *Halsbury's Laws of England.*

The Digest

6–11   *The Digest* (formerly known as the *English and Empire Digest*) contains summaries of cases which have appeared in law reports from the thirteenth century to the present day, arranged in subject order. It enables you to trace cases of any date which deal with your particular subject. In addition to English cases reports of Irish, Scottish and many Commonwealth cases are included, together with cases on European Community law. These are printed in smaller type to enable them to be easily distinguished from English cases.

A summary of the decision in every case is given, followed by

218   VOL. 12—CONTRACT (PART V)

Part V.—Consideration

SECT. 1.   IN GENERAL

LAW.   *See* HALSBURY'S LAWS (3rd Edn.), Vol. 8, pp. 113 *et seq.*

CROSS-REFERENCE.   *See* FRAUDULENT & VOIDABLE CONVEYANCES, Vol. 25 (Repl.), Nos. 108 *et seq.*

1393. Consideration.]—A consideration is a cause or meritorious occasion requiring a mutual recompense in fact or in law. Contracts & bargains have a *quid pro quo.*—CALTHORPE'S CASE (1574), Dyer, 334 b; 73 E. R. 756.

Annotations:—**Consd.** Magdalen College, Cambridge Case (1615), 11 Co. Rep. 66 b; Wain *v.* Warlters (1804), 5 East, 10.

     1394. ——.]—HAMMON *v.* ROLL, No. 1403, *post.*

     1395. ——.]—THOMAS *v.* THOMAS, No. 1560, *post.*

1396. Good consideration.]—There are two manners of gifts on a good consideration, *scil.* consideration of nature or blood, & a valuable consideration.—TWYNE'S CASE (1602), 3 Co. Rep. 80 b.; Moore, K. B. 638; [1558-1774] All E. R. Rep. 302; 76 E. R. 809.

Annotations:—**Refd.** Bennet *v.* Musgrove (1750), 2 Ves. Sen. 51; Ryall *v.* Rowles (1750), 1 Ves. Sen. 348; Holbird *v.* Anderson (1793), 5 Term Rep. 235; Kelson *v.* Kelson (1853), 1 W. R. 143; Corlett *v.* Radcliffe (1860), 14 Moo. P. C. C. 121.

See, further, Nos. 1740, *et seq., post.*

1397. Valuable consideration.]—A valuable consideration, in the sense of the law, may consist either in some right, interest, profit or benefit accruing to the one party, or some forbearance, detriment, loss or responsibility given, suffered or undertaken by the other (*per* CUR.).—CURRIE *v.* MISA (1875). L. R. 10 Exch. 153; 44 L. J. Ex. 94; 23 W. R. 450, Ex. Ch.; *affd. sub nom.* MISA *v.* CURRIE (1876), 1 App. Cas. 554; [1874-80] All E. R. Rep. 686; 45 L. J. Q. B. 852; 35 L. T. 414; 24 W. R. 1049, H. L.

Annotations:—**Consd.** Fleming *v.* Bank of New Zealand, [1900] A. C. 577; Ball *v.* National & Grindlays Bank, Ltd., [1971] 3 All E. R. 485. **Refd.** Jones *v.* Waring & Gillow, [1926] A. C. 670; *Re* Cuthbert, *Ex p.* Monnoyer British Construction Co. *v.* Trustees, [1936] 1 All E. R. 342; Oliver *v.* Davis, [1949] 2 All E. R. 353; Barclays Bank, Ltd. *v.* Astley Industrial Trust, Ltd., [1970] 1 All E. R. 719.

SCOTTISH, IRISH AND COMMONWEALTH CASES

     880. Consideration.]—The definition of "consideration" in Indian Contract Act is wider than the requirement of the English law.—DEBNARAYAN DUTT *v.* CHUNILAL GHOSE (1913), I. L. R. 41 Calc. 137.—IND.

     881. Valuable consideration.]—To constitute a valuable consideration it is not necessary that it should be a money consideration.—CROCKFORD *v.* EQUITABLE INSURANCE CO. (1863), 5 All. 651.—CAN.

     882. ——.]—There is no difference between the French law, which prevails in Lower Canada, & the English law on the subjects of the necessity of valuable consideration for a contract.—MCGREEVY *v.* RUSSELL (1886), 56 L. T. 501.—CAN.

     883. ——.]—To entitle a party to an agreement, other than a donation, to sue thereon, the common law of the Cape Colony requires that such party must have given some *quid pro quo* or valuable consideration under the agreement.—MTEMBU *v.* WEBSTER (1899), 21 S. C. 323.—S. AF.

     884. ——.]—A good cause of action can be founded on a promise made seriously & deliberately & with the intention that a lawful obligation should be established.—CONRADIE *v.* ROUSSOUW, [1919] App. D. 279.—S. AF.

     885. —— *Burden of proof.*]—Where an option states that it is given "for value received" the *onus* of showing there was in fact no consideration is upon the optionor.—BISHOP *v.* GRAY, [1944] 4 D. L. R. 743; O. W. N. 700.—CAN.

SECT. 2.   NECESSITY FOR (NUDUM PACTUM).

LAW.   *See* HALSBURY'S LAWS (3rd Edn.), Vol. 8, p. 113.

CROSS-REFERENCES.   *See* Nos. 5357 *et seq., post* (novation of contract); Nos. 1403, 1758, *post* (promise to pay debt already released); BILLS OF EXCHANGE, PROMISSORY NOTES & NEGOTIABLE INSTRUMENTS, Vol. 6 (Repl.), Nos. 813 *et seq.*; GUARANTEE & INDEMNITY, Vol. 26 (Repl.), Nos. 56 *et seq.* (as requisite of guarantee); DEEDS & OTHER INSTRUMENTS, Vol. 17 (Repl.), Nos. 12 *et seq.*, & FRAUDULENT & VOIDABLE CONVEYANCES, Vol. 25 (Repl.), Nos. 226 *et seq.* (necessity for consideration in deed).

1398. General rule.]—Where there is no consideration, *i.e.* upon *nudum pactum*, there ought to be no more help in Chancery than there is at the common law.—ANON. (prior to 1602), Cary, 5; 21 E. R. 3.

     1399. ——.]—A. delivered £20 to B. to the use of C., a woman, to be delivered her the day of her marriage. Before her marriage A. countermanded it, & called home the money:—*Held:* C. should not be aided in Chancery, because there was no consideration why she should have it.—LYTE *v.* PENY (1541). 1 Dyer, 49 a; 73 E. R. 108; *sub nom.* ANON., Cary, 9.

Annotations:—**Refd.** Rekstein *v.* Severo Sibirsko Gosudarstvernnoe Akcionernoe Olschestro Komseverputj & Bank for Russian Trade, Ltd., [1933] 1 K. B. 47.

     1400. ——.]—CALTHORPE'S CASE, No. 1393, *ante.*

     1401. ——.]—K. was sued in the Exchequer to answer to the Crown for money received by him of the abbot of F. to pay over to the abbot of C. who was attainted of treason. A bill from the abbot of F. to the abbot of C. was shown which was unsealed. On demurrer:—*Held:* the bill was only a chose in action, there was a contract *nudum pactum,* & the action would be dismissed; but if a servant received money to the use of his master, & brought it to the house of the master, who was afterwards attainted, this would be forfeit.—R. *v.* KITCHEN (1582), Sav. 40; 123 E. R. 1000.

     1402. ——.]—On application being made to a widow for payment for goods supplied to her late husband, she promised, in consideration of the creditor supplying her, to pay the amount due from her late husband & the price of goods to be supplied to her by a certain day:—*Held:* the action would lie, & there was a good consideration; for the forbearance of the money was a good consideration in itself, & in every *assumpsit,* he who made the promise ought to have benefit thereby, & the other was to sustain some loss.—HATCH & CAPEL'S CASE (1613), Godb. 202; 78 E. R. 123.

the name of the case, and a list of places where the case is reported. The subsequent judicial history of the case is also shown, in annotations. A list of the abbreviations used for law reports will be found in the front of Volume 1 and also in the front of the *Cumulative Supplement*.

How to Use the Digest to Trace Cases on a Subject

6–12   Let's see how you would use *The Digest* to find out what cases there have been about a particular subject. For example, if you want to look at cases on consideration in contract you can turn to the *consolidated index* and look up the subject. The entry under "consideration" is large, giving references to many different aspects of the law relating to consideration, and referring you to the volume number, the subject heading (contract) and the case numbers for cases dealing with aspects of the doctrine of consideration. Cases with an asterisk in front of the number refer to Scottish, Irish and Commonwealth cases.

Scottish, Irish and Commonwealth cases are always printed in smaller type than English cases on the same subject. In most volumes of *The Digest* all the case numbers, of whatever jurisdiction, are numbered consecutively. Cases 2040 may be an English case while case 2041 is a Canadian case on the same subject. However, in some volumes of the *Digest* the non-English cases have a separate sequence of case numbers, preceded by an asterisk. There are thus two *separate* sequences of case numbers on the same page. (See the above, page 103.) A glance at the top of the page shows the case numbers, both unasterisked (English cases) and asterisked (other jurisdictions) which appear on that page.

Keeping up to Date

6–13   After finding the relevant cases on your subject in the main volumes you should check to see if there have been more recent cases on the subject since the volume was written. To do this update you must consult the *Cumulative Supplement*. Make a note of the volume number, subject heading and case number(s) in the main volumes which contain relevant information. Now turn to the *Cumulative Supplement* and look to see if there is an entry for that volume, subject heading and case number. If there is an entry this will provide information on a later case, in which the case you were consulting in the main work has been referred to, considered, overruled, etc. (A full list of the abbreviations used and their meanings appears at the front of the *Cumulative Supplement*, under the heading "Meaning of terms used in classifying annotating cases"). For example, an entry:

5016 Consd. Podbery v. *Peake* [1981] 1 All E.R. 699

in the *Cumulative Supplement* means that case number 5016 in the main volumes has subsequently been considered in the 1981 case of *Podbery* v. *Peake*.

The *Cumulative Supplement* also includes references to new cases on the same subject matter. These new cases *either* provide a summary, followed by the name of the case (and a reference to where the case will be found in various series of law reports), *or* they refer you to one of the *continuation volumes* where (under the same volume, subject and case number) further details of the case, including a full length summary will be found.

The *Cumulative Supplement* is revised annually; the front cover tells you how recent the information is. If you are looking for new cases on a particular subject, within the last few months, then *The Digest* is not sufficiently up to date and you should consult other publications, such as *Current Law*, the "pink indexes" to the *Law Reports*, or the Current Service to *Halsbury's Laws of England*.

SUMMARY: TRACING CASES ON A SUBJECT IN THE DIGEST

1. Look up the subject in the *consolidated index*. This will refer you to the volume, subject heading and case number where cases on that subject can be found.
2. To see if there have been any more recent cases on the same subject, look in the *Cumulative Supplement* under the relevant volume, subject heading and case number. This will provide you with up to date information. You may be referred to one of the *continuation volumes* for further details. If so, look under the volume number, subject heading and case number in the *continuation volume*.

How to Use Individual Indexes to Series of Law Reports to Trace Cases on a Subject

If the facilities in your library are limited, you may need to use the indexes to individual series of law reports to trace relevant cases on a subject. The most useful are the *Law Reports Indexes* (para. 2–16) because they cover a number of other important series in addition to the *Law Reports*. Indexes are available covering 1951–1960, 1961–1970, and 1971–1980 and supplementary indexes (an annual red index and the latest pink index:

para. 2–16) bring the information up to date to within a few weeks of the present day. The *Law Reports Indexes* are easier to use than *The Digest*, but remember that they only cover cases from 1951 onwards and that foreign cases are not included.

A typical entry from the *Law Reports Index* is given on page 107.

In addition to the *Law Reports Indexes* (and the series of *Digests*, going back to 1865, which preceded them), there are indexes to other series, such as the *All England Law Reports*, which published a *Consolidated Tables and Index* in three volumes, covering 1936–1981. This is kept up to date by supplements (para. 2–16). In addition, there is an index volume to the *All England Law Reports Reprint*, which includes a subject index to selected cases from 1558–1935.

HOW TO TRACE THE SUBSEQUENT JUDICIAL HISTORY OF A CASE

6–14   Judges often rely upon earlier cases to support the reasons which they have given for their decision, and from time to time a judge will review the case law in an attempt to explain the principles stated in earlier cases, or to use them as a springboard to create a new application of the principles. Occasionally a case will be distinguished in order that the judge will not feel obliged to follow it. Less frequently, a superior court will state that an earlier case was wrongly decided, and will overrule it, so that the principles laid down in the case will not be followed thereafter.

The treatment that a case receives when it is subsequently judicially considered has a direct bearing on its importance and reliability. For example, if in a moot or essay you cited as an authority the common law rules relating to compensation for war damage which were laid down in *Burmah Oil Co.* v. *Lord Advocate* [1965] A.C. 75, you would be embarrassed to discover that it was abolished by statute, the War Damages Act 1965. Similarly, you should be aware that the case of *Gillick* v. *West Norfolk Area Health Authority* [1985] 1 All E.R. 533 was reversed on appeal to the House of Lords. Consequently you must be alert to the need to trace the full judicial history of a particular case.

The simplest way to do this is to use the *Current Law Case Citators* (para. 2–14). These will give the citation of any English case which has been judicially considered since 1947 and show its treatment. For instance, the well-known old case *Carlill* v. *Carbolic Smoke Ball Co.*, which was reported in 1892, appears in the *Current Law Case Citators* because it has been considered in

The Weekly Law Reports 19 December 1986

78   **Subject Matter**

NEGLIGENCE—*continued*
  Duty of care to whom?—*continued*
   Occupiers of adjoining premises
     Defendant failing to secure its premises—Vandals entering defendant's premises and causing
     water to escape—Escaping water damaging plaintiff's premises below—Whether defendant
     liable for acts of third party vandals
                   King v. Liverpool City Council, C.A. [1986] 1 W.L.R. 890
   Purchaser of secondhand car
     Defendant purchasing car from dealer with low recorded mileage—No warranty given as to
     mileage and defendant unaware that odometer reading false—Car resold to plaintiff by
     defendant with declaration that odometer reading correct to best of his knowledge and
     belief—Whether declaration made negligently—Whether defendant liable for breach of
     warranty or misrepresentation
                   Hummingbird Motors Ltd. v. Hobbs, C.A. [1986] R.T.R. 276
  Foreseeability of risk
   Local authority's unsafe system
     Local authority carrying out road works involving gas pipes—Negligent system of carrying
     out work—Explosion from damaged gas pipe causing death—Whether reasonably foresee-
     able that accident resulting in personal injury would ensue—Whether local authority liable
     on plaintiff's claim for damages
                   Sullivan v. South Glamorgan County Council, C.A. (1985) 84 L.G.R. 415
  Safe system of work
   Ship
     Vessel lost at sea with all hands—Dependants' claim based on defective construction of
     ship—Whether vessel "equipment"—Employers' Liability (Defective Equipment) Act 1969,
     s. 1(1)(*a*)(3)   **Coltman v. Bibby Tankers Ltd.,** Sheen J. [1986] 1 W.L.R. 751

NUISANCE
  Local authority premises
   Causing nuisance
     Trespassers on educational premises apprehended inhaling solvents—Inhalation of solvents
     in school playground after school hours—School playground left in unfit state—Staff and
     pupils not present—Whether offence caused—Whether inhaling solvents capable of
     amounting to nuisance—Local Government (Miscellaneous Provisions) Act 1982, s. 40(1)(2)
                   Sykes v. Holmes, D.C. (1985) 84 L.G.R. 355
  Noise
   Landlord's liability
     Council letting land to go-kart club for use as go-kart track—Plaintiffs claiming injunction
     against council to restrain continuation of use as go-kart track—Whether council liable for
     nuisance—Whether nuisance ordinary and necessary consequence of operation of track—
     Whether plaintiffs entitled to injunction
                   Tetley v. Chitty, McNeill J. [1986] 1 All E.R. 663

PARTNERSHIP
  Limited partnership
   Partnership losses see REVENUE: **Income tax:** *Loss relief*

PATENT
  Extension
   Transitional provisions
     Existing patent for 16 years—Extension of patent for four years as new existing patent
     endorsed "licences of right"—Application to comptroller to settle terms of licence—
     Effective date of grant of licence—Whether comptroller having power to impose term
     prohibiting importation of patented article—Patents Act 1977, s. 46(3)(*a*), Sch. 1, para.
     4(1)(2)(*c*)—E.E.C. Treaty (Cmnd. 5179–II), arts. 30, 36
             Reg. v. Comptroller-General of Patents, Designs and Trade Marks, *Ex parte*
                   Gist-Brocades NV, H.L.(E.) [1986] 1 W.L.R. 51
  Infringement
   Accrual of cause of action
     Static switch controller for d.c. circuit—Act of infringement after date of publication of
     complete specification but before grant of letters patent—Whether cause of action accruing
     at date of act of infringement or date of grant—Date from which limitation period to
     run—Patents Act 1949, s. 13(4)—Limitation Act 1980, s. 2
                   Sevcon Ltd. v. Lucas CAV Ltd., H.L.(E.) [1986] 1 W.L.R. 462

court several times since 1947. After giving the name of the case, and a reference to where the case is to be found in the *Law Reports*, the following entry appears:

Dicta applied, 67/1745: Applied, 73/1529: Distinguished 73/3095

This means that if you turn to the *Current Law Year Book* for 1967, item 1745 will be found to be the summary of a case in which *Carlill's* case was applied. Similarly, the 1973 *Year Book* contains two reports of cases (items 1529 and 3095) in which the case was considered. The entry in the latest *Current Law Case Citator* shows that *Carlill's* case has been considered subsequently, in 1980 and again in 1984.

The *Law Reports Indexes* contain a heading "Cases judicially considered," and the index to the *All England Law Reports* also includes a list of "Cases reported and considered." *The Digest* (para. 2–15) contains annotations to entries, showing the subsequent judicial history of a case. This is kept up to date by the information in the *Cumulative Supplement*.

HOW TO FIND WORDS AND PHRASES JUDICIALLY CONSIDERED

6–15   The meaning of words is of great importance to lawyers. The interpretation of statutes and documents may hinge upon the meaning of a single word. For example, does "day" in banking terms mean 24 hours, or does it end at the close of working hours? Can a mistress be considered part of a "family"?

Two specialised dictionaries record the courts' decisions on problems such as these. *Stroud's Judicial Dictionary* provides the meaning of words as defined in the case law and in statutes. *Words and Phrases Legally Defined* is a similar publication; both are kept up to date by supplements.

The *Law Reports Indexes* include a heading "Words and phrases" in which full details of cases defining a particular word or phrase are given (see the figure on page 109.)

Current Law, and the *Current Law Year Books,* also include an entry "Words and phrases" and the *Indexes* to the *All England Law Reports* have a similar heading.

6–16   ### HOW TO TRACE STATUTES ON A SUBJECT

Statutes in Force

6–17   Statutes in Force contains the text of all Public General Acts which are at present in force in the United Kingdom, arranged

The Weekly Law Reports 19 December 1986
Subject Matter   103

WILL
  Construction
    Acceleration
      Son of testatrix missing presumed dead during war—Testratrix many years later leaving
      residue of estate to trustees to hold capital and accumulated income on trust for son—If
      son not coming forward to claim by 2020 residue to pass to charity—Perpetuity period to
      be from testatrix's death to 1 January 2020—Whether number of years "specified"—
      Trustees seeking order giving liberty to administer trusts on footing that son predeceased
      testatrix—Whether residuary gift accelerated so as to take effect from testatrix's death—
      Perpetuities and Accumulations Act 1964, s. 1(1)
In re **Green's Will Trusts**, Nourse J. [1985] 3 All E.R. 455

⟶ WORDS AND PHRASES
  "*Abandoned*"—Fair Trading Act 1973, s. 75(5)
Reg. v. Monopolies and Mergers Commission, *Ex parte* **Argyll Group Plc.,**
C.A. [1986] 1 W.L.R. 763

  Absent from work on account of a temporary cessation"—Employment Protection (Consolidation)
  Act 1978, Sch. 13, para. 9(1)(*b*)   **Flack v. Kodak Ltd.,** C.A. [1986] I.C.R. 775
  "*Accommodation*"—Housing (Homeless Persons) Act 1977, s. 17(1)
Reg. v. Hillingdon London Borough Council, *Ex parte* **Puhlhofer,**
C.A. and H.L.(E.) [1986] A.C. 484; [1986] 2 W.L.R. 259

  "*Act or default of some other person*"—Trade Descriptions Act 1968, s. 23
Olgeirsson v. Kitching, D.C. [1986] 1 W.L.R. 304

  "*Agreements between undertakings*"—E.E.C. Treaty, art. 85
Cutsforth v. Mansfield Inns Ltd., Sir Neil Lawson [1986] 1 W.L.R. 558

  "*Alteration*"—Industrial Training (Construction Board) Order 1980, Sch. 1, para. 1(*a*)(i) (as
  amended)   **Construction Industry Training Board v. Chiltern Insulations Ltd.,**
Webster J. [1986] I.C.R. 394

  "*Any*"—Transport Act 1981, s. 19(3)(*a*)   **Reg. v. Yates (Peter),**
C.A. [1986] R.T.R. 68; 82 Cr.App.R. 232

  "*Any proceedings*"—Legal Aid (General) Regulations 1980, reg. 65
Littaur v. Steggles Palmer, C.A. [1986] 1 W.L.R. 287

  "*Armed with*"—Vagrancy Act 1824, s. 4 (as amended)
Wood v. Comr. of Police of the Metropolis, D.C. [1986] 1 W.L.R. 796

  "*As soon as is practicable*"—Police (Discipline) Regulations 1977, reg. 7
Reg. v. Chief Constable of the Merseyside Police, *Ex parte* **Calveley,**
C.A. [1986] Q.B. 424; [1986] 2 W.L.R. 144

  "*As soon as possible*"—Prison Rules 1964, r. 48(1) (as amended)
Reg. v. Board of Visitors of Dartmoor Prison, *Ex parte* **Smith,**
C.A. [1986] 3 W.L.R. 61

  "*Associated employer*"—Employment Protection (Consolidation) Act 1978, s. 153(4)
South West Launderettes Ltd. v. Laidler, C.A. [1986] I.C.R. 455

  "*Attributable to*"—Greater London Council Housing (Compensation) Regulations 1980, regs. 4,
  11(1)   **Fleming v. Wandsworth London Borough Council,** C.A. (1985) 84 L.G.R. 442
  "*Begin to accrue*"—Redundancy Payments Pensions Regulations 1965, reg. 4(1)
British Telecommunications Plc. v. Burwell, E.A.T. [1986] I.C.R. 35

  "*Break-down vehicle*"—Goods Vehicles (Plating and Testing) Regulations 1982, reg. 3(1)
Kennet v. Holding & Barnes Ltd., D.C. [1986] R.T.R. 334

  "*Building . . . work*"—Local Government, Planning and Land Act 1980, s. 20(1)
Wilkinson v. Doncaster Metropolitan Borough Council, C.A. (1985) 84 L.G.R. 257

  "*Business*"—Customs and Excise Management Act 1979, s. 93(2)
Reg. v. Customs and Excise Comrs., *Ex parte* **Hedges & Butler Ltd.,**
D.C. [1986] 2 All E.R. 164

  "*Capital receipts*"—Local Government, Planning and Land Act 1980, s. 75
Reg. v. Secretary of State for the Environment, *Ex parte* **Newham London Borough**
Council, Taylor J. (1985) 84 L.G.R. 639

  "*Carrier*"—Carriage of Goods by Road Act 1965, Sch., art. 27
Elektronska Industrija Oour TVA v. Transped Oour Kintinentalna Spedicna,
Hobhouse J. [1986] 1 Lloyd's Rep. 49

  "*Changes in the workforce*"—Transfer of Undertakings (Protection of Employment) Regulations
  1981, reg. 8(2)   **Bullard v. Marchant,** E.A.T. [1986] I.C.R. 389
  "*Civil or commercial matter*"—Evidence (Proceedings in Other Jurisdictions) Act 1975, s. 9(1)
In re **State of Norway's Application,** C.A. [1986] 3 W.L.R. 452

  "*Collection*"—House to House Collections Act 1939, s. 11(1)
Cooper v Coles, D.C. [1986] 3 W.L.R. 888

  "*Committee*"—Local Government Act 1972, s. 101(1)
Reg. v. Secretary of State for the Environment, *Ex parte* **Hillingdon London**
Borough Council, Woolf J. [1986] 1 W.L.R. 192

  "*Component part*"—Firearms Act 1968, s. 57(1)(*b*)
Reg. v. Clarke (Frederick), C.A. [1986] 1 W.L.R. 209

in subject groups. Each subject is given a number; large subjects are subdivided. The work is issued in looseleaf form, so that alterations and amendments to Acts can easily be incorporated, and new legislation inserted at the appropriate point. *Cumulative Supplements* are issued for each subject group, to keep the information up to date. *Statutes in Force* is issued by HMSO, and is intended to be the definitive edition of the statutes of the realm; unfortunately, inadequate subject indexes, and a failure to keep the work completely up to date make it less useful than *Halsbury's Statutes*. There are alphabetical and chronological indexes of all the Acts included in the work, indicating the group number (and sub-group) where the Act is to be found. Within each group, or sub-group, Acts are arranged in date order. The *Index to the Statutes* (para. 6–18) serves as a subject index to *Statutes in Force*. Following the name of each statute in the *Index to the Statutes*, the group number in *Statutes in Force* is given in heavy type. For instance, under the heading "Dangerous Drugs" in the *Index to the Statutes* there appear the following entries:

Dangerous Drugs
1971 c. 38 Misuse of Drugs (84:)
1977 c. 45 Criminal Law (39: 1)

This indicates that information on dangerous drugs will be found in *Statutes in Force* in the Misuse of Drugs Act 1971, which is printed in group 84 of the work; there is also information on dangerous drugs in the Criminal Law Act 1977, which is printed in group 39, sub-group 1 of *Statutes in Force*.

Index to the Statutes

6–18   A detailed alphabetical index to the statute law on a particular subject will be found in the *Index to the Statutes*. This is unfortunately several years behind in publication, so it will be necessary to consult *Halsbury's Statutes* (para. 6–19) or similar works to ensure that there have not been any recent changes.

The *Index to the Statutes* is comprehensive. It gives a complete list of all the statutes dealing with a particular subject which are still in force. The number which appears in bold type after each Act refers you to the appropriate group, or sub-group, in *Statutes in Force* (para. 6–17) where the Act will be found printed. Following this, there is a detailed analysis of each subject, showing the section and subsections of all statutes which are relevant to that topic. Cross-references are given from one entry to another. (See the figure on page 111.)

LONDON CABS   *See* LONDON GOVERNMENT, 12*(b)*

LONDON CITY

1297 (*Mag.Car.*) c.9 [Confirmation of liberties] (a) **(106:1)**	1963 c.31 Weights and Measures **(131)**
1662 c.3 City of London Militia (b) **(7:2)**	1963 c.33 London Govt. **(81:1)**
1751 c.30 Calendar **(121)**	1963 c.37 Children and Young Persons **(20)**
1820 c.100 Militia (City of London) **(7:2)**	1964 c.42 Admin. of Justice **(82)**
1824 c.74 Weights and Measures	1964 c.48 Police **(95)**
1884 c.70 Municipal Elections (Corrupt and Illegal Practices) (c)	1965 c.45 Backing of Warrants (Republic of Ireland) **(48)**
1888 c.41 Local Govt. **(81:1)**	1969 c.12 Genocide **(39:4)**
1897 c.30 Police (Property) **(95)**	1969 c.19 Decimal Currency **(10)**
1898 c.16 Canals Protection (London) **(102)**	1969 c.33 Housing **(61)**
1907 c.cxl City of London (Union of Parishes) **(103:1)**	1969 c.57 Employers' Liability (Compulsory Insurance) **(43:3)**
1921 c.37 Territorial Army and Militia	1971 c.23 Courts **(37)**
1925 c.49 Supreme Ct. of Judicature (Consolidation) **(37)**	1971 c.48 Criminal Damage **(39:6)**
	1972 c.70 Local Govt. **(81:1)**
1929 c.17 Local Govt. **(81:1)**	1972 c.71 Criminal Justice **(39:1)**
1936 c.49 Public Health **(100:1)**	1979 c.55 Justices of the Peace **(82)**
1945 c.42 Water **(130)**	1980 c.9 Reserve Forces **(7:2)**
1958 c.42 Housing (Fin. Provns.) **(61)**	1980 c.43 Magistrates' Courts
1960 c.67 Public Bodies (Admission to Meetings) **(81:4)**	1982 c.32 Local Govt. Finance **(81:1)**
	1982 c.48 Criminal Justice **(39:1)**
	1984 c.46 Cable and Broadcasting **(96)**

1 *Constitution, etc.*	4 *Finance*
2 *Authorities*	5 *Miscellaneous*
3 *Administration of Justice*	

1 **Constitution, etc.**

(a) POSITION OF CITY WITH REGARD TO GREATER LONDON OR OTHER AREAS

  Inclusion in—
    Greater London: 1963 c.33 s.2(1)
    Bankruptcy High Ct. District   *See* BANKRUPTCY, E&W, 3
    Metropolitan Traffic Area   *See* ROAD TRAFFIC AND VEHICLES, 1*(b)*
  Exclusion from—
    Metrop. Police District   *See* METROP. POLICE DISTRICT, 1
    Tithe Commutation Acts   *See* TITHES, E&W, 2*(l)*
  A county borough for licensing purposes   *See* LICENSING, E&W, 1
  Separate county for purposes of lieutenancies and the militia: 1980 c.9 s.138(2)

(b) LIBERTIES, CUSTOMS, ETC.

  City of London to have all its old liberties and customs: 1297 (*Mag. Car.*) c.9
  Coroners for the City (including the Temples): 1972 c.70 s.220(1)-(3)(5)(6)
  Saving of privileges of Lord Mayor, etc., as to—
    gauging of wines, oil, honey, and other liquors: 1824 c.74 s.25

(c) UNION OF PARISHES

  Union of parishes in city of London into one parish: 1907 c.cxl s.5(1)-(3)
  Common Council to be overseers: 1907 c.cxl s.11
  Precepts to Common Council: 1907 c.cxl s.12
  Transfer of powers of vestry: 1907 c.cxl s.13
  Savings for wards and wardmotes: 1907 c.cxl s.27

2 **Authorities**

(a) CORPORATION

  Application of Representation of the People Act 1983 c.2 to municipal elections in the City   *See* REPRESENTATION OF THE PEOPLE, 4*(b)*
  Vacancy in office caused by decision of election ct.: 1884 c.70 s.35(5)

(**a**) 9 H. 3 in Ruffhead
(**b**) 13–4 c. 2 in Ruffhead
(**c**) Made permanent by Representation of the People Act 1948 (7–8 G. 5) c.64 s.35

Where the law relating to England, Scotland and Northern Ireland is different, under some subject headings the topics are subdivided according to area. For instance, the law relating to agricultural holdings in England and Scotland is different, and there are therefore two main subject headings: Agricultural holdings, England and Wales and Agricultural holdings, Scotland. (denoted by the abbreviations E & W, and S, respectively.)

Halsbury's Statutes of England

6–19 *Halsbury's Statutes of England* is arranged alphabetically by subject. The purpose of the series is to provide the correct and amended text of legislation, of whatever date, which is still in force. It includes all Public General Acts in force in England and Wales, although a few Acts of limited importance have been omitted. The text of each Act is accompanied by Notes which provide, for example, judicial interpretation of words and phrases, details of statutory instruments made under the Act, case law, cross references to other sections, and references to relevant sections of *Halsbury's Laws of England*.

Halsbury's Statutes

The 4th edition is currently being published and will appear in 50 volumes. It is due for completion in 1989, but, in the meantime, readers must consult those volumes of the 3rd edition which have yet to be replaced. A *Cumulative Supplement* and looseleaf *Service* binders keep the information in the 4th edition (and in those volumes of the 3rd edition which are still in use) up to date. The main volumes of the 4th edition will be reissued from time to time as the information in them becomes out of date.

How to use Halsbury's Statutes to Trace Information on a Subject

6–20   1. A *Consolidated Index* to the 4th edition will be issued in 1990. If this is available you should, of course, consult it. This tells you the volume and page number which contains the information you want. Because the volumes of the 4th edition are being reissued, you may occasionally find that the page number given in the index is incorrect. This is because the volume has been reissued to include new law since the *Index* was published. The material is still located in the same volume; and therefore you should look at the index at the back of the volume to discover the new page number. It is anticipated that the *Consolidated Index* will be reissued every three years. It should also be noted that there is an *Index* to the contents

of the looseleaf *Current Statutes Service*. This is reissued
annually.

2. If the *Consolidated Index* to the 4th edition has not yet
been published, you may be able to guess the most
appropriate title (subject heading) which will contain
information on your topic. If so, you can consult the
detailed index at the back of the relevant 4th edition
volume. If this fails, try consulting the *Table of Statutes
and Index for Volumes 1–50* of the 3rd edition. This will
refer you to the appropriate volume and page in the 3rd
edition (if it has not been superseded). If there is now a
4th edition volume dealing with the same subject you
should, of course, consult it.

In many instances, the titles used in the 3rd and 4th
editions are identical: once you have identified the title
used in the 4th edition you can consult the index at the
back of the relevant volume, in order to find the appropriate page. In some cases the titles used in the 4th edition differ from those used in the 3rd edition. For
example, information on betting, gaming and wagers
appeared under the heading of "Gaming and Wagering"
in the 3rd edition. In the 4th edition the same subject
matter is now in the title "Betting, Gaming and Lotter-
ies."

If you know the name of any Act which deals with
your required subject then the easiest way of tracing
other legislation on that topic is to locate the Act which is
known to you (using the *Alphabetical List of Statutes* in
the 4th edition (see the figure on page 114)). Other Acts
on that subject will normally be in the same volume.

Until the *Consolidated Index* is published it will remain
difficult to trace legislation on a particular subject, unless
you already have a clear idea of the general area of law
and can go straight to the appropriate title. The *Tables
and Index* for the 3rd edition can provide some assistance
but, as has already been noted, some titles have been
altered in the 4th edition.

SUMMARY: METHODS OF TRACING ACTS ON A SUBJECT

1. Use the *Consolidated Index* to the 4th edition, if this has
been published. It is due for publication in 1990.
2. If the *Consolidated Index* is not available:
   (a) guess the appropriate title (subject heading) and
   consult the Index at the back of the volume contain-

ing that title or the "Table of Contents" at the beginning of each subject heading, *or*

(b) consult the *Tables of Statutes and Index for Volumes
1–50* of the 3rd edition, and then check to see if the
matter now appears in the 4th edition volumes, *or*

(c) if you know the name of a relevant Act, locate that
Act in the volumes of the 4th edition, using the
Alphabetical List of Statutes. Other Acts on the same
subject should be readily traceable in the same
volume.

How to Check if the Law has Changed
Once you have traced relevant legislation on the subject in the
4th edition (or in those volumes of the 3rd edition which have
not been superseded) it is *essential* that you check that the information you have traced is still up to date.   **6–21**

To do this you should consult:

the *Cumulative Supplement and*
the looseleaf *Noter-up Service* and
the looseleaf *Current Statutes Service*.

Let us take an example to see how this works. Suppose you
want to know if there have been changes to the Police and
Criminal Evidence Act 1984 since it was passed, and also if
there is any case law on the meaning of a particular word or
phrase in the Act.

The text of most of the Police and Criminal Evidence Act is
contained in Volume 12 under the title "Criminal Law." You
can trace it to Volume 12 by using the *Alphabetical List of Statutes*. This shows that part of the Act is printed in Volume 12
commencing at page 941. (See the figure on page 114.) Those
parts of the Act which deal with "Evidence" appear in Volume
17 under that heading. (If you want to see the entire Act it might
be easier to use the *Public General Acts* or *Current Law Statutes*
(para. 3–7, 3–9) where the complete Act is printed in one place.)
Halsbury's Statutes prints Acts under appropriate titles and, in
so doing, sometimes splits one Act up, so that different parts of
it appear in different titles. Make a note of the volume number,
title and page number which contains the information you
require. The figure on page 116 shows part of the Act, as it is
printed in Volume 12 of *Halsbury's Statutes*, under the title
"Criminal Law."

To find out if any part of the Police and Criminal Evidence
Act (as it appears in Volume 12) has been amended, turn first to
the *Cumulative Supplement* and look at the entries for Volume
12, Criminal Law. The *Cumulative Supplement* lists, volume by

Sub-s (1): Practicable. See the note to s 3 ante.
Sub-s (2): Constable. See the note to s 1 ante.
Related provisions; application to Armed Forces. See the notes to s 53 ante.
Definitions. For "fingerprints" and "the terrorism provisions", see s 65 post. Note as to "conclusion" of proceedings, sub-s (4) above.
Immigration Act 1971, Sch 2, para 18(2). See Vol 31, title Nationality and Immigration.

65 Part V—supplementary

In this Part of this Act—

"appropriate consent" means—

- (a) in relation to a person who has attained the age of 17 years, the consent of that person;
- (b) in relation to a person who has not attained that age but has attained the age of 14 years, the consent of that person and his parent or guardian; and
- (c) in relation to a person who has not attained the age of 14 years, the consent of his parent or guardian;

"fingerprints" includes palm prints;

"intimate sample" means a sample of blood, semen or any other tissue fluid, urine, saliva or pubic hair, or a swab taken from a person's body orifice;

"non-intimate sample" means—

- (a) a sample of hair other than pubic hair;
- (b) a sample taken from a nail or from under a nail;
- (c) a swab taken from any part of a person's body other than a body orifice;
- (d) a footprint or a similar impression of any part of a person's body other than a part of his hand;

"the terrorism provisions" means—

- (a) section 12(1) of the Prevention of Terrorism (Temporary Provisions) Act 1984; and
- (b) any provision conferring a power of arrest or detention and contained in an order under section 13 of that Act; and

"terrorism" has the meaning assigned to it by section 14(1) of that Act.

NOTES

Commencement. Up to 1 May 1985, no order bringing this section into force had been made under s 121(1) post.
This Part of this Act. Ie Pt V (ss 53–65) of this Act.
Age of 17 (14) years. See the note "21 years of age" to s 24 ante.
Prevention of Terrorism (Temporary Provisions) Act 1984. See this title ante.

PART VI

CODES OF PRACTICE—GENERAL

66 Codes of practice

The Secretary of State shall issue codes of practice in connection with—

- (a) the exercise by police officers of statutory powers—
  - (i) to search a person without first arresting him; or
  - (ii) to search a vehicle without making an arrest;
- (b) the detention, treatment, questioning and identification of persons by police officers;
- (c) searches of premises by police officers; and

PAGE

Police and Criminal Evidence Act 1984 (c 60)

Section 15

962n   *General Note.* This section and s 16 also have effect, in relation to England and Wales, to warrants for investigating officers, enforcement officers or persons authorised to enforce the Food and Environment Protection Act 1985, authorising entry and search of dwellings; see ss 4, 11, 19 of, and Sch 2, para 7(4) to, that Act, Vol 1, title Agriculture, Vol 18, title Food, Vol 39, title Water.

For the form of warrant to be issued under this section and ss 43 and 44, see the Magistrates' Courts (Forms) Rules 1981, SI 1981/553, r 2, Sch 2, Forms 156 and 157 (as inserted by SI 1985/1945).

Section 16

963–   *General Note.* See the note to s 15, ante.
964n

972–   **Section 24**
973   In sub-s (2)(*c*) the words "14 (indecent assault on a woman)", are repealed by the Sexual Offences Act 1985, s 5(3), Schedule, Vol 12, title Criminal Law.

Section 43

997n   *General Note.* See the General Note to s 15, ante.

Section 44

998n   *General Note.* See the General Note to s 15, ante.

1019–   **Section 66**
1020   *Codes of Practice.* Four codes of practice which the Home Secretary is required to issue under this section have been issued in a single HMSO booklet. The four separate codes, which came into force on 1 January 1986, relate to—

    A The exercise by police officers of statutory powers of stop and search;
    B The searching of premises by police officers and the seizure of property found by police officers on persons or premises;
    C The detention, treatment and questioning of persons by police officers; and
    D The identification of persons by police officers.

Section 113

1023n   *Orders under this section.* The Police and Criminal Evidence Act 1984 Codes of Practice (Armed Forces) Order 1985, SI 1985/1881, bringing the codes of practice referred to in sub-s (3) into operation on 1 January 1986; the Police and Criminal Evidence Act 1984 (Application to Armed Forces) Order 1985, SI 1985/1882 (made under sub-s (1)), applying with modifications in relation to the investigations mentioned in sub-s (1), the following sections: ss 58, 59, 61–65, 117, 118.

Section 114

1024n   *Orders under this section.* The Police and Criminal Evidence Act 1984 (Application to Customs and Excise) Order 1985, SI 1985/1800.

1024–   **Section 116**
1025   *Serious arrestable offence.* A complaint alleging conduct which, if shown to have occurred, would constitute a serious arrestable offence within the meaning of this section, must be referred to the Police Complaints Authority; see the Police (Complaints) (Mandatory Referrals Etc) Regulations 1985, SI 1985/673, reg 4.

Section 121

1028n   *Orders under this section.* Add: the Police and Criminal Evidence Act 1984 (Commencement No 3) Order 1985, SI 1985/1934, bringing into force on 1 January 1986 (with exceptions) the provisions of this Act which are not already in force, namely Pt I (ss 1–7), and Pt II (ss 8–23) (so far as not already in force), Pt III (ss 24–33), Pt IV (ss 34–52) (except s 37(11)–(14), Pt V (ss 53–65) (except

volume, and page by page, changes which have occurred in the law since the main volumes of the 3rd and 4th editions were published. There are a number of entries showing changes to the Police and Criminal Evidence Act, and references are provided to statutory instruments and codes of practice issued under authority granted by the Act. (See the figure on page 117.) There are also references to any cases which have been decided on the interpretation of a particular word or phrase in the Act.

The information in the *Cumulative Supplement* is up to date to the end of the preceding year. For more recent changes to the Act, you must consult the looseleaf *Noter-up Service* under the appropriate volume, subject heading and page number. This will tell you of any changes which have taken place in the law in the last few months. (See the figure on page 119.)

The *Noter-up* may refer you to a particular volume and page number for details of more recent legislation on the same subject. If the letter (S) appears after the volume number, in brackets, this is referring you to the entry in the looseleaf *Current Statutes Service* binders, under the appropriate volume number and subject heading. There you will find printed the text of a recent Act on the same subject, which alters the law as set out in the main volumes.

The entry in the *Noter-up* reproduced on page 119 indicates an amendment to section 69 of the Criminal Justice Act 1982. The main text of the Act appeared in Volume 12, pages 868–903. Section 69 of the Criminal Justice Act appeared on page 888 in the main volume. The entry in the *Noter-up* informs us that section 69, subsection 2 of the Act has been repealed by the Armed Forces Act 1986, section 16(2). The text of the 1986 Armed Forces Act can be seen in the *Current Statutes Service* (indicated by (S), above), amongst the entries for Volume 3, in the title "Armed Forces."

It is essential to consult *both* the *Cumulative Supplement* and the *Noter-up* to see if there have been changes in the law. The *Noter-up* may refer you to the *Current Statutes Service* for further details. If you are looking for recent developments in the law relating to a subject you must remember to look under the appropriate volume and title in the *Current Statutes Service* for details of any new legislation.

SUMMARY: TO CHECK WHETHER THE INFORMATION IS STILL UP-TO-DATE

(1) Note the volume number, title and page number in the main volume which contains the relevant information.

(2) Turn to the *Cumulative Supplement* and look to see if there

PAGE

Criminal Justice Act 1982 (c 48)—*continued*
Section 4
874n   *General Note.* In connection with this section and s 9, see the Drug Trafficking Offences Act 1986, s 6, Vol 12(S), title Criminal Law (imprisonment in default of payment ordered under a confiscation order made under s 1 of that Act), as from a day to be appointed.

Section 9
880n   *Term of imprisonment.* See the General Note to s 4, ante.

886–   **Sections 20–56**
887   S 44 and in s 81(3) the words "section 44", are repealed by the Airports Act 1986, s 83(5), Sch 6, Pt I, Vol 4(S), title Aviation.
     S 45 and in 81(5) the words "section 45", are repealed by the Airports Act 1986, s 83(5), Sch 6, Pt II, Vol 4(S), title Aviation.

888   **Section 69**
     Sub-s (2) is repealed by the Armed Forces Act 1986, s 16(2), Sch 2, Vol 3(S), title Armed Forces, as from a day to be appointed.

892–   **Section 81**
893   In sub-s (3) the words "section 44" are repealed as noted to pp 886–887, ante.
     In sub-s (5) the words "section 45" are repealed as noted to pp 886–887, ante.

Schedule 13
896n   *Treatment of Offenders (Northern Ireland) Order 1976, SI 1976/226.* Other amendments to this Order are noted to the Northern Ireland Act 1974, Sch 1, para 1.

Prevention of Terrorism (Temporary Provisions) Act 1984 (c 8)
Section 17
927n   *Orders under this section.* The Prevention of Terrorism (Temporary Provisions) Act 1984 (Continuance) Order 1986, SI 1986/417, providing that ss 1–13, 14 (except so far as it relates to orders under s 17(2)(a) or (b)) and 17(2)(c) and Schs 1–3 shall continue in force for a period of twelve months from 22 March 1986.

Child Abduction Act 1984 (c 37)
934–   **Section 1**
935   In sub-ss (2)(b), (3)(a) and (5)(a) for the words "a court in England and Wales" there are substituted the words "a court in the United Kingdom", by the Family Law Act 1986, s 65, Vol 6(S), title Children.

Police and Criminal Evidence Act 1984 (c 60)
Section 9
957–   *General Note.* For an example of "excluded material" (press photographs of
958n   riots) for which a judge may make an order for production or access, see *Ex p Bristol Press & Picture Agency Ltd* (1986) Times, 11 November, noted to Sch 1, post.

Section 10
958n   *General Note.* The meaning of "items subject to legal privilege" is applied by the Drug Trafficking Offences Act 1986, s 29(2), Vol 12(S), title Criminal Law, as from a day to be appointed.

Section 11
959n   *General Note.* The meaning of "excluded material" is applied by the Drug Trafficking Offences Act 1986, s 29(2), Vol 12(S), title Criminal Law, as from a day to be appointed.

964–   **Section 17**
965   In sub-s (1)(c)(i) the words from "4" to "peace)", are repealed by the Public Order Act 1986, s 40(2), (3), Sch 2, para 7, Sch 3, Vol 12(S), title Criminal Law, as from a day to be appointed.

is an entry for your title, volume and page number. If there is an entry, then there has been a change in the law, and you should read the information in the *Supplement* in conjunction with the information in the main work. Once you have located this information (or if there is no entry in the *Supplement*) turn to the:

(3) *Noter-up Service.* Look for any entries for your title, volume and page number. Read this information (if there is any) in conjunction with the information in the main volume and in the *Cumulative Supplement*. The *Noter-up* may refer you to other Acts, giving you the appropriate volume number and the title under which the information can be found. If the letter (S) appears after the volume number, look in the looseleaf *Current Statutes Service* (under the volume number and title).

Remember the stages:

    main volume
    cumulative supplement
    noter-up service

and consult them in that order. The Noter-up may refer you to the

    Current Statutes Service

for the text of recent Acts. Once you have checked all these sources you can be sure that your information is complete and up to date.

How to Trace a Specific Statute in Halsbury's Statutes

1. Consult the *Alphabetical List of Statutes* provided with the 4th edition. (See the figure on page 114.) This tells you if the Act has been printed in the 4th edition and refers you to the appropriate volume (in heavy type) and page number. An (S) following the volume number refers you to the *Current Statutes Service*.

    If there is no entry in the *Alphabetical List* the Act has not yet been included in the 4th edition. Consult the list of statutes at the front of the *Tables of Statutes and Index for Volumes 1–50* of the 3rd edition. This will tell you the volume and page number in the 3rd edition where the Act is to be found. Acts passed between 1981–1984 are not included in the *Index* to Volumes 1–50. They can be located by looking at the alphabetical list of statutes at the front of the *Cumulative Supplement* to the 3rd edition (which begins in the middle of the *Cumulative Supplement* volumes).

2. Once you have traced the Act in the main volume, note

the volume, subject heading and page number under which the information appears. Now turn to
(a) the *Cumulative Supplement* and then to
(b) the *Noter-up Service*
and look in *both* under your volume, title and page number. This will tell you of any changes which have occurred in the law, since the main volumes were written. The entries may refer you to the *Current Statutes Service* (indicated by (S) after the volume number) for up-to-date legislation.

Other Sources for Tracing Legislation on a Subject

Halsbury's Laws of England (para. 6–3) contains references to rel-   **6–22**
evant statutes, although the text of the Acts is not printed. *Current Law* and the *Current Law Year Book* (paras. 6–9, 6–10) are arranged by subject and include entries for new statutes as well as for cases on a subject. A brief summary of Acts appears under the appropriate subject heading.
  The full text of statutes still in force on a particular subject will be found in *Statutes in Force* and *Halsbury's Statutes*. The text of statutes will also be found printed in *Statutes of the Realm* (para. 3–21) *Statutes at Large* (para. 3–22), *Public General Acts* (para. 3–7), *Law Reports: Statutes* (para. 3–10) and *Current Law Statutes* (para. 3–12).

CHECKING WHETHER LEGISLATION IS IN FORCE OR HAS BEEN AMENDED

Halsbury's Statutes

The *Alphabetical List of Statutes* enables you to locate a particular   **6–23**
Act which is still in force, in the volumes of the fourth edition of *Halsbury's Statutes*. Once you have done this, a check in the *Cumulative Supplement* and in the *Noter-up* service, under the appropriate subject heading, volume and page number, will enable you to see at a glance if any part of the Act has been repealed or amended since the main volumes were published. (para. 6–21).
  A complementary publication, *Is it in force?*, issued as part of *Halsbury's Statutes*, offers a quick alternative method of check- ing on the current status of Acts passed *since 1961*. (*Halsbury's Statutes*, with the *Supplement* and *Noter-up*, cover Acts of any date which have been repealed or amended recently; whilst *Is it in force?* only covers Acts passed since 1961.) For each Act

passed since 1961 the entry in *Is it in force?* indicates whether it
is currently in force. The statutory instruments which brought
the Act, or part of it, into force are given; this information is
also available in *Halsbury's Statutes*. To find out if an Act which
has recently been passed has come into force, consult *Is it in
force?* and the section *Is it in force?* which is printed in the
Noter-up binder in *Halsbury's Statutes*.

Chronological Table of the Statutes

6–24   The *Chronological Table of the Statutes* is an official publication
which lists every statute which has been passed since 1235, and
shows, for each one, whether it is still law. This is done by the
use of different type faces—an entry in *italic* type indicates that
the statute in question is no longer law, whilst entries in **bold**
type represent Acts which are still wholly or partly in force. The
use of a number of abbreviations can make the entries appear a
little confusing.

The entries are arranged in date order. Let us suppose that
you wish to discover if any part of the Children and Young Persons Act 1956 is still law. Turn to the entries for 1956, and locate
the relevant entry (4 & 5 Eliz. 2, c. 24). The entry, which is reproduced on page 123, is printed in *italic* type. This is an indication
that the Act is *not* in force. The entry tells us that the statute was
repealed (r.) in respect of Scotland (S.) by the Social Work (Scotland) Act 1968 (c. 49), s.95(2) and Schedule 9, Part I; and in England (E.) the Act was repealed by the Children and Young
Persons Act 1969, s.72(4).

The adjoining entry (4 & 5 Eliz. 2, c. 23) for the Leeward
Islands Act, is printed in bold type. This indicates that part of
this Act is still law, although the entry tells you that sections 1,
3, 4 and 5 and the Schedule were repealed by the West Indies
Act 1962, s.10(3). A list of the abbreviations used will be found
at the front of the volume.

The *Chronological Table* also includes a list of Acts of the Parliament of Scotland 1424–1707, and of Church Assembly
Measures, showing if they are still law.

Unfortunately, the *Chronological Table* is usually two or three
years out of date. To see whether there has been a recent change
in the law it will be necessary to check in the annual publication
entitled *The Public General Acts and General Synod Measures:
19—: Tables and Index*, in the section entitled "Effect of legislation." This shows whether the Acts passed during that year
have amended or repealed any previous legislation. Like the
Chronological Table, the entries in this index are arranged by the

1034   CHRONOLOGICAL TABLE OF THE STATUTES

1955 (4 & 5 Eliz. 2).
  c. 9   .. **Rating and Valuation (Misc. Provns.).**
              s. 1–5 **r.**—General Rate, 1967 (c. 9), s. 117 (1), sch. 14.
              6 **r.**—General Rate, 1967 (c. 9), s. 117 (1), sch. 14; S.L. (Repeals), 1975
                (c. 10), s. 1 (1), sch. pt. XIV.
              7–10, 12, 13 **r.**—General Rate, 1967 (c. 9), s. 117 (1), sch. 14.
              14 **r.**—General Rate, 1967 (c. 9), s. 117 (1), sch. 14; S.L. (Repeals), 1975
                (c. 10), s. 1 (1), sch. pt. XIV.
              15, 16 **r.**—General Rate, 1967 (c. 9), s. 117 (1), sch. 14.
              17 **r.** in pt.—Local Govt., 1958 (c. 55), s. 67, sch. 9 pt. V; Local Govt.,
                1966 (c. 42), s. 38 (3), sch. 4 para. 28 (3); S.L. (Repeals), 1975
                (c. 10), s. 1 (1), sch. pt. XIV.
              schs. 1–3 **r.**—General Rate, 1967 (c. 9), s. 117 (1), sch. 14.
              sch. 4 **r.**—General Rate, 1967 (c. 9), s. 117 (1), sch. 14; S.L. (Repeals),
                1975 (c. 10), s. 1 (1), sch. pt. XIV.
              sch. 5–8 **r.**—General Rate, 1967 (c. 9), s. 117 (1), sch. 14.
  c. 10   .. *Validation of Elections.*—**r.**, Representation of the People, 1969 (c. 15),
              s. 24 (4), sch. 3 pt. I.
  c. 11   .. *Sudan (Special Payments)*—**r.**, S.L.(R.), 1971; Superannuation, 1972 (c. 11),
              s. 29 (4), sch. 8.
  c. 12   .. *Validation of Elections (No. 2).*—**r.**, Representation of the People, 1969
              (c. 15), s. 24 (4), sch. 3 pt. I.
  c. 13   .. *Validation of Elections (No. 3).*—**r.**, Representation of the People, 1969
              (c. 15), s. 24 (4), sch. 3 pt. I.
  c. 14   .. *Post Office and Telegraph (Money).*—**r.**, Post Office, 1961 (c. 15), s. 14.
  c. 15   .. *Rural Water Supplies and Sewerage (No. 2).*—**r.**, Rural Water Supplies and
              Sewerage, 1971 (c. 49), s. 2 (2); Rural Water Supplies and Sewerage (S.),
              1970 (c. 6), s. 1 (2).
  c. 16   .. *Food and Drugs.*—**r.**, Food, 1984 (c. 30), s. 134, sch. 11.
  c. 17   .. *Finance (No. 2).*—**r.**, Income and Corporation Taxes, 1970 (c. 10), ss. 538
              (1), 539 (1), sch. 16.
  c. 18   .. **Aliens' Employment.**
              s. 1 trans. of functions—S.I. 1968/1656.
              2 **r.** in pt.—N.I. Constitution, 1973 (c. 36), s. 41 (1), sch. 6 pt. I.
  c. 19   .. **Friendly Societies.**
              ss. 1, 2 **r.**, in pt., 4 **r.**—Friendly Societies, 1974 (c. 46), s. 116 (4),
                sch. 11.
              5 **r.**—S.L.(R.), 1978 (c. 45), s. 1 (1), sch. 1 pt. XVII.
              7 **r.**—Adoption, 1958 (7–8 Eliz. 2. c. 5), s. 59 (2), sch. 6.
              8 **r.**—Friendly Societies, 1974 (c. 46), s. 116 (4), sch. 11.
              9 **r.** in pt.—S.L.R., 1965; Social Security, 1973 (c. 38), s. 100 (2) (*b*),
                sch. 28 pt. I; Friendly Societies, 1974 (c. 46), s. 116 (1) (4), sch. 9
                para. 16, sch. 11; Social Security (Consequential Provns.), 1975
                (c. 18), s. 1 (2), sch. 1 pt. I.
              am.—Social Security, 1973 (c. 38), s. 100 (2) (*a*), sch. 27 para. 17;
                Friendly Societies 1974 (c. 46), s. 116 (4), sch. 9 para. 16.
              10 **r.**, 11 **r.** in pt.—Friendly Societies, 1974 (c. 46), s. 116 (4), sch. 11.
  c. 20   .. **Agriculture (Improvement of Roads).**
              r. (S.) (1.1.1985)—Roads (S.), 1984 (c. 54), s. 156 (3), sch. 11.
              s. 1 **r.** in pt.—Highways, 1959 (c. 25), s. 312 (2), sch. 25; Local Govt.,
                1972 (c. 70), s. 272 (1), sch. 30.
              3 **r.** in pt.—Local Govt., 1972 (c. 70), s. 272 (1), sch. 30.
              5 am.—Highways, 1980 (c. 66), s. 343 (2), sch. 24 para. 6.
  c. 21   .. *Diplomatic Immunities Restriction.*—**r.**, Diplomatic Privileges, 1964 (c. 81)
              s. 8 (4), sch. 2.
  c. 22   .. *E.L.C.*—**r.**, S.L.R., 1963.

1956 (4 & 5 Eliz. 2).
  c. 23   .. **Leeward Islands.**
              s. 1, 3–5, sch. **r.**—West Indies, 1962 (c. 19), s. 10 (3), sch.
  c. 24   .. *Children and Young Persons.*—**r.** (S.) Social Work (S.), 1968 (c. 49), s. 95
              (2), sch. 9 pt. I; (E.), Children and Young Persons, 1969 (c. 54), s. 72 (4),
              sch. 6.
  c. 25   .. **Therapeutic Substances.**
              r. (*prosp.* except s. 1 pt., ss. 2, 8–15, pt. sch. 1)—Medicines, 1968 (c. 67),
              s. 135 (2), sch. 6.

[*See next page.*]

STATUTE CITATOR 1972–86   **1973**

1973—cont.

8. Coal Industry Act 1973—*cont.*
s. 7, order 76/494; repealed: 1977, c.39,sch.5.
s. 8, order 76/492.
s. 8, repealed: 1983,c.60,s.2,sch.
s. 9, repealed: 1977,c.39,s.8,sch.5.
s. 12, orders 76/492–494.
s. 12, amended: 1985,c.9,sch.2; repealed in pt.: 1977,c.39,sch.5.
sch. 1, repealed in pt.: *ibid.*

9. Counter Inflation Act 1973.
Royal Assent, March 22, 1973.
see *London Transport Executive* v. *Gray Brothers (East Finchley)* (1981) 259 E.G. 629, Forbes J.
order 73/967.
Pts. I (ss. 1, 2), II (ss. 3, 4), V (ss. 15–23), repealed: 1980,c.21,sch.2.
s. 1, orders 77/1078; 79/795.
s. 2, see *British Leyland U.K.* v. *Pay Board* [1974] I.C.R. 134.
s. 2, orders 73/658, 1785; 74/661, 785; 2113, 2158; 75/864, 1293; 76/71, 630, 1170, 2207; 77/1272; 78/1082.
s. 5, orders 73/662, 664, 1786, 1788, 2118; 74/184, 543, 775, 840, 933, 1500, 1793, 2114, 2195; 75/1294, 1583, 1947, 2208; 76/73, 496, 1378; 77/1281; 78/1083; 79/60, 178, 568; continued: orders 76/228, 1161; amended: 1977,c.33,ss.14,21, sch.2.
s. 6, continued: orders 76/228, 1161; amended: 1977,c.33,ss.7,14,21; repealed in pt.: *ibid.,*sch.3.
s. 7, continued: order 76/1161.
s. 8, orders 73/616, 620, 646, 675, 810; 74/2116; 77/1302; continued: orders 76/228, 1161; 77/1302; amended: 1977,c.33,s.14.
s. 9, continued: orders 76/228, 1161; amended: 1977,c.33,s.14.
s. 10, orders 73/659, 1801; 74/1223; 75/615, 1081, 1674; 77/1302; 78/1454; continued: orders 76/228, 1161; 77/1302; 1978,c.54,s.1; amended: 1977,c.33.s.14.
s. 11, orders 73/682, 741, 1717, 1741, 2118; 74/184, 380–383, 434, 1030, 1294, 1482, 1924, 1928, 1988; 75/21, 590; 76/73.
ss. 11, 12, repealed: 1977,c.33,schs.2,3.
s. 13, order 73/619.
s. 14, repealed: 1977,c.42,sch.25.
s. 15, orders 73/662–664, 778, 784, 968, 1786–1789, 1840; 74/543, 775, 776, 840, 933, 1500, 2114, 2115; 75/865, 1294, 1295, 1948, 2209; 76/72, 1172, 1377; 77/1281; 78/1083; 79/60, 178, 568.
s. 23, regs. 77/1222; orders 73/645, 682, 741, 1065, 1717, 1741; 74/380–383, 434, 1030, 1294, 1482, 1924, 1928, 1988; 75/21, 590; 77/1223, 1225.

1973—cont.

9. Counter Inflation Act 1973—*cont.*
sch. 1, amended: 1977,c.33,s.1,sch.2; repealed in pt.: 1975,c.24,sch.3;c.25, sch.3; 1977,c.33,s.1,schs.2,3.
sch. 2, orders 73/616, 620, 646, 661, 662, 664, 784, 1786, 1788, 2118; 74/184, 543, 775, 840, 933, 1500, 2114; 75/1294; 76/73; 77/1281.
sch. 3, orders 73/659, 682, 741, 1717, 1741, 1801; 74/380–383, 434, 543, 775, 840, 933, 1030, 1223, 1294, 1482, 1500, 1793, 1924, 1928, 1988, 2114, 2116, 2195; 75/21, 590, 615, 1081, 1294, 1583, 1674, 1947, 2208; 76/496; 77/1225, 1281; 78/1083, 1454; 79/60, 178, 568; regs. 73/621, 660; 77/1222; amended: 1977,c.33,s.14; regs. 77/1220; repealed in pt.: 1977,c.33,sch.3.
sch. 4, orders 73/645, 1065; 77/1223; amended: regs. 77/1220; repealed in pt.: 1977,c.33,schs.2,3; c.42,sch.25.
sch. 5, repealed: 1977,c.42,sch.25.

10. Consolidated Fund (No. 2) Act 1973.
Royal Assent, March 29, 1973.
repealed: 1975,c.44,sch.C.

11. Fire Precautions (Loans) Act 1973.
Royal Assent, March 29, 1973.
s. 1, order 73/1271.

12. Gaming (Amendment) Act 1973.
Royal Assent, April 18, 1973.

13. Supply of Goods (Implied Terms) Act 1973.
Royal Assent, April 18, 1973.
ss. 1–7, repealed: 1979,c.54,sch.3.
s. 3, see *Smith* v. *Park,* 1980 S.L.T. (Sh.Ct.) 62.
s. 4, see *White Cross Equipment* v. *Farrell* (1983) 2 Tr.L. 21, Garland Q.C.
ss. 8, 9, amended: 1974,c.39,sch.4.
s. 10, see *Laurelgates* v. *Lombard North Central* [1983] 133 New L.J. 720, Webster J.
s. 10, amended: 1974,c.39,sch.4; 1982,c.39,s.17.
ss. 10, 12, see *McCann* v. *Patterson* [1984] 16 N.I.J.B., Lord Lowry L.C.J.
s. 11, amended: 1974,c.39,sch.4.
s. 12, see *Robotics* v. *First Co-Operative Finance,* November 1, 1982, Assistant Recorder G. G. Brown, Poole County Ct.
s. 12, amended: 1974,c.39,sch.4; repealed in pt.: 1977,c.50,sch.4.
s. 13, repealed: 1977,c.50,sch.4.
s. 14, repealed in pt.: 1981,c.19,sch.1.
s. 15, amended: 1977,c.50,sch.3; 1979,c.54,sch.3; repealed in pt.: 1977,c.50,sch.4.
s. 17, amended: 1973,c.36,sch.6.
s. 18, repealed in pt.: 1979,c.54,sch.3.

date of the original Act, so that it is possible to tell at a glance if there has been any change to a particular statute. The *Public General Acts: Table and Index* is published separately by HMSO and it is also printed at the end of the annual volumes of the *Public General Acts and Measures.*

A quicker method of bringing the information in the *Chronological Table* up to date is to look in the latest *Current Law Legislation Citator* (para. 6–25)

Current Law Statute Citator and Current Law Legislation Citator

The *Current Law Statute Citator 1947–1971* enables you to check   **6–25** whether any statute has been repealed or amended by legislation between 1947 and 1971 and also to trace cases on the interpretation of a statute. The period from 1972 to the end of last year is covered by the *Current Law Legislation Citator.* (If your library has the Scottish edition of *Current Law*, this is called the *Scottish Current Law Legislation Citator.* Despite the name, it includes all English statutes.)

Changes made during the current year are given in a supplementary *Statute Citator* which is issued as part of the looseleaf *Current Law Statutes* service. Changes too recent to be included in here can be found by looking under the appropriate heading in the monthly issues of *Current Law.* The statutes service also contains a list of "Legislation not yet in force."

Entries in the *Citators* are arranged by date, and cover Acts passed since the thirteenth century, showing, for each one, whether there have been any alterations or amendments to the text since 1947, or whether the Act has been repealed since 1947. Any statutory instruments made under a particular Act are also shown, together with any cases on the meaning of words or phrases used in the statute. There is a very useful alphabetical list of statutes, at the front of the *Legislation Citator.* This enables you to look up the name of an Act and find out the date of the Act, and the chapter number. It is then easy to locate the Act in the *Public General Acts* or similar collections of statutes.

The entry from the *Statute Citator* on page 124 shows that the Supply of Goods (Implied Terms) Act 1973, which was Chapter 13 in the Statute book, received the Royal Assent in April 1973. Sections 1–7 of the Act were repealed in 1979, by 1979, c. 54, Schedule 3. There have been cases on the meaning of sections 3 and 4 of the Act. Sections 8, 9, 10 and 11 have been amended by subsequent legislation, in 1974. If any statutory instruments had been passed under the Act, the year and the statutory instrument number would be given, preceded by the words "Commencement order," "order" or "regs."

Very recent changes in the law can be traced in *Current Law*, or by consulting the weekly practitioners' journals, such as the *New Law Journal* and *Solicitors' Journal*.

6–26   HOW TO TRACE STATUTORY INSTRUMENTS ON A SUBJECT

Halsbury's Statutory Instruments

6–27   *Halsbury's Statutory Instruments* is a series which covers every statutory instrument of general application which is in force in England and Wales. It reproduces the text of a selected number and provides summaries of others. The series is arranged alphabetically by subject. The volumes are currently being reissued to incorporate new material: the revised volumes are in grey bindings. The series is kept up to date by looseleaf *Service* binders containing, in Binder 1 notes of changes in the law and, in Binder 2 the text of selected new instruments.

If you know the year and number of a statutory instrument then the easiest place to locate it is in the bound volumes of *Statutory Instruments*. If these are not available you can locate the instrument in *Halsbury's Statutory Instruments* by consulting the *Chronological List of Instruments* which appears in Binder 1. This is a complete list of all statutory instruments currently in force. The entry gives you the name of the statutory instrument, followed by the title (subject heading) under which it is found in the main work. Whilst the main volumes are being reissued the entry may give *two* titles, which are bracketed. The first of these is the title (or subject heading) under which the statutory instrument appeared in the original (black) volumes. The second title (in italics) refers to the subject heading under which the instrument appears in the reissued (grey) volumes. (The *Title key* in Binder 1 shows, at a glance, whether the black or the grey volume contains the latest information). If only one title is given then that refers you to the appropriate grey volume.

Once you have used the *Chronological List of Instruments* to locate the correct volume of the main work, consult the list of statutory instruments which appears at the front of the relevant title. This tells you the page number. If the instrument is too recent to have been included in the main volumes it will be traced by looking at the list at the front of the appropriate title in the *Annual Supplement* (in Binder 1). The *Monthly Survey—*

Summaries (in Binder 1) summarises, in numerical order, statutory instruments passed during the last few months.

If you are unable to find a particular statutory instrument in the *Chronological List* in Binder 1, this may mean that the instrument is no longer law.

If you are looking for statutory instruments dealing with a particular subject you should start by looking up your subject in the latest *Consolidated Index*. This is reissued annually, and covers the contents of all the main volumes, and also the information in the *Annual Supplement* (in Binder 1). The entries give you the volume number (in heavy type) and page number in the main work and the number of the statutory instruments, in brackets. Where "S" appears instead of a volume number you should refer to the *Chronological List* in Binder 1, which will refer you to the appropriate title in the *Annual Supplement*.

Once you have traced relevant statutory instrument on your subject in the main volumes it is important to turn to Binder 1 to find out if the information you have traced is still up to date. To do this turn first to the *Annual Cumulative Supplement* in Binder 1 and look up the relevant title. This shows new statutory instruments on that subject which have appeared since the main volume was compiled. It tells you which statutory instruments printed in the main volumes are no longer law and provides you with a page by page guide to changes made since the main volume was published.

For the most recent changes in the law you should consult the *Monthly Survey-Key and Index* (in Binder 1). Under appropriate titles this lists new statutory instruments and any amendments or revocations of earlier instruments. Summaries of the new instruments are given in numerical order in the *Monthly Survey-Summaries*.

If you know the name of a particular Act and want to find out if any statutory instruments have been made under authority granted by that Act, consult the *Table of Statutes* in Binder 1. This shows you where to locate any statutory instruments which are currently in force which were made under authority granted by a particular statute. Remember to check the *Annual Cumulative Supplement* and the *Monthly Survey-Key* (in Binder 1) for more up to date information.

SUMMARY: HOW TO USE HALSBURY'S STATUTORY INSTRUMENTS

[A *User's Guide* to *Halsbury's Statutory Instruments* is available from the publishers, Butterworths.]

(A) Tracing a particular statutory instrument number, *e.g.* S.I. 1985/1787.

1. The Chronological List of Instruments (in Binder 1) tells you the appropriate title (subject heading) to look under in the main volumes. Where there are two headings, bracketed together, the first gives the title in the old (black) volumes and the second the title in the reissued (grey) volumes.
2. Check the *Title Key* in the *Service* volume to find out if you are looking for a grey or black volume. Find the volume, and consult the chronological list of instruments at the front of the appropriate title. This tells you the page number in the volume. If the instrument is too recent to be included in the main volumes look at the beginning of the appropriate title in the *Annual Supplement* (in Binder 1).
3. To see if there have been any changes to that instrument consult both the *Annual Supplement* and the *Monthly Survey-Key* (in Binder 1) under the relevant title.

(B) To find statutory instruments on a subject.

1. Consult the *Annual Consolidated Index*. This tells you the volume, page number and statutory instrument numbers you require. Where "S" appears instead of a volume number, the instrument appears in the *Annual Supplement* (in Binder 1).
2. To check if there have been any changes in the law look
   —in the *Annual Supplement* and in
   —the *Monthly Survey-Key*
   under the appropriate title.

Index to Government Orders

6–28   The *Index to Government Orders* is published every two years. It is arranged alphabetically by subject and enables you to trace statutory instruments which were in force at the time the *Index* was issued and which deal with a particular subject. Where there are a large number of entries under a subject heading, the subject is divided into a number of subsections. For instance, under the heading "Legal Aid and Advice" there are a number of sub-divisions,—"Persons eligible for advice and assistance, Scope of advice, Representation in proceedings," etc.

Every entry gives the statute under which a power to make statutory instruments was conferred, and the instruments which have been made under the provisions of that statute. If

INDEX TO GOVERNMENT ORDERS 1983

ANIMALS—*cont.*

1 Prevention of cruelty—*cont.*

(4) SPRING TRAPS—*cont.*

Power (S.)
1948 (as am. 1954)   Secy. of State may by O. withdraw any authority granted under *Agric. (S.) Act 1948 (c.45)* s. 50 (4), if satisfied that it is expedient having regard to quantities of approved traps available at reasonable prices and other relevant considerations
O. to be by S.I. .. .. Agric. (S.) Act 1948 (c. 45) s. 50 (5) (*a*) (8)
Pests Act 1954 (c. 68) s. 10
1948 (as am. 1954)   Secy. of State may by regs. withdraw all such authorities then subsisting if satisfied that power to grant them is no longer necessary
Regs. to be by S.I., and to be subject to annulment on resolution of either House
Agric. (S.) Act 1948 (c. 45) ss. 50 (5) (*b*), 85
Pests Act 1954 (c. 68) s. 10

Exercise
Power not yet exercised

Power (S.)
1948 (as am. 1954)   Secy. of State may by O. specify descriptions of spring traps for exclusion from application of *Agric. (S.) Act 1948 (c. 45)* s. 50, as being adapted solely for the destruction of rats, mice or other small ground vermin
O. to be by S.I., and to be subject to annulment on resolution of either House
Agric. (S.) Act 1948 (c. 45) s. 50 (7) (8)
Pests Act 1954 (c. 68) s. 10

Exercise
1958/1779   Small Ground Vermin Traps (S.) O.

Power (E. & W.)
1954   Min. of Agric. and Fisheries (E.), Secy. of State (W.) by O. to approve types and makes of traps as approved traps, either generally or subject to conditions as to the animals for which or circumstances in which they are to be used
O. to be by S.I. .. .. Pests Act 1954 (c. 68) s. 8 (3) (8)
S.I. 1978/272

Exercise
1975/1647   Spring Traps Approval O.
1982/53   Spring Traps Approval (Variation) O.

Power (E. & W.)
1954   Min. of Agric. and Fisheries (E.), Secy. of State (W.) may by O. specify descriptions of spring traps for exclusion from application of *Pests Act 1954 (c. 68)* s. 8, as being adapted solely for the destruction of rats, mice or other small ground vermin
O. to be by S.I., and to be subject to annulment on resolution of either House
Ibid. s. 8 (5) (8)
S.I. 1978/272

Exercise
1958/24   Small Ground Vermin Traps O.
1982/53   Spring Traps Approval (Variation) O.

Power (E. & W.)
1954   Min. of Agric. and Fisheries (E.), Secy. of State (W.) may by regs. authorise the use of spring traps for killing or taking hares or rabbits elsewhere than in a rabbit hole, in circumstances, and subject to conditions, prescribed by the regs.
Regs. to be by S.I. .. .. *Ibid.* s. 9
S.I. 1978/272

Exercise
Power not yet exercised

(5) USE OF POISONS

Power
1962   Secy. of State, if satisfied that a poison cannot be used for destroying animals without causing undue suffering, and that other, adequate, methods of destroying them exist, may by regs. made by S.I. prohibit or restrict use of that poison for destroying animals, or animals of any description
S.I. to be subject to annulment on resolution of either House
Animals (Cruel Poisons) Act 1962 (c. 26) s. 2

Exercise
1963/1278   Animals (Cruel Poisons) Regs.

the power conferred by the Act has not yet been exercised (*i.e.* if no statutory instruments have been made under a particular "Act) this is stated. Suppose, for instance, that you were interested in locating the law relating to the use of poisons for killing animals regarded as pests. Under the heading "Animals" there are a large number of entries, which have been subdivided. A relevant entry is found under "Animals—prevention of cruelty" in the sub-section "Use of poisons." (See the figure on page 129.) This indicates that the powers conferred under section 2 of the Animals (Cruel Poisons) Act 1962 were exercised by Statutory Instrument number 1278, passed in 1963. This will be found in the 1963 volumes of *Statutory Instruments.*

Tracing Recent Statutory Instruments and Amendments

6–29   Statutory instruments on a subject which have been passed since the latest *Index to Government Orders* was published may be traced by consulting the indexes in the bound volumes of *Statutory Instruments*, and, for more recent changes, the monthly and annual *Lists of Statutory Instruments*, which contain entries in subject order. If you suspect that there has been a very recent change, it may be necessary to go through the *Daily List of Government Publications* (para. 5–18) for the past few weeks, which will bring the information in the latest monthly *List* up to date. However, students will probably seldom need to go to these lengths. Recent instruments can also be traced by looking in *Current Law*, or in the *Monthly Reviews* filed in the looseleaf *Service* binder issued with *Halsbury's Laws of England*, (under the appropriate subject heading) or by using *Halsbury's Statutory Instruments*, where the information is kept up to date by the looseleaf service Binders (para. 6–27). New instruments are also noted weekly in the *Solicitor's Journal* and the *New Law Journal.*

If you suspect that the text of an instrument has been changed or amended, *Halsbury's Statutory Instruments*, or one of the specialist looseleaf encyclopedias (if there is one available covering your subject field), is probably the easiest place to trace the up-dated version of the instrument. Amendments to the text can be traced in the *Table of Government Orders* (para. 6–31). The *Current Law Legislation Citator* contains a numerical list of statutory instruments passed since 1947, showing, for each one, whether it has been amended or revoked.

Tracing Statutory Instruments made under a Particular Act

6–30   If you know the name of an Act, and you wish to find out if any statutory instrument has been made under that Act, you should consult the *Table of Statutes* which appears at the front of the *Index to Government Orders*. This will indicate under which subject heading(s) entries relating to that Act appear in the Index. For instance, suppose you wish to trace what instruments were made under the powers conferred by the Local Government Act 1972, section 184(2). If you look in the *Table of Statutes* at the front of the volume, this informs you that the powers conferred under this Act are dealt with under the heading "Countryside", section 3. The relevant entry in the *Index* is reproduced on page 132. The information can be brought up to date by consulting the latest issue of the *Current Law Legislation Citator* (para. 6–25) under the Act *i.e.* the Local Government Act 1972, c. 70. *Halsbury's Statutory Instruments* provides a similar guide in its *Service* binder.

Finding out if a Statutory Instrument is Still in Force

If you know the number of a statutory instrument you can check **6–31** whether it is still in force by consulting the *Table of Government Orders*. This is a list, in date order, of all instruments passed since 1671, and it shows, for each one, whether it was still in force when the volume was published. If the entry is in bold type then it is wholly or partly in force; if it appears in italics then the instrument is no longer law. Entries in bold type indicate whether any changes have been made to the instrument since 1948 (the text as it stood in December 1948 will be found in *Statutory Rules and Orders and Statutory Instruments Revised*). Full details of the abbreviations used will be found in the Introduction to the volumes. The *Table* is produced annually, and the information is brought up to date between editions by a Noter-up. A typical entry is produced on page 133.

Halsbury's Statutory Instruments (para. 6–27) collects together all S.I.'s which are still in force. The information in *Halsbury's* is likely to be more up to date than the information provided in the *Table of Government Orders*.

FINDING BOOKS ON A SUBJECT

Your first task should be to find out what suitable books are **6–32** available in your own library. We have already explained that the classification scheme (para. 1–3) is intended to bring together on the shelves books dealing with the same subject. You need to consult the *subject index* to find out what classification number has been given to books on your topic. This is an

COUNTRYSIDE—*cont.*

3 Access to open country

Power
1949, 1972   Min. may by regs. prescribe scale, manner of describing land, etc., (*a*) of maps for purpose of notification to Min. by county planning authorities of action taken to secure public access; (*b*) of maps to be contained in access orders; (*c*) of maps to be kept by county planning authorities showing land subject to public access; and descriptive matter to be included in access orders   ..   Nat. Parks and Access to the Countryside Act 1949 (c. 97) ss. 63 (1), 65 (3), 78 (1)
Local Government Act 1972 (c. 70) s. 184 (2)

Exercise
1950/1066   National Parks and Access to the Countryside Regs.

Power
1949   Min. may by regs. prescribe manner and time for making applications for compensation for depreciation due to the making of an access order; payment of compensation; recording of claims; rate of interest, etc.   .. National Parks and Access to the Countryside Act 1949 (c. 97) s. 72

Exercise
1950/1066   National Parks and Access to the Countryside Regs.

National Parks, suppty. grant for   *See* LOCAL GOVERNMENT. E. & W., **6** (6) (*c*) (v)
Public rights of way   *See* RIGHTS OF WAY, **1** (2) (3)
Traffic regulation O. for roads in special areas in the countryside   *See* ROAD TRAFFIC, **3** (1) (*a*)

4 Adaptation of enactments

Power
1949, 1972, 1973   Secy. of State may by regs. prescribe adaptations of ss. 201–4 of *Local Government (S.) Act 1973* (*c*. 65) in their application to byelaws made by Nature Conservancy under 1949 Act
National Parks and Access to the Countryside Act 1949 (c. 97) s. 106 (1) (4)
Local Government Act 1972 (c. 70) s. 184 (2) sch. 30
Local Government (S.) Act 1973 (c. 65) sch. 27, para. 105, sch. 29
1965   Activities of Nature Conservancy taken over by Natural Environment Research Council
Science and Technology Act 1965 (c. 4) s. 3 (3)
1973   Nature Conservancy Council subst. for National Environment Research Council
Nature Conservancy Council Act 1973 (c. 54) sch. 1 para. 2 (2)

Exercise
1975/1543   Nature Conservancy Council (Byelaws) (S.) Regs.
1975/1970   Nature Conservancy Council (Byelaws) Regs.

Power
1968   Min. may by O. repeal or amend provisions in local Acts passed before Act of 1968 relating to local authorities, if inconsistent with, or unnecessary because of, provisions of that Act. Before making O., Min. to consult with local authorities affected
O. not to rep. or am. enactments relating to water undertakings of local authorities, may contain transitional, supptl., etc. provisions
O. to be by S.I., subject to annulment on resolution of either House
Countryside Act 1968 (c. 41) s. 44

Exercise
Power not yet exercised

5 Procedure

Power
1949   Min. may by regs. prescribe form of notices as to effect of orders under 1949 Act
National Parks and Access to the Countryside Act 1949 (c. 97) sch. 1 Pt. I paras. 1 (1), 3, 4 (3)
1949   Min. may by regs. provide for procedure as to submission and confirmation of orders to which sch. 1, Pt. I, applies; and may provide for proceedings preliminary to confirmation of extinguishment orders to be taken concurrently with similar proceedings for public path or diversion orders   ..   ..   *Ibid.* sch. 1 Pt. I para. 4

Exercise
1950/1066   Nat. Parks and Access to the Countryside Regs. Pt. IV

Service of notices   *See* TOWN AND COUNTRY PLANNING, E. & W., **10** (2)
See also RIGHTS OF WAY, **1** (3)

1980

2023   *Milk (N.I.) (No. 2) O.* **r.**, 1981/1854
2024   *Torts (Interference with Goods) Act* 1977 *(Commencement No. 3) O.* spent
2025   **Merchant Shipping (Certification of Marine Engineer Officers) Regs.**
2026   *Merchant Shipping (Certification of Deck Officers) Regs.* **r.**, 1985/1306
2027   **Motor Vehicles (Designation of Approval Marks) (Amdt.) (No. 2) Regs.**
2028   *Hill Livestock (Compensatory Allowances) (Amdt.) Regs.* **r.**, 1984/2024
2030   *Sports Grounds and Sporting Events (Designation) (S.) O.* **r.**, 1985/1224
2031   **Companies (Winding-up) (Amdt.) Rules**
2032   **Customs Duties (ECSC) (Quota and Other Reliefs) (No. 2) O.**
2035   **Employment Appeal Tribunal Rules**
       rule 3 am., 1985/29
             25A inserted, 1985/29
             32 am., 1985/29
       sch., Forms 1, 3 replaced, 1985/29
2036   *Domestic Proceedings and Magistrates Cts. Act* 1978 *(Commencement No. 2) (S.) O.* spent
2038   **Harbours, Piers and Ferries (Scotland) Act (Variation of Financial Limit) O.**
2040   **Assistance for House Purchase and Improvement (Qualifying Lenders) (No. 2) O.**
2044   **Bankruptcy (Amdt.) Rules**
2047   **Rate Support Grant (Principles for Multipliers) O.**
2048   **Rate Support Grant (Increase) O.**
2049   **Rate Support Grant (Increase) (No. 2) O.**
2050   **Local Government (Rate Product) (S.) Amdt. Regs.**
2051   **Domestic Water Rate Product (S.) Amdt. Regs.**
13 Feb.   **Proclamation Calling in all Coins of the Denomination of Two and a Half New Pence (I p. 2173)**
,, ,,   **Proclamation Determining the Specifications and Design for, and giving Currency to Cupro-nickel Coins in Our Colony of the Falkland Islands (I p.2174)**
24 June   **Proclamation Determining the Specifications and Design for the Twenty- Five New Pence Coins Commemorating the Eightieth Birthday of Her Majesty Queen Elizabeth the Queen Mother (II p. 4281)**
23 July   **Tasmania Additional Instructions (II p. 4283)**
28 July   **Proclamation Determining the Specifications and Design for, and giving Currency to Silver and Cupro-nickel One Crown Coins in Gibraltar (II p. 4284)**
,, ,,   **Proclamation Calling in all Coins of the Denomination of Two and a Half New Pence in the Falkland Islands and the British Antarctic Territory (II p. 4286)**
,, ,,   **Tasmania Letters Patent (II p.4288)**
22 Aug.   **Hong Kong Additional Instructions (II p. 4289)**
13 Oct.   **Proclamation Determining the Specification and Design for, and giving Currency to Silver and Cupro-nickel Coins in Our Colony of the Falkland Islands (III p.7342)**

1981

1   *Gaming (Small Charges) (Amdt.) O.* **r.**, 1984/246
2   **Gaming Act (Variation of Monetary Limits) O.**
       art. 3 am., 1985/575
       sch. am., 1983/1740, 1984/247, 1985/575
5   **Matrimonial Causes (Amdt.) Rules**
6   **Guarantee Payments (Exemption) (No. 21) O.**
7   *Diseases of Animals (Approved Disinfectants) (Amdt.) O.* **r.**, 1983/1071
8   **Disease of Animals Act 1950 (Metrication) Regs.**

alphabetical list of subjects, giving the classification number which has been assigned to each one. If you cannot find the desired subject try some alternative headings, or look under a more general, or a more specific, subject. For instance, suppose that you require information on negligence, which is part of the law of torts. There will be a chapter on negligence in any general textbook on the law of torts; but, in addition, there may be books specifically on negligence, or even on one specialised aspect of negligence, *e.g.* professional negligence. Remember that if your topic is not exclusively legal, there may be books on the subject in other parts of the library. You should therefore consult the main library catalogues as well as any catalogues in the law library. If you have any difficulty in finding relevant entries in the subject index ask the library staff for help.

Once you have found the classification number or numbers, you can go to the shelves at that number to see what is available. However, this means that you will inevitably miss some relevant material which is not on the shelves. For instance, some of the most useful books may already be on loan to other students. You should therefore look in the *subject catalogue* under the classification number. There you will find a record for *every* book which the library possesses on that subject. Remember that more general books may also contain a chapter or substantial sections on your topic.

Footnotes and bibliographies (lists of books) in textbooks and periodical articles will refer you to other books, journals and cases on the subject. You can check in the library catalogue to find out if these are available in your library. Remember that government reports on the subject may not be entered in the library catalogues. You may need to consult the separate indexes to government publications (para. 5–18) to trace these in the library.

6–33 **Legal Bibliographies**

To find out what books have been published on a subject, both in this country and abroad, you need to consult bibliographies. A number of possible sources of information are given below. Not all of them may be available in your library, and you will probably only need to use one or two of them in order to trace relevant books. You will also find details of how to discover whether a book is still in print (that is, whether it can easily be obtained from a bookseller), and the approximate cost.

BUSINESS NAMES

See also Trade Marks.

Encyclopaedias

Statutes in Force. Group: Partnerships and Business Names.
Halsbury's Laws of England. 4ed. see index vol.
Halsbury's Statutes of England. 3ed. vol. 37.
Encyclopaedia of Court Forms in Civil Proceedings (Atkin). 2ed. vols. 30,38.
Encyclopaedia of Forms and Precedents. 4ed. vol. 5.

Texts

CHOWLES, V.G., WEBSTER, G.C. & PAGE, N.S.
South African law of trademarks, company names and trading styles. 2ed. Butterworths (S.Africa), 1973.

JOSLING, J.F.
Registration of business names. 3ed. Oyez, 1955 (Practice notes no.2).

KERLY, Sir D.M.
The law of trade marks and trade names. 11ed. Sweet & Maxwell, 1983.

STONE's Justices' manual. Butterworths. 3 vols. Annual.

BUSINESS TENANCIES

See also Landlord and Tenant.

Encyclopaedias and periodicals

Statutes in Force. Group: Landlord and Tenant.
Halsbury's Laws of England. 4ed. vol. 27.
Halsbury's Statutes of England. 3ed. vol. 18.
Encyclopaedia of Court Forms in Civil Proceedings (Atkin). 2ed. vol. 24.
Encyclopaedia of Forms and Precedents. 4ed. vol. 11.

Estates Gazette. 1858–

Texts

ALDRIDGE, T.M.
Letting business premises. 4ed. Oyez, 1981.

ALDRIDGE, T.M. & JOHNSON, T.A.
Managing business property: a legal handbook. Oyez, 1978.

ENVIRONMENT, DEPARTMENT OF THE
Security of tenure of business premises: how landlord and tenant are affected. 5ed. HMSO, 1977.

FOX-ANDREWS, J.
Business tenancies. 3ed. Estates Gazette, 1978.

MAGNUS, S.W.
Business tenancies. Butterworths, 1970.

RUSSELL-DAVIES, M.
Letting and managing residential or business premises: a legal and practical outline. R.I.C.S., 1978.

BY-LAWS

See also Delegated Legislation; Local Government.

Encyclopaedias

Halsbury's Laws of England. 4ed. see index vol. 4ed.
Encyclopaedia of Forms and Precedents. 4ed. see index vol.

D. Raistrick—Lawyers' Law Books (2nd ed.)

6–34   *Lawyers' Law Books* (published by Professional Books, 1985) is probably the quickest and easiest way for students to find out what has been written on a particular subject. It is alphabetically arranged by subject (see the figure on page 135). Under each subject heading it gives a list of textbooks written on that topic. There are also references to relevant government publications, such as reports issued by the Law Commission. At the beginning of each subject heading there are references to alternative headings, and a list of the major legal reference works and journals which contain information on that topic. Full details of the authors, titles, publishers and dates of books are provided. This information enables you to look in your own library catalogue to see if the books mentioned are available in the library.

Information Sources in Law

6–35   *Information Sources in Law*, edited by R. G. Logan, and published by Butterworths in 1986, provides a detailed guide to sources of legal information. There are chapters, written by leading experts, on sources of information for each of the major areas of law, *e.g.* revenue, criminal, social and welfare law, etc. The work covers sources of information on the law of the United States of America, the Commonwealth, international law and European Community law, as well as English, Scottish and Irish law. There are useful references to historical sources of information. The book is particularly helpful for anyone starting research on a particular subject.

Law Books Published

6–36   *Law Books Published* is issued in several parts during the year, and these parts are then replaced by an annual volume, giving details of all books on law and allied topics published during a particular year. It covers British and American books and some foreign books written in English. There are entries under authors and under titles, in a single alphabetical sequence. The second half of each volume is a list of books published on particular subjects during the year. The subject headings are American as is the spelling, *e.g.* railroads, labour.

Law Books in Print

6–37   *Law Books in Print* is published at intervals, and gives a list of all law books which are still in print at the time of publication. Entries are arranged in the same way as in the companion *Law Books Published* (*i.e.* under authors, titles and subjects).

Current Law
At the back of each monthly issue of *Current Law* is a list of new   **6–38**
books published during that month (mainly British, with a few
foreign works in English). Unfortunately, the publishers are not
given, although the price is stated. When the monthly issues of
Current Law are replaced by the *Current Law Year Book*, a list of
books published during the year is printed at the back of the
Year Book, arranged in subject order.

A useful list of recently published books also appears in the
front of current issues of the *Modern Law Review*, and *Law Quarterly Review*.

Current Publications in Legal and Related Fields
Current Publications in Legal and Related Fields is published in   **6–39**
looseleaf parts which are replaced by annual volumes. There are
entries under authors and titles in the looseleaf volume.

In the annual volume, a detailed subject index at the front of
the volume guides you to relevant entries in the main (alphabetically arranged) part of the work. Each item has its own individual number.

Law Books 1876–1981
The first three volumes of this work are arranged by subject,   **6–40**
and cover books published in English (mainly in the U.S.A.)
between 1876 and 1981. British and foreign publications are
included, but the coverage of foreign material is less comprehensive. The fourth volume contains entries under authors,
under titles, under serials, and a list of the names and addresses
of legal publishers in the U.S.A.

Bibliographical Guide to the Law
This is based on international, foreign and English language   **6–41**
publications received by the American Library of Congress. It
appears annually, and has entries for authors, titles and subjects
in one single alphabetical sequence. It is particularly useful for
tracing books on law written in languages other than English.

Other Sources
Raistrick's *Lawyers' Law Books* (para. 6–34) contains a useful list   **6–42**
of more specialised legal bibliographies (under the heading
"Bibliographies") and Logan's *Information Sources in Law*
(para. 6–35) is likewise very helpful. The catalogues of specialised law libraries, such as the Squire Law Library (at the
University of Cambridge), the Institute of Advanced Legal
Studies Library, (London University), the Radzinowicz Library
of Criminology, (University of Cambridge), and the Harvard

Law School Library (on microfiche) are valuable sources of information.

Two detailed bibliographies are Sweet & Maxwell's *Legal Bibliography of the British Commonwealth* (especially useful for tracing older British books) and C. Szladits, *Bibliography on Foreign and Comparative Law* (which covers books and articles in English only).

Many more specialist legal bibliographies are also published, *e.g.* R. W. M. Dias, *Bibliography of Jurisprudence*; B. A. Hepple, *Bibliography of the Literature on British and Irish Labour Law*, P. O'Higgins and M. Partington, *Social Security Law in Britain and Ireland: a bibliography*.

The library staff will help you to trace relevant bibliographies. Remember that many textbooks will also contain a bibliography on their subject.

Non-Legal Bibliographies

6–43   If your library does not possess the specialised legal bibliographies, or if you are trying to trace information on a non-legal topic, you can use a number of more general bibliographies, which cover law in addition to other topics.

General Bibliographies and Guides to Books in Print

6–44   The main source of information for British books which have been published since 1950 is the *British National Bibliography*. This is published weekly. The last issue of each month has a green cover, and this issue contains an index to all the books published that month. Every few months the information is cumulated. At the end of the year an annual volume is produced containing details of all British books published during that year.

The main arrangement is by subject: entries for law books will be found at the numbers 340–349. There is an alphabetical list of all authors and titles of books included.

British Books in Print is published annually, and lists all the books published in this country which are still in print. Entries appear under authors and under titles. In some cases the title order is slightly changed, so that the entry appears under the most important words, *e.g.* Law of the Sea, Developments in. Details of the current price, publisher and date are given. A microfiche version is also available, which is more up to date.

Books in Print is an American publication listing all books published or distributed in the U.S.A. which are still in print. There are entries under authors and under titles (in separate volumes). There is also a *Subject Guide to Books in Print*. Similar guides to books in print in other countries are available. Ask a member of the library staff to help you locate them.

The catalogues of large general libraries can also provide very useful lists of books on a subject. The catalogues of some major law libraries are available (para. 6–42) in printed form, or on microfiche. The American Library of Congress published a *National Union Catalog* giving details of books published in the U.S.A., and foreign books, on all subjects, in both author and subject orders. The British Library has published a *General Catalogue of Printed Books* listing, in author order, all the books in the British Library. This is kept up to date by supplements, and by the *British National Bibliography* (para. 6–44). The national libraries in several other countries have produced similar catalogues. Your librarian can tell you which of these are available locally.

In addition to printed sources of information, your library may have access to *computer databases* which can tell you what books and periodical articles have been written on a subject. The library staff can tell you about the availability of such databases, and can suggest many other possible sources of information. Never be afraid to ask them for help and guidance.

THESES

If you are undertaking a comprehensive piece of research, you **6–45** may need to find out if any theses have already been written on that subject. The Institute of Advanced Legal Studies (University of London) has published a complete list of all theses on legal topics—*Legal Research in the United Kingdom 1905–1984*. This is kept up to date by *Lists of Current Legal Research topics*, issued annually by the Institute, which show research in progress in universities and polytechnics in the United Kingdom.

These publications cover theses submitted for higher degrees in law at universities and polytechnics throughout the United Kingdom. Theses which have been completed at your own institution are normally available for consultation in the library. It may be possible for the library staff to borrow, on interlibrary loan, copies of theses completed in other universities in this country and abroad.

Other sources of information about (non-legal) theses are the *Index to Theses* and *Dissertation Abstracts*. The library staff can help you to find out what theses have been written on subjects of interest to you.

CHAPTER 7

Using Computers to Find the Law

LEXIS

7-1 More and more lawyers are using computers and word processors for various office tasks such as accounting, time costing and drafting legal documents. Within the last few years much of the law of the United Kingdom (and other countries) has become available in computer databases. It is now possible to instruct a computer to find, for example, all cases and all legislation dealing with a particular legal problem. Eventually this may be the normal way in which solicitors and barristers will solve legal problems—by turning, not to the printed book, but to something resembling a television screen. Therefore, it is important that law students should know something about the "new technology" as it affects the law. Most law schools now have access to computer databases and instruction in their use is available.

The most widely available legal database in the United Kingdom is *Lexis*. The information is obtained by using a "dedicated" terminal—that is, a machine which can only be used for this purpose (although it is now possible to obtain access through a personal computer). The terminal consists of three items:

   (i) a keyboard (similar to a typewriter keyboard but with a number of extra keys) (see the figure on page 141)
   (ii) a television screen (visual display unit, VDU) which displays the information which the computer has found, and

LEXIS

SELECT SERV | EXIT SERV | PRINT CASE | MAIL IT | FULL | CITE | SEGMTS | NEXT CASE | PREV CASE | FIRST CASE | DISP DIF LEVEL

CHG LIB | CHG FILE | NEW SEARCH | VAR KWIC

KWIC

NEXT PAGE | PREV PAGE | ROLL UP | ROLL DOWN | FIRST PAGE

INS CHAR | DEL CHAR

HOME | END | CLEAR

SIGN OFF | ! 1 | " 2 | # 3 | $ 4 | % 5 | & 6 | ' 7 | * 8 | (9 |) 0 | = _ | · | STOP

Q | W | E | REQST R | TIME T | YES Y | U | I | O | PAGES P | ([|)] | £ :

LOCK | A | SORT .S | D | F | G | HELP H | J | K | L | + ; | TRANSMIT

SHIFT | Z | X | CLINT C | V | B | NO N | MODFY M | < , | > . | ? / | SHIFT

PRINT

(iii) a printer, which can print out the information on to a roll
of paper.

What does Lexis include?

7–2   Lexis includes the full text (*i.e.* every single word, not summaries) of many thousands of cases, statutes and statutory instruments. Briefly, Lexis covers:

1. All the cases reported in the major general series of English law reports (*All England Law Reports, The Law
Reports, Weekly Law Reports,* etc.) plus all cases reported
in many more specialised series (*Building Law Reports,
Family Law Reports, Criminal Appeal Reports, Estates
Gazette, Insurance Law Reports, Lloyds Reports* and many
others). The case is reported in its entirety.
2. Some unreported cases from superior courts (excluding
the Court of Appeal Criminal Division) and from some
tribunals since 1980. Cases which have only been
reported briefly in *The Times,* the *Solicitors Journal* and
other publications can thus be read in full by using Lexis.
3. All Public General Acts which are currently law in England and Wales. If an Act has been amended the latest
version of the Act is given.
4. All statutory instruments currently in force.
5. Tax material, including double taxation agreements,
Inland Revenue documents, and the text of the latest
Finance Bill.
6. A file giving details of damages awarded for all forms of
personal injuries.
7. European law: cases heard in the European Court of Justice, European Commercial cases and cases on the European Convention on Human Rights.
8. Commonwealth materials: Australian and New Zealand
cases.
9. American law reports, (both Federal and State), and the
full text of some legal journals published in the United
States.
10. French cases and legislation (in the French language.)
11. Scottish and Irish cases.

New material, covering new areas of law, is being added constantly. This means that the list (items 1–11) may be incomplete
when you read this. A complete list of all the *libraries* (as these
sources are called in Lexis) is available in the red looseleaf
folder which should be available near the Lexis terminal. When

you go "online," *i.e.* connect with the computer, you are immediately provided with a full list of available material.

New cases and legislation are added on a weekly basis. It takes on average about six to eight weeks from the date of the court hearing until the time that Lexis carries a full report. Thus, Lexis can be considered a good source of recent information.

How does Lexis Work?

The computer which contains the information (the database) is located in the U.S.A. Access to the computer is through an ordinary telephone which is specially connected to the computer by a modem. The call is made to a London telephone number which then links to the computer. The cost is that of a telephone call to London coupled with a charge for the use of Lexis.

In order to make the most economical use of computer time you should plan, in advance, what you are going to do when connected to the computer. This is known as planning the *search strategy*. You should also be familiar with the functions of all the different keys on the keyboard (see the figure on page 141.)

Lexis allows you to search quickly through thousands of cases, statutes and statutory instruments. It can rapidly trace cases in which a particular case or Act has been mentioned and find, within seconds, *all* cases or statutes which mention a particular word, or words. Let us suppose, for example, that you want *all* cases on terrorism. Because the computer contains the full text of each case, you need to think how judges, in talking about terrorism, would phrase their judgments. They might talk about "terrorist" and about "terrorism," and cases using either of these words would probably be of interest to you. You can instruct the computer to look for:

TERRORIST or TERRORISM

How do you issue these instructions? Start by turning on the terminal (by pressing the "power" button) and then dial the London telephone number which gives you access to the computer. When the ringing tone is replaced by a high pitched squeak, press the "data" button on the top of the telephone and replace the handset. You are welcomed by the computer and asked to identify yourself.

Each user, when he or she has been trained, is given a "password" which must be typed in at this point. The password prevents unauthorised use. Training in the use of Lexis is required

7–3

and we do not go into detailed explanations here of the operating procedures for the computer. These are set out in the *Lexis Users' Guide* which is available to those who have received a training programme. Contact your librarian, law teacher, or Butterworth Telepublishing Ltd., 4–5 Bell Yard, London WC2 for details of the training programme.

After you have entered in your password the computer displays a list of all the different "libraries" (see para. 7–2) on the screen and invites you to select one. Probably the most useful library for law students is the English general library (*ENGGEN*). This contains cases and statutory material on all subjects. If you are going to use this library type in ENGGEN on the keyboard and press the "transmit" key (see page 141) which sends the message to the computer.

Next, the screen shows a list of different "files" and asks you to choose between them. Do you want cases, statutes, statutory intruments, or a combination of both statutes and statutory instruments? Let's suppose you want cases. You type in CASES, and press the transmit key. The computer informs you that it is ready for you to begin your search.

Let's return to the search for information on terrorism. You will have decided before operating the terminal that you are searching for all cases which mention terrorism or terrorist. So you type in

TERRORISM or TERRORIST

and press the transmit key. The computer searches through *all* the cases in its files looking for any mention of *either* of these two words. It will also pick up references to "terrorists" as the plural, if formed by adding "s," is automatically retrieved. After a few seconds the computer informs you that it has found a certain number of cases which mention the stated words. You can look at these cases (to see if they are relevant) by pressing the button marked "KWIC" (Key Word in Context). This shows you the search word (terrorism/terrorist) together with the surrounding sentences in the law report. This gives you the context in which the word is found. Normally, this is enough to let you decide whether the case is relevant. If you want a list of the cases then press the "CITE" button and a complete list of the citations of all the cases which the computer has retrieved will be displayed on the screen. By pressing the "PRINT" button the list is printed out on the roll of paper. You can then go to the actual reports in the library to read the cases.

If the printed report is not available in your law library then

Lexis can be used to print the full report. It is possible that the case is a transcript and therefore not reported in any law reports. Again, a printout can be obtained from Lexis.

What if you have a more complicated problem? Suppose you wish to find out what cases there are dealing with the negligence of surveyors. Prepare your research strategy by deciding what words judges use for this issue. The words "surveyor" or "valuer" might be used in the judgment so you must tell the computer to search for both terms:

SURVEYOR or VALUER

By typing in these terms Lexis will discover all cases which mention *either* of these words. But this information is far too general for your problem. You want to know about negligence of surveyors. Here the judges might use words such as:

NEGLIGENCE or NEGLIGENT or NEGLIGENTLY

So you can type in these words as alternatives for Lexis to work on. You can see that they have a common stem "Negligen. . . . " As a short cut you can instruct the computer to search for any words which begin Negligen. . . . This is done by use of the "truncation mark." The truncation mark is ! (an exclamation mark). If you type in NEGLIGEN! the computer searches for *any* word beginning with "negligen" . . . You must be careful with this method or you may end up with many words that you do not want, or simply had not thought about. For instance, if you put in TERROR! in the search for terrorism/terrorist it would also retrieve cases mentioning "terrorstricken," "terrorise" and, of course, "terror."

You can instruct the computer to link the two parts of the search by telling it to search for cases in which surveyor or valuer *and* negligence (or the alternative words) are mentioned in the same case. You can do this by typing in:

(SURVEYOR or VALUER) and NEGLIGEN!

The computer will respond by informing you of the number of cases which mention surveyor or valuer *and* negligen . . . in the same case. This technique helps you to narrow down the number of cases that you might want to read.

You can refine this strategy further by looking for words which appear close together in the law report. For instance, let's suppose that you want to find all cases which mention *Laker Airways* v. *Department of Trade*. If you type in:

LAKER W/5 TRADE

you are asking the computer to find every mention of Laker within five words of Trade. So W/ . . . followed by a number instructs the computer to search for words which occur within so many words of each other.

You can use this technique to link negligence more closely with surveyor. This will make sure that there is a relevant connection between the two words "negligence" and "surveyor." Otherwise both the words may appear somewhere in the same case but be unassociated with the issue of the negligence of surveyors. If you specify that the two words should appear fairly close to each other, say within 20 words, then you are likely to find that there is a relevant connection for your purposes.

SURVEYOR W/20 NEGLIGEN!

Of course, this short cut also runs the danger of missing relevant cases where the key words do not occur within the stated 20-word proximity! Practice, and a certain instinct, will help you to develop a search strategy which will retrieve all the relevant cases and avoid picking up too many irrelevant cases.

SUMMARY: RESEARCH STRATEGY

7–4   The four most useful words and symbols that you are likely to need when planning your research strategy are:

OR: This tells Lexis to look for alternative words. Doctor OR Surgeon; Surveyor OR Valuer; Negligence OR Negligently OR Negligent. It has the effect of *widening* the search and increasing the number of possible cases which may be relevant.

AND: This tells Lexis to link together two (or more) words and to refer you only to the cases which contain *both* words.
Surveyor AND Negligence
Elephant AND Circus
Both words must appear in the same case. Lexis will not report on cases which deal only with an elephant or only with a circus. "And" has the effect of *narrowing down* (or limiting) your research. "And" retrieves fewer cases than the word "or."

W/5: W/ . . . means "Within so many words of." This example instructs Lexis to find two words when they are located in the case within five words of each other. You can choose any number between 1 and 100. Do not bring the words too close together or you will miss relevant cases. The effect of using "W/ . . . " is again to *narrow down* (or limit) your search.

!: This means "truncation mark." This instructs the computer to search for words which have the same beginning (stem) but different endings—negligent, negligence etc. Its effect is to *widen* the search. It may, if you are not careful, result in the retrieval of irrelevant words and therefore irrelevant cases.

There are other commands which you may need to use from time to time. For instance, each law report and statute is divided up into parts (or *segments*). Law reports, for instance, can be searched looking for all cases heard in a particular court, or all judgments by a particular judge. The most common segment search is to ask the computer to retrieve a specific case. Let's suppose you want to see the case of *Gillick* v. *West Norfolk and Wisbech Area Health Authority*. A search for *Gillick W/4 West Norfolk* will retrieve the *Gillick* case itself, and also other cases in which the *Gillick* case has been referred to. If you only want to retrieve the *Gillick* case itself, the best way to do this is with a segment search. Our search would be: NAME (*Gillick W/4 West Norfolk*). This would retrieve *only* the *Gillick* case. Full details of segment searches are found in the Lexis *User's Guide*.

Modifying Your Search Strategy
It could be that, at your first attempt, you are unsuccessful with   7–5
your research strategy, and fail to find the information you need. If, for example, you key in a command which produces 5,000 cases which refer to the word you are searching for then obviously you must rethink your strategy. You have defined the search far too widely. You must limit the search by adding another word or words to your command. For example if you put in NEGLIGEN! on its own then you would be informed of thousands of cases which are concerned with various aspects of negligence. So you must narrow the search by asking for negligence *and* surveyors. This command will reduce the number of cases significantly.

To modify your search, press "M" (for modify) and then the "transmit" button. You can now type in a new search word or words. Your modified search would begin with the word "and." For instance, if you have retrieved too many cases using the search word "negligence" you can modify the search by transmitting "M," followed by: "and surveyor or valuer." The computer will search through all the negligence cases and retrieve only those which mention surveyors or valuers. If you are still having difficulty in retrieving helpful material you must reconsider your research strategy. This is best done by "signing off" from Lexis as time thinking as opposed to researching still costs money. Press the "sign off" button, answer Lexis' question as to whether you intend to return to the search later and then rethink your commands to the computer. If you have instructed the computer that you will return, when you rejoin the computer your original material reappears. You can then modify your search, or you can erase the search by pressing the "new search" button, which allows you to start again. You can always obtain advice on search strategy by telephoning the Customer Service Department at Butterworths Telepublishing. (The number should be available at the terminal).

This section only provides a brief outline of the types of searches that Lexis can undertake. Further details are found in the Lexis *User's Guide* which you should consult before starting a search. The *Guide* will tell you, for example, how to find all cases discussing the interpretation of a particular section of an Act; what statutory instruments brought sections of an Act into force; or it will enable you to discover in which cases named barristers, solicitors or judges were involved. If a statute has been amended by subsequent legislation it will display the amended, up-to-date version of the Act. It will retrieve all references to statutes or statutory instruments on a subject, and provide you with the full text of the Act or statutory instrument. If you remember the facts of a case but not its name; or if you know only the name of one of the parties in the dispute, Lexis can find the case. Sometimes such a search would be impossible with conventional printed sources. Almost always Lexis is faster than conventional methods.

Remember that Lexis does not contain any information about what books, periodical articles and theses have been written about the law in this country (although it does have the text of some American journals). It contains only *primary* sources. Some other databases exist which contain background material relevant to lawyers. Your librarian can tell you which of these are available and can, where relevant, get access to the information on your behalf.

7–6   There have been other recent developments in new technology. Most people are familiar with Ceefax and Oracle, which can provide printed information about holidays, sports results, weather, news headlines, etc., on your home television screen. Prestel is a similar system and included on this is a legal database called Lawtel.

LAWTEL

Lawtel is a digest of legal information that is accessed via   7–7
British Telecom's Prestel Videotex Service. The information is
displayed on a screen and is indexed as it would be in a legal
encyclopedia—instead of turning the pages of a book you press
keys on a keyboard, which in turn changes the "page" of information on the screen.

What is Needed to Use Lawtel?

To use Lawtel you need (i) to become a registered user of both
Prestel and Lawtel and (ii) suitable terminal equipment, which
may consist of either a videotex terminal, a television with an
adaptor, or a micro computer with a modem and appropriate
software. Many libraries are now equipped with Lawtel and
should contain the Lawtel *User Guide* booklet, which any user
may obtain on request.

What Does Lawtel Contain?

The Lawtel Service consists of various facilities the majority of
which are designed to help you in your legal research:

The Database

This comprises a cumulative and continuously updated store of
legal information. A glance at the *subject titles index* on Lawtel or
in the *User Guide* indicates its scope. It includes summaries of
leading cases, statutes, Bills in progress, statutory instruments,
significant subsidiary legislation, practice directions, white and
green papers, commencement dates, DHSS commissioners'
decisions, damages awards, and references to legal articles. All
this information is traditionally arranged, referenced and
indexed, while extensive cross-indexing takes you directly to
summaries of the precedents upon which later decisions were
based.

The Daily Update

This page is updated every working day. It routes the user to
the most significant material added to the database during the
previous 24 hours. The 24 most recent updates are always available.

The Research Bureau

This service can assist you with any research problem concerning the laws of England and Wales by directing you to the relevant authorities. To use the service you simply complete a
"response frame" on screen and the reply appears, also on

screen, within 24 hours. At the time of writing no additional charge is made for this service, though it is only available to those who subscribe at the standard business rate.

As a result of a special arrangement with Butterworth (Telepublishing) Ltd., indirect access is available to the unique libraries of legal materials available on Lexis. By this means printouts may be obtained of the full text of precedents and legislation, including thousands of otherwise unreported cases.

Other Services
These include the HMSO publication buying and ordering facility, the courts and tribunal calendar, and the London law courts directory. Details of these services are given on Lawtel.

How is Lawtel Used?

7–8   Assuming that access to Prestel is possible, you should key in *25190#. This will take you to the Lawtel Main Index. You will only be able to gain access to the Lawtel Main Index if the terminal you are using belongs to a registered member of the Lawtel Closed User Group. However, any Prestel user can get the feel of using Lawtel by keying in *251#, which is the opening page of the Lawtel Magazine. The Magazine contains a digest of recent developments, updated daily, together with general information about the use of Lawtel.

The Main Index has a series of numbers running down the left hand side of the screen. For example, if you want to see the latest Daily Update just key in the number 6. Assuming that you have just done this and that today's Daily Update page is now on-screen you can turn to the Main Index in one of three different ways:

1. You can key in the number 0. This will take you back to the Main Index page because it is so "indexed" from the Daily Update page. Keying 0 from any page in Lawtel will take you to either the Main Index or a "local" index—in the latter case you can return to the Main Index by continuing to key 0.
2. You can key in *#. This always takes you back to the last page you looked at *unless* you arrived at the page on-screen by keying a two digit index number, in which case key in *# twice.
3. You can key in *25190#. This is because the page number of the Main Index is 25190. The number of any page always appears at the top right of the screen and *page

number# will always take you to that page from anywhere in Prestel.

Throughout the Lawtel database a simple system of moving
forward and backward through a subject is used. The user is
taken forward through the pages by keying 9, or back by keying
8. Assume you are looking at today's Daily Update: key 8 and
yesterday's Update appears on the screen, key 8 again and you
will see the previous day's Update and so on.

How Do I Find What I Want?

The Lawtel database is divided into several hundred subjects.   7–9
These may be found by consulting the Subjects Index on
p. 25189. A list of subject titles is given in the Lawtel User
Guide. These subjects are constantly updated. A flashing
number indicates the most recent entry on any subjects page,
while a white arrow pointed to a number indicates the next
most recent.

Suppose you are looking for a case—you could find it either

1. by its title, through the Table of Cases on p. 251190, or
2. by the point or points of law involved, through the
   appropriate Subjects Index heading, or
3. by the statutory provisions cited in the case, through the
   Statute Citator.

All case summaries now have the title and citation of the case at
the head of the first page of the summary, though some pre-
1984 summaries still have the title at the end. Cases are cross-
referenced to other material by use of the indexing system—a
yellow "LTS" appears in the text preceded by a number to be
keyed in.

If you are having problems with your research you can try
asking the Lawtel Research Bureau. The Bureau is there to help
you with research problems by directing you to the appropriate
authorities—it does not give legal advice. There is a Research
Bureau Index on p. 251333102.

To send the Lawtel Research Bureau details of a problem via
Prestel you must use the response frame provided. An on-
screen answer appears within 24 hours (during weekdays). To
use the response frame follow the steps below:

(a) Go to p. 25100000 and wait for the screen to fill up.
(b) A flashing cursor appears after NAME:
(c) Enter your name and key #.

(d) Enter the text of your problem clearly and briefly and key
#.

(e) EITHER enter a Prestel Account Number (nine digits) and then key # *or* just key #. If you enter an account number then the Bureau's reply will be sent via Prestel Mailbox (*i.e.* it will be sent to the Prestel Mailbox of the subscriber whose number you give—to find out more about Mailbox go to p. 7).

If you just key # the reply will be indexed from tomorrow's Daily Updates—this is safer if you are using someone else's library.

(f) Finally, a message appears at the bottom of the screen which tells you how to send, or not to send, your question. To return to the Lawtel Main index key #.

(g) Replies to Research Bureau questions are indexed from the relevant subjects and are thus continuously incorporated into the main body of the database.

It is possible to authorise the Lawtel editors to carry out a Lexis search on your behalf. Information about Lexis is given on p. 2517191; details of the additional cost involved are given on p. 251333195. Printouts of the results of a Lexis search can be sent to users through the post, the London Document Exchange or, for an additional charge, by fax.

Questions regarding the Lawtel Service can be sent via any Prestel terminal with a suitable keyboard. The question should be sent on the response frame on p. 251744763. First, type in the question, then key # and finally 1 to send. Messages to Lawtel may be sent on the response frame on p. 2517013.

CHAPTER 8

Scots Law

INTRODUCTION

England and Wales, Northern Ireland and Scotland each have 8–1
their own legal systems. The law of the first three countries is
similar but that of Scotland is markedly different in many ways.
This fact must be borne in mind when considering questions of
law and where you look to find the answers. Throughout the
United Kingdom, of course, the law is uniform in a number of
respects and, broadly speaking, it is within the area called
private law that the differences are greatest.

The history and development of Scots law is included in the
introductions to most general textbooks on law. The most popular account, published in 1949, has now attained the status of a
classic. This is Lord Cooper's *The Scottish Legal Tradition* (Saltire
Society) which has frequently been reprinted and which is now
in its 4th edition, 1977. *Cooper* should be read by anyone interested in Scots law or in Scottish history.

The rest of this chapter describes briefly the main categories
of printed information which will be of help to you, in the following order—law reports, statutes, reference books, textbooks
and casebooks, and periodicals.

LAW REPORTS

Chapter 2 contains detailed information on English law reports 8–2
and how to use them; it should be noted that these are often
cited in Scotland so that it is necessary to be familiar with them.

A helpful summary of the citations of the chief Scottish reports, old and modern, is contained in D. M. Walker's *The Scottish Legal System* (5th ed., 1981), pp. 417–422.

The most important series of Scottish reports is *Session Cases* (more correctly, *Cases decided in the Court of Session*). Five series appeared between 1821–1906 and these are known by the name of the five respective editors (see Walker, p. 419).

First Series	Shaw	16 vols. 1821–38
Second Series	Dunlop	24 vols. 1838–62
Third Series	Macpherson	11 vols. 1862–73
Fourth Series	Rettie	25 vols. 1873–98
Fifth Series	Fraser	8 vols. 1898–1906.

These are cited by the volume number, the initial of the editor, and the page number. For example, if your reference is 6 M. 321, this indicates that you need to consult *Session Cases*, third series, Vol. 6, edited by Macpherson, at page 321. The year, in this instance 1867, is occasionally mentioned and certainly helps to avoid confusion.

After 1906 the editor's name was no longer used and the citation became S.C. It is important to note that there are three *separate* sets of page numbers within each bound volume of *Session Cases*. The first deals with cases which have gone to appeal in the House of Lords; these are cited, *e.g.* 1956 S.C. (H.L.) 48. The second series of page numbers in each volume covers criminal cases, decided in the Court of Justiciary; these are cited, *e.g.* 1956 J.C. 59. The third sequence consists of cases decided in the Court of Session itself, *i.e.* civil cases, which are cited, *e.g.* 1956 S.C. 394.

The House of Lords series began to be issued with separate paginations as far back as 1850, so that an 1852 case is cited, *e.g.* 15 D.(H.L.) 28; and Justiciary Cases similarly are separately paged from 1874, *e.g.* 2 R.(J.) 22.

The other major series of Scottish law reports is the *Scots Law Times*. This has been published weekly since 1893 and is divided into two chief sections (a) *Notes* and (b) *Reports*. The weekly parts are cumulated into an annual volume. The *Reports*, which form the major part of each volume, include cases heard in the Court of Session, the High Court of Justiciary, and the House of Lords. Unlike *Session Cases*, there are *not* three separately paged sections. The citation is straightforward, *e.g.* 1975 S.L.T. 133. The *Reports* part also contains the following which *are* paged separately.

(1) *Notes of Recent Decisions* which, as implied, is devoted to

a page or two on current cases of interest. These may appear later as fuller reports.

(2) *Sheriff Court Reports,*
(3) *Scottish Land Court Reports,* and
(4) *Lands Tribunal for Scotland Reports.*
These are cited, *e.g.* 1975 S.L.T. (Sh.Ct.) 32. Care should be taken when using either the thin weekly parts or the bulky annual volumes to ensure that you are looking in the right portion.

Older Cases

Session Cases covers cases from 1821 onwards. The most import- **8-3**
ant collection of earlier cases is contained in *Morison's Diction-ary of Decisions.* This is in 38 volumes. It claims to mention all important cases up to 1820, is arranged by subject, and the pages throughout the volumes are numbered continuously, from page 1 to 17074. Thus, a typical citation might be (1743) M. (*or* Mor.) 11274. Various appendices, supplements and synopses were added and, most importantly, an index was issued in 1823.

Old House of Lords Reports, known as *Appeal Cases,* for the period 1707–1873 are contained in 35 volumes, again cited by one of the ten editors (see Walker, *Scottish Legal System* (5th ed.), p. 420). Early Justiciary Cases date from 1819–1916 in 28 volumes, again with ten separate editors (see Walker, p. 421). After a long gap a new set of criminal reports began in 1981, namely *Scottish Criminal Case Reports,* cited, *e.g.* 1981 S.C.C.R. 219. A noteworthy feature at the end of most reports is a brief commentary on their particular points of interest.

Two other sets of older reports are often consulted. They are:

(1) The *Scottish Law Reporter,* issued in 61 volumes from 1865–1924 and cited, *e.g.* 22 S.L.R. 116 (do not confuse with the *Scottish Law Review,* also S.L.R.); and
(2) *Sheriff Court Reports* in 79 volumes from 1885–1963 cited, *e.g.* 1951 Sh.Ct.R. 196. Note that these were published as part of the *Scottish Law Review* and may be bound with that set.

Indexes to Law Reports

Scotland suffers in not having an index to its main sets of older **8-4**
law reports. This means that if you do not know the exact date of a case you have to look through the indexes to as many indi-vidual volumes as is necessary, a laborious task. However, there

are short cuts for the more important cases, contained in two sets of digests (which are arranged by subject-matter). The *Scots Digest* covers 1800–1873 with subsequent volumes for 1873–1944; and the *Faculty Digest* covers 1868–1922 with five further volumes from 1923–1963. The indexes to these will often reveal the case you are after and in the instance of the *Faculty Digest* inform you if it has been judicially referred to later. For more recent cases, the *Scottish Current Law Case Citators* (para. 2–14) can be consulted, if you know the name of a case and want to find a citation for it. D. Raistrick's *Index of Legal Citations and Abbreviations* (para. 1–8) is invaluable for checking both Scottish and English abbreviations.

Scottish Current Law (monthly) and the *Scottish Current Law Year Books* (annually) enable you to see, at a glance, all recent developments in the law of a particular subject; new cases, statutes and official documents are summarised, under appropriate subject headings, and periodical articles relating to Scottish law are noted. The green pages in *Scottish Current Law* contain information on Scottish matters; in the *Scottish Current Law Year Book* the information relating to the law in Scotland forms a separate sequence, at the back of the *Year Book*, with its own index.

STATUTES

8–5   Acts of Parliament are described and dealt with in Chapter 3; the position in Scotland differs as follows.

Before 1707 Scotland had its own Parliament and enacted its own laws. Some of these are still in force and are to be found in the *Acts of the Parliament of Scotland 1424–1707* (HMSO), (2nd ed., 1966). Since 1707 many Acts have applied to Britain, but there are a number each year pertaining to Scotland only. These are published by HMSO, as part of the *Public General Acts* (para. 3–7). Those which were Scottish only were collected together by the Edinburgh publishing firm of Blackwood, which issued three volumes covering 1707–1847, then produced annual volumes from 1848–1946. These are known as *"Blackwood's Acts."* Since 1948, the *Scottish Current Law Statutes* have been issued and these are now the most consulted set; issued in loose-leaf form from 1984, it should be noted that they include *all* public Acts, not just Scottish ones.

Local Acts effectively appeared first in 1801 and during Victoria's reign in particular, were produced in vast quantities. They relate especially to the building of railways and harbours.

Not many sets are available and a visit to a good law library is necessary to consult them.

A complete set of *Statutes in Force* (para. 6–17) will contain all British Acts. In Scotland you will often find that libraries subscribe only to those applicable to Scotland.

REFERENCE BOOKS

Reference books, such as dictionaries and encyclopedias, can be   **8–6** of considerable assistance when you are looking for information on a subject. D. M. Walker's *Oxford Companion to Law* (1980), is a very useful source of information. It refers to all sorts of legal topics including persons and institutions. As it is written by a Scottish professor of law, there is much Scottish material which would not be found in a similar work compiled south of the border. It is often worth looking at the *Companion* first, if you are trying to find information on a particular topic.

Scotland formerly had two legal encyclopedias, the *Encyclopaedia of the Laws of Scotland* and its companion, *Encyclopaedia of Scottish Legal Styles*, but these have long been out of date and are not now much use for most subjects. They are being replaced by a major new legal encyclopedia *The Laws of Scotland: Stair Memorial Encyclopaedia* which is currently being published in 25 volumes. When complete this will fill a large gap.

A mini-encyclopedia which should not be overlooked is the loose-leaf *Parliament House Book*; this covers many topics, especially court practice and procedure. Two small books which will aid the newcomer to law are A. D. Gibb's *Students' Glossary of Scottish Legal Terms* (2nd ed.) and J. A. Beaton's *Scottish Law Terms and Expressions*, both issued by Green (1982). These complement each other, rather than overlap; Gibb gives only brief definitions and consequently contains more than Beaton, who enlarges on meanings, sometimes considerably. The *Scottish Law Directory* (often known as "the *White Book*") contains useful addresses and will help you trace an individual or firm.

TEXTBOOKS

There are several books which are essential reading for the   **8–7** beginner in Scottish law. D. M. Walker's *The Scottish Legal System* (5th ed., 1981), explains in depth much of the background to, and working of, our present-day system. Such chapters as those on the development of Scots law, the judicial system, the personnel of the law, and its sources and its repositories, help you to understand their complexity.

The standard textbook has long been W. M. Gloag and R. C. Henderson, *Introduction to the Law of Scotland*, now in its 8th edition (1980). Its 50 chapters encompass most Scots law subjects and treat them in straightforward fashion. Designed for university students, you will find you use Gloag and Henderson a lot both as an undergraduate and in your later career. A parallel text is Enid Marshall's *General Principles of Scots Law*, (4th ed., 1982) which is designed for students attending Scottish technical and commercial colleges. This is also a very useful title. *Introductory Essays on Scots Law*, by W. A. Wilson (2nd ed., 1984) is meant for students commencing their studies; this is worth consulting for the information given in such chapters as Law and language, Dealing with decisions, Reading and interpreting statutes, Appeals and so on.

Perhaps the most comprehensive modern text is *Principles of Scottish Private Law* by D. M. Walker, the third edition of which was published in four volumes in 1982–1983. This is expensive and is probably too detailed for the absolute beginner but it is likely to be the place where you will find up-to-date information not mentioned in more elementary texts. It is worth listing the contents of each volume, especially as there is no comprehensive index which will lead you easily to a particular topic.

Volume I has an introductory and general section which includes such subjects as the civil courts and their jurisdiction, arbitration, and authentication of deeds. This is followed by a section on international private law, and the remainder of the volume deals with the liability of persons. This includes domestic relations (husband and wife, parent and child), friendly societies and trade unions (unincorporated associations), and companies, building societies, etc. (incorporated bodies).

Volume II is devoted to the law of obligations and deals with the various ramifications of contract law and delict and reparation, in each instance giving both principles and their practical application.

Volume III covers the law of property, and comprises chapters on rights in both corporeal and incorporeal, and moveable and heritable property. (Corporeal property consists of things that can can be seen or handled, *e.g.* clothes, while incorporeal property consists of rights, *e.g.* company shares. Heritable property consists of land and buildings while moveable property comprises all other property.)

Volume IV comprises five chapters dealing respectively with

the law of trusts; succession; civil remedies; diligence; and insolvency.

Although Scotland has far fewer legal textbooks than England, the position has improved a good deal during the last 15 years and nearly every subject now has at least one reasonably up-to-date work devoted to it. Most will be of use to you only when you have been in practice for some time but there are others, rather less scholarly in approach, which you may find valuable. Space does not allow elaboration of their contents but their titles are usually sufficient to indicate their scope. They include *Scots Mercantile Law* by Enid Marshall (1983), covering such topics as sale of goods, consumer credit, bankruptcy, etc.; *Constitutional Law* by J. D. B. Mitchell (2nd ed., 1968), written from a Scottish standpoint; *Conveyancing Manual* by A. J. McDonald (3rd ed., 1986); *The Succession (Scotland) Act 1964* (3rd ed., 1982) by J. A. Meston, one of several such concise guides to various acts; and *A Practitioner's Guide to the Criminal Courts* by J. Ross Harper (1985) which is a racy account of a lifetime's experience.

Although English in scope and intent it is often worth consulting *Halsbury's Laws of England* (para. 6–3). This is especially useful for those subjects which are broadly similar in the two countries.

CASEBOOKS

A recent development in Scottish legal publishing has been the appearance of a series of casebooks, issued by W. Green & Son. Most of the titles contain excerpts from statutes, law reports and books, covering both law and procedural matters, with commentaries. A full list of the available casebooks can be found in the publisher's catalogues. **8–8**

PERIODICALS

There are not many legal periodicals published in Scotland. The main one is the *Scots Law Times*, the weekly parts of which include the latest news, an article on a current topic of interest and various reports of cases (para. 8–2). The monthly *Journal of the Law Society of Scotland* is devoted chiefly to articles and professional news. The *Juridical Review* is given over to learned papers and appears twice a year; in contrast *Scolag*, issued monthly by the Scottish Legal Action Group, sets out to be topical and occasionally controversial. **8–9**

CHAPTER 9

Northern Ireland Law

INTRODUCTION

9–1 The student of Northern Ireland law, having read a statement of the law on a particular topic in a standard English textbook, has to determine the extent to which this law applies in Northern Ireland. As regards statute law, it may be that a particular Westminster Act applies completely, *e.g.* the Child Abduction and Custody Act 1985 (c. 60); or only certain sections may apply, *e.g.* The Administration of Justice Act 1985 (c. 61); or the Act may not apply at all, *e.g.* The Housing Act 1985 (c. 68). Usually the last or penultimate section of a recent Act will tell you whether, or to what extent, the Act applies in Northern Ireland. If a Westminster Act does not apply to Northern Ireland, and there is a Northern Ireland equivalent, then the Northern Ireland legislation may be similar, but with significant differences, or it may be virtually the same. In either case, the point is that if there is a separate piece of Northern Ireland legislation it constitutes a different source, and the Westminster Act cannot be quoted as being the relevant legislation.

For a general introduction to Northern Ireland law read Brice Dickson's book *The Legal System of Northern Ireland* (2nd ed., 1987).

THE CONSTITUTIONAL BACKGROUND

9–2 For a full explanation of the constitutional position of Northern Ireland up to 1981, read Brigid Hadfield's "Committees of the House of Commons and Northern Ireland affairs" in (1981) 32 *Northern Ireland Legal Quarterly* 199.

In brief, the Northern Ireland jurisdiction came into existence in 1921, established by the Government of Ireland Act 1920 (10 & 11 Geo. 5, c. 67) which set up a parliament for Northern Ireland with power to legislate on many aspects of civil and criminal law, *e.g.* law and order, local government, health and social services, education, planning, agriculture. For some 50 years the Parliament of Northern Ireland legislated on these transferred matters, taking a line independent of Westminster in some fields and following "step by step" in others, until the system of government was suspended on March 30, 1972, by virtue of section 1(3) of the Northern Ireland (Temporary Provisions) Act 1972 (c. 22). The last Act of the Northern Ireland Parliament received the Royal Assent on March 28, 1972.

During the first phase of "direct rule," *i.e.* from the end of March 1972 to the end of 1973, the Queen in Council legislated on transferred matters by means of Orders in Council (which were Statutory Instruments), while executive powers were vested in a Westminster Secretary of State.

The Northern Ireland Constitution Act 1973 (c. 36) abolished the Northern Ireland Parliament on June 18, 1973, and established the Northern Ireland Assembly with a power-sharing Executive from January 1, 1974. The Assembly was given authority to legislate by Measure on a wide range of matters of Northern Ireland concern. Four Measures were passed before the Assembly, as a result of the collapse of the power-sharing executive, was prorogued by Order in Council and its legislative power returned to Westminster in May 1974.

After a brief interim period, the second (and present) phase of "direct rule" was introduced in July 1974 by the Northern Ireland Act 1974 (c. 28). Under the present system, laws may be made for Northern Ireland by Order in Council on all matters which had fallen within the legislative competence of the Assembly.

A second Assembly was set up in 1982, under the Northern Ireland Act 1982 (c. 38), with "scrutiny, consultative and deliberative powers," not with legislative powers. It was dissolved in June 1986 by virtue of the Northern Ireland Assembly (Dissolution) Order 1986 (S.I. 1986/1036).

PRIMARY MATERIALS   9–3

Legislation

The statute law which affects, or has affected Northern Ireland   9–4
comes from more than one source and in more than one form,

comprising: Acts passed by the Irish Parliament in Dublin from 1310 to 1800; Acts passed by the Parliaments of England (1226 to 1707) and Great Britain (1707 to 1800) and by the United Kingdom Parliament thereafter; Acts passed by the Parliament of Northern Ireland from 1921 to March 1972; Orders in Council made in 1972 and 1973 under section 1(3) of the Northern Ireland (Temporary Provisions) Act 1972 (c. 22); Measures passed by the Northern Ireland Assembly in 1974; Orders in Council made from 1974 onwards under para. 1 of Schedule 1 to the Northern Ireland Act 1974 (c. 28). While the Northern Ireland Orders in Council, being Statutory Instruments, are delegated legislation in form, they are not so in substance.

This body of statute law is indexed, in four separate sequences, in the *Chronological Table of the Statutes, Northern Ireland* which is published triennially by Belfast HMSO. There is a companion volume, arranged by subject, the *Index to the Statutes, Northern Ireland* which is also published triennially.

9–5   Editions of Statutes
As regards the editions of the statutes affecting Northern Ireland, the most comprehensive edition of the statutes of the Dublin Parliament 1310 to 1800 is *The Statutes at large passed in the Parliaments held in Ireland from AD 1310 to 1786 inclusive* (13 volumes), continued to 1800 in seven additional volumes, printed in Dublin by George Grierson, 1786 to 1810.

The Statutes, Measures and Orders in Council of Northern Ireland were published by Belfast HMSO, singly at first and later in annual bound volumes from 1921 to 1981.

The first edition of *The Statutes Revised Northern Ireland* was published in 1956 in 16 volumes, covering all the legislation in force at 1950, revised to 1954. This included both Dublin and Westminster legislation. The second edition of *The Statutes Revised Northern Ireland* was published in 1982 in 13 looseleaf binders for convenience in updating. The Dublin Acts (up to 1800) are included, but the Westminster Acts after 1920 are omitted, as these are already available in their revised version in *Statutes in force* (para. 6–17). So far this second edition (originally revised to 1981) has been updated annually by a spiral-bound cumulative supplement which covers not only the 13 volumes of *Statutes Revised 2nd ed.* but also subsequent Northern Ireland Orders in Council, *i.e.* 1982 inclusive onwards, up to the end of the precurrent year.

From 1982 Belfast HMSO ceased to produce annual bound volumes of Orders in Council. Instead they have supplied looseleaf binders matching those of the 1981 revision. You may find that your library, while filing the majority of sets in the looseleaf binders, will have had one or more sets bound. This is because, although readers will usually be looking for updated versions of legislation, some readers will sometimes require a piece of legislation in its original version as at the date of Royal Assent.

Identifying the Source of Legislation   9–6
Sometimes it is possible to tell by the date whether an Act was passed at Westminster, Dublin or in Northern Ireland (Belfast to 1932 and Stormont thereafter), since the all-Ireland Parliament was abolished in 1800, and the Northern Ireland Parliament was prorogued in 1972 and abolished the following year.

However, the indicator of source is generally the position of the words "Ireland" or "Northern Ireland" in relation to the word "Act." If "Ireland" or "Northern Ireland" in the title comes *before* "Act" the source is Westminster, *e.g.* The Bills of Exchange (Ireland) Act 1828; The Social Security (Northern Ireland) Act 1975. If "Ireland" appears *after* "Act," and directly *before* the date, the source is Dublin, *e.g. The Landlord and Tenant Act (Ireland) 1741.* If "Northern Ireland" appears *between* "Act" and the date, the source is the Northern Ireland Parliament, *e.g.* The Factories Act (Northern Ireland) 1949.

Orders are dealt with under delegated legislation (para. 9–7).

Delegated Legislation   9–7
The Rules, Regulations and Orders made by Northern Ireland rule making authorities are called *Statutory Rules and Orders* (S.R. and O's) up to the end of 1973 and *Statutory Rules* (S.R.'s) thereafter. From 1973 onwards they occupy two bound volumes per year, the annual indexes being available only upon publication of the second volume. Recently published *Statutory Rules* (S.R.'s) are listed both in Belfast HMSO's monthly catalogues and in the London HMSO *Daily Lists* (para. 5–18). They are listed by subject in the Belfast HMSO annual catalogues.

The triennial *Index to the Statutory Rules and Orders of Northern Ireland in force on 31st December 19 . . .* like its counterpart the *Index to Government Orders* (para. 6–28), indicates the statutory powers under which the S.R. and O.'s or S.R.'s are made. (See figure on page 164.)

Identifying the source of delegated legislation   9–8
To distinguish between a Westminster Statutory Instrument applying solely to Northern Ireland (which may or may not be a Northern Ireland Order in Council) on the one hand, and a Northern Ireland Statutory Rule, whether an "Order," "Rule" or "Regulation," on the other: one is generally guided by the

NAVAL COURTS *See* Index to Govt. Orders

NAVAL DISCIPLINE *See* Index to Govt. Orders—DEFENCE, 4(3)

NAVAL MEDICAL COMPASSIONATE FUND *See* Index to Govt. Orders—DEFENCE 4(9)

NAVIGATION *See* CANAL AND NAVIGABLE RIVER; ECONOMIC DEVELOPMENT, DEPT. of; Index to Govt. Orders—CIVIL AVIATION, 2; HARBOURS, DOCKS, PIERS AND FERRIES, 1(1)(*c*)(*d*); MERCHANT SHIPPING, 6, 9, 10

NAVIGATION OF AIRCRAFT *See* Index to Govt. Orders—   CIVIL AVIATION, 2

NAVY *See* Index to Govt. Orders—DEFENCE, 4

NETS *See* FISHERIES

NETS INDUSTRIES (DEVELOPMENT) *See* INDUSTRIAL AID AND DEVELOPMENT

NEW TOWNS
  Power
    1965. Dept of the Environment may by an O., made with the concurrence of the Dept. of Finance and Personnel, designate site of new town. Draft O. to be approved by resolution of N.I. Ass. (subject to mods. and adaptations)
                                                    New Towns Act (N.I.) 1965 (c. 13) s. 1

  Exercise

1965, July 9	New Town Designation Order (N.I.) 1965 (No. 147)	1965, p. 529
1966, July 7	New Town (Antrim) Designation Order (N.I.) 1966 (No. 161)	1966, p.523
1967, Aug. 22	New Town (Antrim and Ballymena) Designation Order (N.I.) 1967 (No. 232)	1967, p. 824
1969, Feb. 5	Londonderry Area Designation Order (N.I.) 1969 (No. 23)	1969, p. 133

  Power (not yet exercised)
    1965. Dept. may make O. for compulsory acquisition of land
                                                    New Towns Act (N.I.) 1965 (c.13) s. 4

  Power
    1965. Where an O. is made under s. 1 of the Act with respect to a proposed new town, the Dept. may by O. establish a new town commn. to secure the laying out and development of the new town in accordance with proposals approved by the Dept. and to exercise such further functions as may be confirmed upon the new town commn. by virtue of an O. made under s. 28 of the Act
                                                    New Towns Act (N.I.) 1965 (c. 13) s. 7(1)

  Exercise

1966, Dec. 1	Antrim Development Commission Order (N.I.) 1966 (No. 282)	1966, p. 922
1969, Feb. 5	Londonderry Development Commission Order (N.I.) 1969 (No. 24)	1969, p. 135

    O. of a local character made under this power are excluded from this Index. Summaries are given in classified lists of Local O. in the annual vols.
  Power (not yet exercised)
    1965. Dept. may by regs. make such mod. or alteration in such further provn. with respect to the procedure to be followed by a local govt. auditor acting under s. 10 of the Act as the circumstances require
                                                    New Towns Act (N.I.) 1965 (c. 13) s. 10(4)

    1965. On application by the new town commn. the Dept. may make an O. in respect of the compulsory acquisition by them of land
                                                    New Towns Act (N.I.) 1965 (c. 13) s. 15(3)

  Power
    1965. Dept may make an O. directing that a new town commn. shall, in relation to an area designated as the site of a new town, exercise the functions of a county borough or district council: supplementary provns. Draft O. to be approved by a resolution of N.I. Ass.
                                                    New Towns Act (N.I.) 1965 (c. 13) ss. 28, 29
                                                    New Towns (Amdt.) Act (N.I.) 1968 (c. 33) s. 1, sch.

    1965. Dept may, by either a municipal functions O., or an O. (subject to affirmative resolution) made under s. 30, make such adaptations of or mods. in any transferred provn. as appear to be necessary or desirable to meet the circumstances of a new town commn. or otherwise for the purpose of giving full effect to the Act
                                                    New Towns Act (N.I.) 1965 (c. 13) s. 30
                                                    New Towns (Amdt.) Act (N.I.) 1968 (c. 33) s. 1, sch.

Power (not yet exercised)

1965. Where the Dept. is satisfied that the construction of the new town has been substantially achieved, the Dept. shall by O., subject to affirmative resolution, provide for the termination and winding up of the new town commns.

New Towns Act (N.I.) 1965 (c. 13) s. 33

1965. Dept shall by regs. make provn. for the payment of compensation under s. 35 of the Act and such regs. may include provn. as to the manner in which and the person to whom any claim for such compensation is to be made, for the determination of all questions under the regs.

New Towns Act (N.I.) 1965 (c. 13) s. 35(5)

Power

1965. Dept may make regs. prescribing anything that is under this Act to be prescribed and providing for any matter in regard to which regs. may be made under the Act and generally for carrying the Act into effect. Regs. made under s. 43 (1) to be subject to negative resolution

New Towns Act (N.I.) 1965 (c. 113) s. 43

Exercise

| 1966, Apr. 18 | New Towns (Extinguishment of Public Rights of Way) 1966, Apr 18 New Towns Way) Regs. (N.I.) 1966 (No. 83) | 1966, p. 275 |
| 1971, Sept. 1 | New Towns and Town Development (Municipal Functions—Compensation) Regs. (N.I.) 1971 (No. 282) | 1971, p. 1352 |

Power

1965. Dept may by O., subject to negative resolution, determine the value of contracts or instruments to be made under seal.

New Towns Act (N.I.) 1965 (c.13) sch. 4 para. 14, *as amended by*
Financial Provns.
(N.I.) Order, S.I. 1976/1212 (N.I. 21) art. 8(3)

Exercise

1980, Aug. 18 Sealing of Contracts (Financial Limits) Order   (N.I.) 1980 (No. 283) *See also* Bye-Laws; Local Govern ment, 9

NEW TOWNS COMMISSION *See* New Towns

NEW UNIVERSITY OF ULSTER

Power

1970. Dept. may by O. appoint a day for the transfer of certain property from Trustees to University Magee University College Londonderry Act (N.I.) 1970 (c. 15) s. 1

Exercise

1970, Sept. 21 Magee University College Londonderry (Appointed Day) Order (N.I.) 1970 (No. 248)
1970, p. 1265

Power (not exercised)

1970. Dept., with the approval of the Dept. of Finance and Personnel, may after the appointed days by regs., subject to affirmative resolution, make provn. for the payment compensation to staff who suffered loss of emoluments or employment by reason of not being employed by the University: supplementary provns.

Magee University College Londonderry Act (N.I.) 1970 (c. 15) s.6

See also University of Ulster

relative positions of "Northern Ireland" and "Order." The
same principle applies as in the case of Acts, *e.g.* The Export of
Sheep (Prohibition) (No. 2) Order (Northern Ireland) 1986 is a
Statutory Rule, its citation being S.R. 1986/325. The Local Elections (Northern Ireland) Order 1985 is a statutory instrument,
its citation being S.I. 1985/454. The Social Need (Northern Ireland) Order 1986 is a statutory instrument which is also a
Northern Ireland Order in Council. This is revealed by its having a double citation, *i.e.* S.I. 1986/1302 (N.I.14). The difference
in the two numbers is accounted for by the fact that only about
one statutory instrument in one hundred is a Northern Ireland
Order in Council.

Law Reports

9–9   Although the Northern Ireland jurisdiction came into existence
in 1921, the Incorporated Council of Law Reporting for Northern Ireland only started publishing the *Northern Ireland Law
Reports* in 1925. Reports of cases in the Northern Ireland courts
between 1921 and 1924 can be found in the *Irish Reports* and the
Irish Law Times Reports.

Because of the inconvenience caused by the time-lag before
publication of the official law reports, the *Northern Ireland Law
Reports Bulletin of Judgments* (which has had several minor
changes of title over the years) has been produced from 1970
onwards. The bulletins consist of collections of recent judgments within blue paper covers. They are sometimes carelessly
referred to as the "blue bulletins," or, even more carelessly, as
the "blue books," thereby causing confusion with government
publications. They are cited as; [year] number NIJB.

9–10 **Indexes to law reports**
The *Index to cases decided in the Courts of Northern Ireland and
reported during the period 1921 to 1970*, edited by Desmond Greer
and Brian Childs, (I.C.L.R.N.I., 1975) covers Northern Ireland
cases reported in the *Northern Ireland Law Reports, Irish Law
Times Reports, Irish Jurist Reports, Irish Reports, Law Reports:
Appeal Cases, Criminal Appeal Reports* and *Tax Cases.* The sections consist of: alphabetical table of cases reported; subject-
matter titles; subject-matter index; statutes judicially considered, (in four separate sequences: public and general Acts of
the Parliaments of England, Great Britain and the United Kingdom, 1215–1970; Parliament of Ireland to 1800; Parliament of
Northern Ireland; parliaments outside the United Kingdom);
private and local Acts judicially considered (again four

sequences); Statutory Rules and Orders judicially considered; Rules of the Supreme Court judicially considered; cases judicially considered; words and phrases judicially considered.

The *First Interim Supplement, 1971 to 1975* to the above index was published in 1976. It covers *Northern Ireland Law Reports* from 1971 to 1974. For 1975 it covers the *Northern Ireland Judgments Bulletin/Northern Ireland Law Reports Bulletin of Judgments* only, as the official law reports had not appeared by the date of compilation. Also covered are Northern Ireland cases in *Criminal Appeal Reports, Tax Cases* and *Taxation Reports*.

No second supplement has yet been published, but at least two unofficial supplements are in (limited) circulation.

The *Bulletin of Northern Ireland Law* (1981 onwards) digests cases in the official law reports and in the judgments bulletins. In addition, it has digested some otherwise unreported cases. (See the figure on page 172.)

The *Irish Digest* is the name of a number of volumes published in Dublin and covering the years 1867 to 1983. Coverage includes the *Northern Ireland Law Reports*.

Decisions of Tribunals

Reports of decisions of the [Northern Ireland] Industrial Tribunals **9-11** were published with a limited circulation from 1966 to 1978, originally by the Ministry of Health and Social Services for Northern Ireland and later by the Department of Manpower Services. An example of their citation is I.T.R. 135 (N.I.). They are now distributed only to a chosen few but may be consulted by callers at the Central Office of the Industrial Tribunals, in Belfast. Selected decisions have been digested in the *Bulletin of Northern Ireland Law* since 1981.

Industrial Court (Northern Ireland) Awards have been published since 1963. At present they are appearing at the rate of three or four per year. They are available from the Belfast office of HMSO and are also digested in the *Bulletin of Northern Ireland Law*.

The Lands Tribunal for Northern Ireland has produced reports in typescript since 1965. From 1981 all of these have also appeared, in digested form, in the *Bulletin of Northern Ireland Law*.

The Planning Appeals Commission, which was set up in 1973, has been producing a *Bulletin* since April 1974. It is issued monthly and distributed on an informal basis to interested persons.

Reported decisions of the Umpire under the Family Allowances, National Insurance and Industrial Injuries Acts (N.I.) 1948 to 1961, published for the Northern Ireland Ministry of Labour and National Insurance by Belfast HMSO in 1963, was followed by *Reported Decisions of the Commissioners under the Family Allowances, National Insurance and Industrial Injuries Acts (N.I.) and the Social Security Acts (N.I.) April 1961 to December 1977*, published for the Northern Ireland Department of Health and Social Services by Belfast HMSO in 1978. The more recent Decisions are, as yet, unbound.

Decisions of the Commissioner under the Supplementary Benefits (N.I.) Order 1977 are also still unbound.

From 1981 all the printed Commissioners' Decisions are digested in the *Bulletin of Northern Ireland Law*, and recently some unpublished Decisions have also been appearing in the *Bulletin*.

Annual Reports and Statements of Accounts

9–12 The various Northern Ireland government departments and quangos (*i.e.* quasi-autonomous governmental organisations) are obliged to publish annual reports of their activities and statements of accounts. Some reports are published by the Belfast office of HMSO on behalf of the relevant department. Others are published as House of Commons papers or Command papers (see paras. 5–5, 5–14) by HMSO in London. In the case of a quango with a statutory obligation to report to Parliament (*e.g.* the Fair Employment Agency for Northern Ireland) the annual reports and/or statements of accounts will appear as House of Commons papers.

These reports can be traced through the HMSO printed lists and catalogues. (para. 5–18).

SECONDARY MATERIALS

Books and Pamphlets (Monographs)

9–13 As already stated, the student of Northern Ireland law is faced with the problem as to whether, or not, a statement of the law which he/she has just read in one of the standard English text books, is applicable to Northern Ireland.

Until 1981, practitioners, teachers and students of Northern Ireland law were nearly always obliged to use the primary materials in order to determine the law on any point. The only secondary sources available were a handful of books and pamphlets, the *Northern Ireland Legal Quarterly* (the main source) the *Gazette of the Incorporated Law Society of Northern*

Ireland, and various articles thinly scattered throughout United Kingdom, foreign and Commonwealth legal journals.

However, in 1980 the Council of Legal Education for Northern Ireland set up S.L.S. Legal Publications (N.I.) which is producing monographs and periodical publications on various aspects of the Northern Ireland legal system. It has published books and pamphlets on areas of Northern Ireland law and practice which differ substantially from English law and practice. The books include the Law in Action series, primarily intended for the general public. The pamphlets include the Recent Developments series, designed to keep readers informed of recent changes in the law. In areas where the Northern Ireland material, though considerable, does not justify a separate textbook, S.L.S. has produced Northern Ireland Supplements to major English textbooks, *e.g.* to *Cross on Evidence* (5th ed.) and to *Smith and Hogan's Criminal Law* (5th ed.). A useful starting point for the general reader or law student is a title in the Law in Action series: Brice Dickson, *The Legal System of Northern Ireland* (2nd ed., 1987).

The latest S.L.S. publisher's catalogue serves as a useful bibliography on Northern Ireland law. For the works of other publishers, consult the heading "Northern Ireland" in *Lawyers' Law Books* (2nd ed.) (para. 6–34). Other bibliographies are listed on pp. 245–246 of *Information Sources in Law*, edited by Robert Logan, Chapter 16 by Elizabeth Gleeson (para. 6–35).

The Belfast Law Centre has published pamphlets in the welfare law field. Their journal, *Welfare Rights News*, from time to time lists names and addresses of pressure groups and agencies in the province, many of whom produce relevant pamphlets, *e.g.* the Rape Crisis Centre, which is campaigning for changes in the law relating to rape. Among other presure groups, the Belfast-based Committee on the Administration of Justice has produced a number of pamphlets, policy documents and leaflets in the human rights field—on criminal justice, police powers, etc.

Government publications can be traced through the monthly and annual lists published by Belfast HMSO. However, note that government departments now produce some of their material internally, by use of word processors, etc., and such material does not appear on HMSO lists.

The various Northern Ireland quangos produce pamphlets as well as annual reports. As they are obliged to report their activities and submit their accounts annually to Government, their annual reports and statements of accounts appear in the HMSO lists, (para. 9–12) but their miscellaneous other publications do not all appear there. The quangos include: the Standing Advisory Commission on Human Rights, the Fair Employment Agency for Northern Ireland, the Equal Opportunities Commission for Northern Ireland, the Labour Relations Agency, the Northern Ireland Housing Executive.

Journals

9–14 *The Northern Ireland Legal Quarterly* (1936–1961, 1964–), published by S.L.S., is a general legal journal containing articles, notes, comments and book reviews on a wide variety of legal topics. It does not confine itself to Northern Ireland law, but contains articles of world-wide legal interest.

The *Gazette of the Incorporated Law Society of Northern Ireland* was published irregularly between 1964 and 1982. It is succeeded by *The Writ; Journal of the Law Society of Northern Ireland* (August 1986–), primarily for members of the Society, but containing items of interest to the keener student, particularly the post-graduate professional student.

Welfare Rights News has been published by the Belfast Law Centre since December 1983. It normally appears quarterly, and contains articles and news on various aspects of welfare law. It regularly lists Northern Ireland voluntary welfare advice and/or campaigning agencies, giving their current addresses and telephone numbers.

Fortnight: an Independent Review published since 1970, is primarily concerned with local politics and current affairs but frequently contains articles or commentary relevant to the study of the Northern Ireland legal system.

Articles on Northern Ireland law appear, from time to time, in journals published outside Northern Ireland, *e.g.* "Supergrasses and the legal system in Britain and Northern Ireland" by Steven Greer in (1986) 102 L.Q.R. 198.

Indexes to Journals

9–15 *A Bibliography of Periodical Literature relating to Irish Law* by Paul O'Higgins is an invaluable guide to articles published up to 1981. The original volume was published in 1966 and was followed by two supplements in 1973 and 1983. It covers articles in journals published anywhere in the world, non-legal journals, and articles on foreign law by Irish authors.

The *Index to Legal Periodicals*, *British Humanities Index*, and other periodical indexes mentioned in Chapter 4 may also contain relevant articles on Irish law.

Encyclopedic Works   9–16

General Encyclopedic Works   9–17

The Digest of Northern Ireland Law, to be published by S.L.S., is due in late 1987/early 1988. It will be in looseleaf form, regularly up-dated. It is intended particularly for use by non-lawyers (*e.g.* staff of Citizens' Advice Bureaux) who require information about specific areas of law. It explains, clearly and simply, aspects of Northern Ireland law which are of general interest, *e.g.* legal services, children and the law, family law, consumer finance, employment law, etc. Differences between the law in Northern Ireland and in England and Wales are highlighted.

S.L.S. also publishes the *Bulletin of Northern Ireland Law* (1981 onwards) (see the figure on page 172.) Published ten times a year, it provides up to date legal information under broad subject headings arranged alphabetically. Coverage consists of: summaries of all new legislation applicable to Northern Ireland; commencement dates for legislation; digests of written judgments in the Northern Ireland Court of Appeal, High Court and County Court; digests of selected decisions of the Lands Tribunal, Planning Appeals Commission, Industrial Court, Industrial Tribunals and Social Security Tribunals; digests of selected tax cases; summaries of jury awards in the High Court; summaries of selected County Court awards in criminal damage and criminal injury claims; practice directions; Northern Ireland court service notices; relevant developments in E.E.C. law; and selected legal developments in England and the Republic of Ireland.

Current Law (para. 6–9) uses "Northern Ireland" as one of its subject headings, further subdivided alphabetically by subject. (See the figure on page 173.)

Specialised Encyclopedias   9–18

Encyclopedia of Northern Ireland labour law and practice, published by the Labour Relations Agency, is a three-volume looseleaf work up-dated regularly.

(noted 81/7/16) and the Companies (NI) Order 1982 (noted 82/9/5) relating to the names under which persons may carry on business in NI.
Commencement: 24 September 1986 (£1.40)

8   Consequential provisions - legislation - consolidation

COMPANIES CONSOLIDATION (CONSEQUENTIAL PROVISIONS) (NI) ORDER 1986 (SI 1986/1035 (NI 9))
The Order makes provision, in connection with the consolidation of the Companies Acts 1960 - 1983 and other statutory provisions relating to companies, for transitional matters and savings, repeals and consequential amendments of other statutory provisions.
Commencement: 24 September 1986 (£4.40)

9   Insider dealing - legislation - consolidation

COMPANY SECURITIES (INSIDER DEALING) (NI) ORDER 1986 (SI 1986/1034 (NI 8)
The Order consolidates provisions in the Companies Act (NI) 1960, the Companies (NI) Order 1981 (noted 81/7/16) and the Companies (NI) Order 1982 (noted 82/9/5) relating to insider dealing in company securities.
Commencement: 24 September 1986 (£2.40)

10   Winding up - fraudulent preference

UNFAIR PREFERENCES IN COMPANY LIQUIDATIONS
An article by Gerard McCormack, Lecturer in Law at the Queen's University of Belfast, concerning s 288 of the Companies Act (NI) 1960 has been published at (1986) 37 NILQ 86.

CONSTITUTIONAL LAW

11   United Kingdom - relationship with Republic of Ireland

THE ANGLO-IRISH AGREEMENT 1985 - BLUE PRINT OR GREEN PRINT?
An article by Brigid Hadfield, Senior Lecturer in Law at the Queen's University of Belfast, concerning the Agreement in the perspective of constitutional developments in and relating to NI, has been published at (1986) 37 NILQ 1.

CONSUMER LAW

12   Consumer credit - period of standard licence

CONSUMER CREDIT (PERIOD OF STANDARD LICENCE) (AMENDMENT) REGULATIONS 1986 (SI 1986/1016)
The Regulations vary the 1975 Regulations by extending from ten to 1 years the period during which a standard licence, as defined by s 22(1)(a) of the Consumer Credit Act 1974, is to have effect.
Commencement: 1 August 1986 (45p)

CONTRACT

13   Option to purchase land - specific performance - document not under seal - damages - whether action out of time

YOUNG v LAVERY, Magherafelt Cty Ct (Judge Hart QC), 25 March 1986
The defendant, L, was the registered owner of 3.7 acres of land situated at Ballymaguigan, Magherafelt. He had purchased the land for

result the load-bearing capacity of the land on which the spine road was to be constructed was adversely affected.

Held, by the Lands Tribunal, on a preliminary point of law, that the compensation, if any, must be assessed in accordance with art. 55 of the 1973 Order which applies s.38 of the Mineral Development Act (Northern Ireland) 1969.

LANSON HOMES *v.* DEPARTMENT OF THE ENVIRONMENT FOR NORTHERN IRELAND (R/26/1985).

261. Company law—winding up—transfer of funds by liquidator for "advantage" of creditors

[Companies (Northern Ireland) Order 1978 (S.I. No. 1040), art. 75(2).]

In Northern Ireland a transfer of funds by a liquidator is permissible once a relevant advantage (including financial) to creditors is proved to exist.

The liquidation of the company raised a sum which was lodged in an Insolvency Account maintained by the Department of Economic Development. Interest at $3\frac{1}{2}$ per cent. was credited. An application was made to transfer $\frac{3}{4}$ of the sum into a separate deposit account with a commercial bank paying interest at $11\frac{1}{2}$ per cent. The department rejected the application. The applicant contended that art. 75(2) of the 1978 Order was wide enough to cover this situation.

Held, granting the orders, the Department could not withhold authorisation once a relevant advantage to creditors had been proved to exist, which (unlike English Law) included financial advantage).

P.X. NUCLEAR, *Re* [1987] PCC 82, Murray J, Northern Ireland.

262. Compulsory purchase

COMPULSORY ACQUISITION (INTEREST) ORDER (NORTHERN IRELAND) 1987 (No. 147) [45p], made under the Public Health and Local Government (Miscellaneous Provisions) Act (Northern Ireland) 1955 (c.13), s.12, the Administrative and Financial Provisions Act (Northern Ireland) 1956 (c.17), s.14, and the Local Government Act (Northern Ireland) 1972 (c.9), Sched. 6, para. 18; operative on April 22, 1987; decreases to $11\frac{1}{4}$ per cent. per annum the rate of interest on compensation payable under specified enactments for compulsorily acquired land; revokes the 1985 (No. 313) Order.

263. Compulsory purchase—construction of reservoir—whether interest payable on compensation

The Department of the Environment compulsorily acquired part of C's land for the construction of a reservoir. Subsequently the Department constructed the reservoir and laid a water main. During the execution of the works a gravity flow of water from a well to a tap in an outhouse owned by C was cut off. Compensation was agreed at £1,500 for the land acquired, £225 for temporary disturbance, £2,000 for the loss of the water supply and £275 for the laying of the water main.

Held, by the Lands Tribunal, that interest was payable on the compensation for the land and the temporary disturbance but not on the compensation for the loss of the water supply or the laying of the water main.

McBRIDE *v.* DEPARTMENT OF THE ENVIRONMENT FOR NORTHERN IRELAND (R/15/1986).

264. Criminal law—Public Order (Northern Ireland) Order 1987 (S.I. 1987 No. 463 (N.I. 7))

This Order repeals and re-enacts with amendments the Public Order (Northern Ireland) 1981. The principal amendments require not less than seven days advance notice to be given of a public procession, add to the matters to be notified, widen the grounds on which conditions may be imposed by the police on public processions and on which the Secretary of State may prohibit public processions and open-air public meetings and confer on the police new powers to impose conditions on open-air public meetings. The Order also amends the law on incitement to hatred and repeals the Flags and Emblems (Display) Act (Northern Ireland) 1954) (c.10).

The Order came into operation on April 2, 1987.

265. Criminal law

PUBLIC ORDER (EXCEPTIONS) ORDER (NORTHERN IRELAND) 1987 (No. 126) [45p], made under S.I. 1987 No. 463 (N.I. 7), art. 3(4)(*b*); operative on April 1, 1987; excepts public processions customarily held along particular routes by the Salvation Army from the requirement to give advance notice under art. 3(1) of the 1987 S.I.

265a. Criminal Law—Crossbows Act 1987 (c.32). See CRIMINAL LAW, § 73b.

266. Education

PAYMENT OF TEACHERS' SALARIES AND ALLOWANCES REGULATIONS (NORTHERN IRELAND) 1987 (No 127) [45p], made under S.I. 1986 No. 594 (N.I. 3), arts. 69(3), 134(1); operative on April 15, 1987; make provision for the payment of teachers' salaries and

CHAPTER 10

Republic of Ireland

INTRODUCTION

10–01 Having the complex historical background that Ireland does, it is generally accepted that Irish law is difficult to find. Irish legal history very much consists of English law in Ireland, as with the importation of English law from the twelfth century onwards, the existing Brehon law was effectively eradicated. Apart from the few brief intervals of legal independence, until 1922 the Irish legal system was heavily influenced by English authority. In 1800, after the Act of Union, the Irish Parliament was dissolved. In 1920, the Government of Ireland Act provided for devolved governments in both the North and South, but this was never implemented in the South. The Anglo-Irish Treaty of 1922 established the Irish Free State with dominion status within the British Commonwealth. A considerable amount of nineteenth century English law is still in force in Ireland. It is only within the last 20 years or so that there has been a move away from dependence on English law and legal literature. This divergence from English law has seen a new era of Irish legal publishing, with the production of textbooks in all the main subject areas. However, as with many former Commonwealth countries, early editions of secondary materials published in the United Kingdom are frequently of great interest. The later editions which contain current United Kingdom legislation are now too far removed to be of very much importance. Consequently, many secondary sources now amended in England are still relevant to the law in Ireland.

① *Number 1 of* 1986

② **COURTS ACT, 1986**

③ AN ACT TO AMEND THE COURTS OF JUSTICE ACT, 1936.
   [*27th February*, 1986] ④

⑤ BE IT ENACTED BY THE OIREACHTAS AS FOLLOWS: 5

⑦ Amendment of
Courts of Justice
Act, 1936.

1.—(1) The Courts of Justice Act, 1936, is hereby amended by—

(*a*) the insertion in the Second Schedule of

Galway	Galway County Borough

after

Galway	Galway county

10

   and

(*b*) the insertion in section 33, with effect as on and from the 1st
day of January, 1986, of the following paragraph after
paragraph (*a*) of subsection (2):

   "(*aa*) alter the composition of a High Court Circuit by 15
   adding to or removing from the Circuit a county
   or counties, a county borough or county boroughs
   or a county or counties and a county borough or
   county boroughs, or".

⑥ (2) (*a*) Galway is hereby deemed to be the appeal town, within 20
   the meaning of Part IV of the Courts of Justice Act, 1936,
   for the purposes of appeals from judgments or orders of
   the Circuit Court given or made in actions or matters
   heard and determined before the passing of this Act in
   the County Borough of Galway or before the 1st day of 25
   January, 1986, in the area that, upon that date, constituted
   the said County Borough.

   (*b*) A notice of appeal served before such passing in respect of
   a judgment or order referred to in *paragraph (a)* of this
   subsection shall not be invalid by reason only of the fact 30

2

10–2   PRIMARY SOURCES

Bunreacht na hEireann (the Constitution)

10–3   The written constitution of Ireland embodies the most important constitutional laws. Legislation which conflicts with the
constitution may be declared invalid by the courts. If a Bill is
introduced to amend the constitution, it can only become an
Act after a public referendum.

In 1922, the Constitution of the Irish Free State, or Saorstat
Eireann, was enacted and established the foundations for the
machinery of government for the new state. In 1937, a new constitution was adopted by plebiscite. This constitution in the
main provided a stabilising and reforming continuation of that
of 1922, but also established a constitution free from all
elements of subservience to the British crown.

The latest edition of the Constitution was published in
bilingual format by the Stationery Office in 1980. It contains a
list of amending acts up until 1979, along with the dates of their
signature. Subsequent amendments appear on inserted slips.
There is an alphabetical subject index at the rear.

10–4   Legislation

10–5   Primary Legislation
Before a Bill can become law, it must be approved by both
Houses of the Irish Parliament—Dáil and Seanad Eireann—and
signed by the President. Once this has happened, the Bill
becomes an Act immediately. Unless otherwise specified, the
date of commencement is the date of signature by the President.

10–6   *Parts of an Act*
The various parts of an Act can be seen on the copy reproduced
in the figure on p. 175, and are as follows:

1. official citation
2. short title
3. long title
4. date of signature by the President
5. enacting formula
6. section and sub-section
7. marginal note

10–7   *Citation*
Acts are commonly referred to by their short title and the year of
publication, *e.g.* The Finance Act 1985. Acts are numbered
within the year, and may also be cited in this way. Thus the

Finance Act 1985 is cited officially as 10/1985. Prior to 1922 the British method of citation in use at that time applies, so that statutes are referred to by regnal year and by chapter number. (para. 3–3)

Publication of Irish Acts   10–8

The *Acts of the Oireachtas* are the official source of Irish legislation and are published by the Stationery Office. They are available in two formats:

1. A4 format which is a reprint of the Bill as passed by both Houses, with the addition of an Act title, number, and date of signature by the President.
2. Bilingual format produced in quarto. It is this version that eventually appears as the official annual bound volume.

However, as there is such a delay in the production of bilingual texts, the Stationery Office now issue annual volumes of the A4 size Acts in English only.

More recently, Sweet and Maxwell have produced an annotated edition of the Irish Acts entitled *Irish Current Law Statutes Annotated*. This is a looseleaf publication which commenced in 1984. It is issued in several parts each year, each part covering several Acts, and is published several months after the Acts included have been passed. Not all Acts have full annotations, but all come with detailed general notes. There is a subject index at the rear which is updated with each issue. The table of contents at the front of the volume lists the Acts both alphabetically and chronologically within each year.

Tracing an Irish Act   10–9

At the front of each volume of the *Acts of the Oireachtas* can be found both an alphabetical and a chronological list of statutes passed during that year. A consolidated index for the years 1922–1982 has been produced. This contains a complete chronological table of the statutes detailing:

1. year and number of the Act
2. short title
3. how the Act has been affected
4. the affecting provision relating to 3. (see the figure on page 178)

There is also a subject index which cites the statutes by number, year and subsection. The following chronological tables are also included:

1. List of Irish private Acts.
2. Pre-Union Irish statutes, English statutes, pre-Union

272   CHRONOLOGICAL TABLE OF THE STATUTES

Year and Number	Short Title	How Affected	Affecting Provision
1977 32—*contd.*	**Finance (Excise Duty on Tobacco Products) Act, 1977**—*contd.*	S. 10, new rate of duty. Ss. 10 (4) (5), 11 appl. with mods. S. 11 appl. with mods.	14/1980, s. 77 (4), sch. 7, pt. 4. S.I. No. 57 of 1979, par. 21 (3)–(5) S.I. No. 152 of 1979, par. 12; S.I. No. 153 of 1979, para. 3
33.	*Gaeltacht Industries (Amendment) Act, 1977.*	r.	5/1979, ss. 3,4
34.	**International Development Association (Amendment) Act, 1977.**		
35.	**Nítrigin Éireann Teoranta Act, 1977.**		
36.	*Appropriation Act, 1977.*	Spent.	
37.	**Industrial Development Act, 1977.**	S. 2 am. S. 2 am.	13/1981, s. 6. 13/1981, s. 7.
1978 1.	**Consumer Information Act, 1978.**	Ss. 9(6)(h), 18 constr.	16/1980, ss. 1(2), 57.
2.	**Agricultural Credit Act, 1978.**	S. 12 am. S. 14 am. S. 28, limitation on recovery of cert. interest.	24/1982, s. 2. 24/1982, s. 3. 6/1957, s. 42.
3.	**Shannon Free Airport Development Company Limited (Amendment) Act, 1978.**	S. 3 r., new provn.	28/1980, s. 3.
4.	**Medical Practitioners Act, 1978.**		
5.	*Social Welfare Act, 1978*	r., continuance of instrs., etc.	1/1981, ss. 310–312, sch. 6, pt. 2.
6.	*Health Contributions (Amendment) Act, 1978.*	r.	4/1979, ss. 3, 19.
7.	**Landlord and Tenant (Ground Rents) Act, 1978.**	Saving provn. S. 2(1), applic, rstrct.	21/1981, s. 16(1). 10/1980, ss. 2, 30 (3).
8.	**Road Transport Act, 1978.**		
9.	Rates on Agricultural Land (Relief) Act, 1978.	S. 1, "agricultural land" ext. S. I (2)(3) r.	20/1980, s. 4. 20/ 1980, s. 5.
10.	**Local Loans Fund (Amendment) Act, 1978.**	S.1 r., new provn.	41/1980,. 1.
11.	**Restrictive Practices (Confirmation of Order) Act, 1978**		

* *See* Interpretation Act, 1937, s. 20 (1).

British statutes and the Local Government (Application of Enactments) Order 1898, affected by the Acts 1922–1975, or by Regulations made under section 3 of the European Communities Act 1972.

3. Provisions contained in pre-Union Irish statutes, British statutes and Saorstat Eireann statutes which have been specifically adapated or modified by orders made under the Adaptation of Enactments Acts 1922 and 1931 and the Constitution (Consequential Provisions) Act 1937.

4. Table of expressions used in British statutes or in Saorstat Eireann statutes which have been adapted by orders made under the Adaptation of Enactments Act 1922 or the Constitution (Consequential Provisions) Act 1937.

5. List of Regulations made under section 3 of the European Communities Act 1972.

A supplement covering the years 1983 to 1985 can be found at the back of this index, and follows the same format. Subsequent to this, a separate index is issued annually.

Older Irish Acts   10–10
Prior to 1922 there are two principal sources of legislation:

A. *Irish or pre-Union* statutes passed in the parliaments held in Ireland between 1310 and 1800 were published by Grierson in the nineteenth century in two editions:

1. Folio edition of 20 volumes entitled *The Statutes at Large Passed in the Parliaments Held in Ireland.*
2. Octavo edition of 12 volumes, entitled *Statutes Passed in the Parliaments Held in Ireland.*

A two volume subject index accompanying the octavo edition contains a table showing the correspondence between the two.

These Acts were presented in a much more convenient one volume format by HMSO as the *Irish Statutes Revised 1310–1800.* This contains a chronological table which gives details of:

1. the regnal year, statute title and chapter number
2. subject matter
3. reason for total or partial omission (usually that it has been repealed in full or in part)

There is a subject index at the back of the volume.

B. *United Kingdom of Great Britain and Ireland 1801–1921.* During this period Ireland, being governed directly from Westminster, had no separate legislation. The sources for the years 1801–1921

S.I. No. 422 of 1985   (2)

Waterford City Management (Reserved Functions) Order, 1985   (1)

(4)

(3) The Minister for the Environment in exercise of the powers conferred on him by subsection (2) of section 11 of the Waterford City Management Act, 1939 (No. 25 of 1939), hereby directs and orders as follows:-

1. This Order may be cited as the Waterford City Management (Reserved Functions) Order, 1985.

2. This Order shall come into effect on the 1st day of January, 1986.   (6)

3. The power of Waterford County Borough Corporation to make charges for services provided in respect of domestic premises by virtue of section 2 of the Local Government (Financial Provisions) (No. 2) Act, 1983 (No. 21 of 1983) shall be exercisable and performable directly by the Waterford City Council.

4. The power of Waterford County Borough Corporation to make charges for water supplied for domestic purposes by virtue of section 65A of the Public Health (Ireland) Act, 1878 (inserted by section 7 of the Local Government (Sanitary Services) Act, 1962 (No. 26 of 1962)), as amended by section 8 of the Local Government (Financial Provisions) (No. 2) Act, 1983 (No. 21 of 1983) shall be exercisable and performable directly by the Waterford City Council.

5. In this order "domestic premises" means a premises used wholly or mainly as a dwelling.

(5) GIVEN under the Official Seal of the Minister for the Environment this/7th day of December, 1985.

L.S.

LIAM KAVANAGH

Minister for the Environment.

are therefore the same as for British statutes and have been described in Chapter 3.

Oulton's *Index to the Statutes at present in force in, or affecting Ireland, from the year 1310 to 1835 inclusive,* with eleven annual supplements from 1836 to 1846, is a useful guide to early Irish legislation.

Another source of Irish legislation which should be mentioned is "The Green Book" or *Reading made easy of the Irish Statutes* by Vance. Published in 1862, it contains an account of the principal decisions of Irish statutes, Rules and Orders of Court from 1224 to 1860, and any amendments made to them. A subject index is found at the rear of the volume.

Secondary Legislation   10–11
In order to avoid the necessity of passing a huge amount of primary legislation, certain Ministers or government departments are given powers under various Acts to make detailed rules and regulations. These are known as *Statutory Instruments,* and fulfil the same function as their British counterparts.

Parts of a Statutory Instrument   10–12
The following elements can be seen on the statutory instrument reproduced on page 180:

- (1) Title
- (2) Statutory Instrument number
- (3) Enabling Act
- (4) Minister responsible
- (5) date of signature
- (6) date from which Statutory Instrument is effective

Citation   10–13
During the year, every Statutory Instrument published is given its own number; for example, the Army Pensions Regulations, 1985 is cited as S.I. No. 359 of 1985

Publication   10–14
Statutory Instruments are available in three formats:–

- (1) Loose typescript A4 issued by the relevant department.
- (2) Printed quarto format—English only, published by the Stationery Office.
- (3) Printed quarto format—bilingual (later bound in volumes and published by the Stationery Office)

Bound volumes of *Statutory Instruments* were published annually from 1948 to 1981. They are arranged numerically within each year, and there may be more than one volume for

each year. From 1982 onwards they are only available individually. Prior to 1948, Statutory Instruments were known as
Statutory Rules and Orders. These were published by the
Stationery Office in 1948 as a subject collection of 39 volumes,
entitled *Statutory Rules, Orders and Regulations.*

10–15   *Tracing Statutory Instruments*
Printed indexes are available only up until 1979. Entitled *Index
to the Statutory Instruments*, they are published in eight volumes
and cover the following years:–

> 1922–1938
> 1939–1945
> 1946–1947
> 1948–1960
> 1961–1963
> 1964–1970
> 1971–1974
> 1975–1979

From 1948 onwards, each index is divided into two parts. The
first part is an alphabetical arrangement by title of the enabling
Act or statutory authority. Within this arrangement, the titles of
the Statutory Instruments made under these authorities are
listed along with their year and number (see the figure on page
183.) The second part of the index is the reverse of the first, and
lists the Statutory Instruments alphabetically by title, with their
corresponding enabling Acts (see the figure on page 184.)

If you know the title of the Statutory Instrument you are looking for, look in the alphabetical list of Statutory Instruments.
This will give you the year and number so that you can then
find the correct volume. If you have an idea of the year this will
be a help, otherwise it will mean looking in all eight volumes of
the index. You must also remember that the pre-1948 Statutory
Instruments are arranged by subject so that you must take note
of the volume within the subject collection in order to trace the
Statutory Instruments made during this period.

If you do not have a title, but you have an idea of the statutory
authority, or, if you want to find out if any Statutory Instruments have been made under a particular Act, you will then use
the alphabetical list of statutory authorities or enabling Acts.

10–16   Case Law

10–17   Reported Judgments of the Superior Courts
Irish law reporting dates from 1615 with the publication of *Irish
Equity Cases 1604–1612* by Sir John Davies, Attorney General.

Statutory Authority	Section	Statutory Instrument	Year and Number or Volume of I.O.
Ministers and Secretaries (Amendment) Act, 1956 (No. 21)	2	Gaeltacht Areas Order, 1974	1974 [192]
Ministers and Secretaries (Amendment) Act, 1973 (No. 14)	2	Ministers and Secretaries (Amendment) Act, 1973 (Appointed Day) Order, 1973	1973 [293]
Motor Vehicles (Registration of Importers) Act, 1968 (No. 15)	1(2)	Motor Vehicles (Registration of Importers) Act, 1968 (Definition of Motor Vehicle) Regulations, 1973	1973 [2]
National College of Art and Design Act, 1971, (No. 28)	3	National College of Art and Design Act, 1971 (Establishment Day) Order, 1972	1972 [108]
Noxious Weeds Act, 1936 (No. 38)	2	Noxious Weeds (Wild Oat) Order, 1973	1973 [194]
Nuclear Energy (An Bord Fuinnimh Núicléigh) Act, 1971 (No. 12)	2	Nuclear Energy (An Bord Fuinnimh Núicléigh) Act, 1971 (Commencement) Order, 1973	1973 [319]
Offences against the State Act, 1939 (No. 13)	36	Offences against the State (Scheduled Offences) Order, 1972	1972 [142]
	,,	Offenders against the State (Scheduled Offenders) (No. 2) Order, 1972	1972 [282]
	41(1)	Special Criminal Court Rules, 1972	1972 [147]
Oil Pollution of the Sea Act, 1956 (No. 25)	19(1)	Oil Pollution of the Sea (Convention Countries and Convention Amendment Countries) Order, 1971	1971 [323]
Oireachtas (Allowances to Members) and Ministerial and Parliamentary Offices (Amendment) Act, 1964 (No. 14)	5(1)	Oireachtas (Allowances to Members) (Travelling Facilities) (Amendment) Regulations, 1971	1971 [1C0]
	,,	Oireachtas (Allowances to Members) (Travelling Facilities) (Amendment) Regulations, 1972	1972 [156]
	,,	Oireachtas (Allowances to Members) (Travelling Facilities) (Amendment) Regulations, 1974	1974 [167]
Patents Act 1964 (No. 12)	80, 96	Patents (Amendment) Rules, 1974	1974 [20]
Pensions (Increase) Act, 1964 (No. 10)	29	Pensions (Increase) Regulations, 1971	1971 [280]
	,,	Pensions (Increase) Regulations, 1972	1972 [261]
	,,	Pensions (Increase) Regulations, 1973	1973 [271]
	,,	Pensions (Increase) Regulations, 1974	1974 [76]
Pigs and Bacon Act, 1935 (No. 24)	8, 28(1)	Pigs and Bacon Act, 1935 (Part II) (No. 4) Regulations, 1973	1973 [217]
Pigs and Bacon Act, 1937 (No. 23)	58	Pigs and Bacon Acts, 1935 to 1961 (Pigs and Bacon Commission) Insurance Allowance (No. 1) Order, 1971	1971 [39]
	,,	Pigs and Bacon Acts, 1935 to 1961 (Pigs and Bacon Commission) Insurance Allowance (No. 2) Order, 1971	1971 [231]
	,,	Pigs and Bacon Acts, 1935 to 1961 (Pigs and Bacon Commission) Insurance Allowance (No. 1) Order, 1973	1973 [282]

184   *Republic of Ireland*

Statutory Instrument	Year and Number or Volume of I.O.	Statutory Authority	Section
Mines (Fire and Rescue) Regulations, 1972	1972 [226]	Mines and Quarries Act, 1965 (No. 7) —*contd.*	11, 68, 127
Mines (Locomotives) Regulations, 1971	1971 [238]		11, 18, 76, 127
Mines (Mechanically Propelled Vehicles) Regulations, 1973	1973 [153]		18, 41, 76, 127
Mines and Quarries (General Register) Regulations, 1974	1974 [97]		127
Mines and Quarries Inquiries (Draft Regulations) Rules, 1971	1971 [219]		Sch. 2, Art. 8
Mines and Quarries (Notification of Diseases) Order, 1971	1971 [61]		100
Minimum Notice and Terms of Employment Act, 1973 (Commencement) Order, 1973	1973 [242]	Minimum Notice and Terms of Employment Act, 1973 (No. 4)	2
Minimum Notice and Terms of Employment (Reference of Disputes) Regulations, 1973	1973 [243]	Redundancy Payments Act, 1967 (No. 21)	39 (19)
		Minimum Notice and Terms of Employment Act, 1973 (No. 4)	11, 14
Ministers and Secretaries (Amendment) Act, 1973 (Appointed Day) Order, 1973	1973 [293]	Ministers and Secretaries (Amendment) Act, 1973 (No. 14)	2
Monaghan Traffic and Parking Bye-laws, 1973	1973 [352]	Road Traffic Act, 1961 (No. 24)	89, 90
Money Order Amendment (No. 19) Regulations, 1971	1971 [35]	Post Office Act, 1908	23
		Post Office (Amendment) Act, 1969 (No. 18)	3
Money Order Amendment (No. 20) Regulations, 1974	1974 [283]		,,
Motor Vehicles (Registration of Importers) Act, 1968 (Definition of Motor Vehicle) Regulations, 1973	1973 [2]	Motor Vehicles (Registration of Importers) Act, 1968 (No. 15)	1 (2)
Mullingar Traffic and Parking Bye-Laws, 1970	1971 [178]	Road Traffic Act, 1961 (No. 24)	89, 90
Naas Traffic and Parking Bye-Laws, 1972	1972 [126]		,,
National College of Art and Design Act, 1971 (Establishment Day) Order, 1972	1972 [108]	National College of Art and Design Act, 1971, (No. 28)	3
National Drugs Advisory Board (Establishment) Order, 1966, (Amendment) Order, 1974	1974 [176]	Health (Corporate Bodies) Act, 1961 (No. 27)	3-6
5% National Loan, 1962–1972 (Conversion) Regulations, 1972	1972 [195]	Government Loans (Conversion) Act, 1951, (No. 12)	9

125

Originally in Norman French (*Le Primer Report des Cases en Ley en les Courts de Roy en Ireland*) it was reprinted in London in 1628 but was not published in English until 1762. Little else was published until the mid-eighteenth century. 1782–1800 saw a brief period of independence of the Irish courts and Parliament and an increase in the publication of reports, including Ridgeway's three-volume work on cases in the Irish House of Lords 1784–1792. From this date until the mid-nineteenth century over 50 series of reports were published covering case law in Ireland. In 1866 the Incorporated Council of Law Reporting in Ireland was established and in 1867 began publication of "official" reports:–

The Irish Common Law Series
The Irish Reports Equity Series

These two series later joined to become *The Law Reports (Ireland)* in 1878 after the Judicature (Ireland) Act 1877. In 1894 they were to become the *Irish Reports* and the volume numbers were replaced by the year of issue.

Hence the reporting of Irish case law goes back to the seventeenth century and is continued with varying levels of coverage down to the two major series of today—the *Irish Reports* and the *Irish Law Reports Monthly*, the latter providing coverage from 1980.

Citation of Reports **10–18**
This resembles the British method of citation:

e.g. *Gillespie*[1] v. *Attorney General*[2] [1976][3] I.R.[4] 233[5]

1. Plaintiff or Appellant
2. Defendant or Respondent
3. Year in which the case is reported
4. Abbreviated name of reports series
5. Page number at which report begins

Format of Law Reports **10–19**
The various parts of a law report (see the figure on page 186) are:

1. Names of the parties
2. Name of the court(s) in which the case was heard, and the date
3. Summary in italics
4. Headnote
5. Ruling of the court
6. Cases mentioned during the hearing
7. Names of Counsel appearing for the parties
8. Judgment(s)

Waterford Glass Ltd v Controller of Patents Designs and Trade Marks: Supreme Court 1982 No. 166 (O'Higgins CJ, Henchy and McCarthy JJ) 2 March 1984

Trade Mark - Application to register - Distinctiveness - Geographical name - Mark factually distinctive of goods - Whether 'inherently capable of distinguishing' - Trade Marks Act 1963 (No. 9), ss. 17, 18(2) (b), 58(3).

Facts Waterford Glass Ltd sought registration of the word 'Waterford' as a trade mark for its crystal. The Controller of Patents, Designs and Trade Marks refused registration on the ground that the word 'Waterford' lacked an inherent capacity to distinguish glassware. The company appealed to the High Court, where Hamilton J (whose judgment is reported at [1982] ILRM 91) allowed the appeal. The Controller of Patents, Designs and Trade Marks thereupon appealed to the Supreme Court. Argument hinged on whether the words 'capable of distinguishing' used in s. 18 of the Trade Marks Act, 1963 should be construed as meaning 'capable in law of distinguishing'.

Held by the Supreme Court (*per* O'Higgins CJ and McCarthy J: Henchy J dissenting) in dismissing the appeal that the mark 'Waterford' had achieved one hundred per cent factual distinctiveness in relation to the products of Waterford Glass Ltd, and that the company was entitled to have the mark registered; and that the words 'capable of distinguishing' were to be understood in their plain sense: *York Trailer Holdings Ltd v Registrar of Trade Marks* [1982] 1 All ER 257 not followed.

Cases referred to in judgment
Baglin v Cusenier (1910) 221 US 580
In re California Fig Syrup Co [1910] 1 Ch 135
In re Joseph Crosfield & Sons Ltd (the 'Perfection' case) [1910] 1 Ch 118
In re Liverpool Electric Cable Co Ltd Application 46 RPC 99
Lauritzers Application (1931) 48 RPC 392
York Trailer Holdings Ltd v Registrar of Trade Marks [1981] FSR 33; and (upon appeal to the House of Lords) [1982] 1 All ER 257

Brian McCracken SC and Fidelma Macken for the plaintiff/respondents.
R. C. Sainsbury for the controller/appellant

O'HIGGINS CJ (McCarthy J concurring) delivered his judgment on 2 March 1984 saying: This appeal comes before the court pursuant to leave granted in the High Court by Hamilton J under the provisions of s. 58(3) of the Trade Marks Act 1963. It is concerned with the meaning and effect of the words 'is in fact capable of distinguishing' contained in s. 18(2) (b) of the Act which deals with registration under Part B of the register. Before expressing my opinion, I think it may be useful to look at the manner in which Part B of the register was introduced into trade mark law.

This introduction was effected by the Trade Marks Act 1919. Prior to that Act eligibility for registration of trade marks was provided for, exclusively, in s. 9 of the Trade Marks Act 1905. The main features of this section have been

Often the High Court and the Supreme Court judgments will be reported together.

Recent and Unreported Judgments   **10–20**
Until recently, law reports in Ireland were sadly lacking in both coverage and currency, with only a very small percentage of the judgments delivered annually actually appearing in the reports. Those which were published often appeared several years after they had been decided. It must therefore be emphasised that although the situation with regard to reporting has improved recently, the written judgment itself is of primary importance with regard to case law in Ireland. In 1976, following a recommendation of the Committee on Court Practice and Procedure, the superior courts began to distribute copies of the Written Judgments delivered by the High Court, Court of Criminal Appeal and Supreme Court, to the following:

The judiciary
Government bodies
The Law Reform Commission
The Garda Siochana
The Attorney General
Director of Public Prosecution
The legal profession
Universities and third level institutions

Citation of Unreported Cases   **10–21**
These are cited by:

1. names of parties
2. judge
3. record number
4. date

e.g. McMillan v. *Carey*[1] *McWilliam J.*[2] 1978/4122p[3] 18.12.78[4]

Where the judgment is delivered in the Supreme Court, "Supreme" appears instead of the name of the judge.

Format of Unreported Judgments   **10–22**
Unreported judgments are produced in typescript format on foolscap, and more recently, on A4 paper (see page 188).

1. plaintiff
2. defendant
3. judge
4. record number
5. court
6. date

THE HIGH COURT (5)

1980 No. 10121p (4)

BETWEEN:

IRISH MICROFORMS LIMITED (1)

Plaintiffs

AND

SEAN BROWNE AND ANN CLUNE (2)

Defendants

(3)

Judgment of Mr. Justice Murphy delivered the 3rd day of April 1987. (6)

In July last this action was heard as against the first named Defendant alone. Due to the indisposition of the secondly named Defendant the trial as against her was adjourned. When the matter was re-entered last November the Court was informed that all differences between the Plaintiffs and the secondly named Defendant had been resolved. Regretfully I must accept responsibility for the delay which has occurred since then.

The association between the Plaintiffs and Mr. Browne goes back for approximately twelve years. From the incorporation of the Plaintiff company on the 8th January 1974 and for six years thereafter Mr. Browne was involved with the Plaintiff company as a director, shareholder and employee. In the next six year period commencing with the institution of these

Indexes and Digests   **10–23**
Irish Digests are available covering the period up until 1983:

O'Donnell and Brady, *Analytical Digest of all the Reported Cases in Equity* 1840
Brunker, *Digest of all the Unreported Cases Decided in the Superior courts of Common Law in Ireland and in Admiralty* 1865
Gamble and Barlow, *Index to Irish Equity Cases* (2v) ... 1838–1867
Green and Manders, *The Law Reports Digest of Cases* 1890
Stubbs, *Irish Law Times Digest of Cases* 1867–1893
Murray and Dixon, *Digest of Cases* 1867–1893
Maxwell, *Digest of Cases* 1894–1918
Ryland, *Digest of Cases* 1919–1928
Ryland, *Digest of Cases* 1929–1938
Harrison, *Digest of Cases* 1939–1948
Harrison, *Digest of Cases* 1949–1958
Ryan, *Digest of Cases* 1959–1970
de Blaghd, *The Irish Digest* 1971–1983

These provide access in the following ways:

1. By name of parties
2. By subject matter
3. Citator approach—this lists case law and legislation followed, overruled or considered by the reports so
   digested.

In addition to these digests, a publication entitled *Ryan's Notes of Cases* covers the period 1969–1978. This however, includes selected cases only.

Pink Lists. since 1976, a subject index to the Written Judgments   **10–24**
has been published, entitled *Index to Supreme and High Court Written Judgments*, or "Pink Lists," as they are commonly referred to. These are produced on average three times a year, the third part being a consolidation of parts one, two and three. This index was produced by the Incorporated Council of Law Reporting in Ireland until 1985. From 1986 onward, its produc-tion has become the joint responsibility of the General Council of the Bar of Ireland and the Incorporated Law Society of Ire-land. It is issued as a supplement to the *Gazette of the Incorpor-ated Law Society*. This Index provides subject access only, in the following format:

1. Main subject heading
2. Secondary subject heading
3. Summary of the case
4. Record number

>   5. Judge or court
>   6. Date
>   7. Parties

10–25 *Red Index*. The Irish Association of Law Teachers have produced a consolidated index entitled *Index to Irish Superior Court Written Judgments 1976–1982* which covers all the written judgments of the superior courts which were available for circulation from the beginning of 1976 to December 1982. The first part is an alphabetical index by party to all the cases summarised in the subject index which forms the second part. This subject index forms a consolidation of all the entries in both the "Pink Lists" for 1976–1982, and a supplemental index prepared by Anthony Kerr on behalf of the I.A.L.T. and published by the Incorporated Law Society of Ireland. The subject index follows the format of the "Pink Lists." The alphabetical index lists information about the judgments alphabetically by plaintiff in the following format:

Flynn v. **Buckley**[1]
PRACTICE: Action.[2] PRACTICE: Lis Pendens
SALE OF LAND: Contract.
1978/5515p[3] H.C. (McWilliam J.[4]) 30.11.79
169/1978 Supreme Court 24.4.80
1980 I.R. 423[5]
1979   9   1593;
1980   5   999[6]

>   1. Plaintiff and Defendant
>   2. Subject Headings (relating to the subject index)
>   3. Record Number
>   4. Judge/Court
>   5. Report reference (where one exists)
>   6. Reference to volumes bound in-house by the Law Library and the Law Society Library

This index is commonly referred to as the "Red Index"

10–26 *Tracing a Judgment*
If you have the title of the case:

>   1. Look in the *Digests* up to 1983
>   2. *Ryan's Notes of Cases* 1970–1978
>   3. Red Index 1976–1982

If you have an idea of the year in which the case was heard, this will save you looking through all of the Digests.

For judgments delivered after 1983, you will have to check individual volumes of the *Irish Reports* and the *Irish Law Reports*

Monthly. However, your own library may have devised an in-house index which will help you to locate these and other unreported judgments. Ask your library staff about this.

If you do not know the name of the case in question, or you are looking for case law on a particular subject, you will use the subject index in the *Digests* and in the red index. For the years 1983 onwards, unbound "Pink Lists" are available, and again, individual libraries will have their own methods of making these available for consultation. Ask the library staff.

SECONDARY SOURCES   10–27

Official Publications

Acts, Bills and Statutory Instruments   10–28
These have already been dealt with in an earlier section.

Parliamentary Debates   10–29
Debates are issued in daily parts which are unrevised. Corrections or amendments may be included in the bound volume a year later. The bound volumes are each indexed and contain a list of ministers, deputies and senators. Each volume is assigned a running number. At the start of 1986 The Dáil Debates had reached volume 363 and the Seanad Debates volume 113, so it should not be assumed that the volume number for the Dáil Debates would be the same in the Seanad Debates of the same date. Consolidated indexes are published for the years:

Dáil Debates:

1922–1927	Vols. 1–19
1927–1937	Vols. 20–68
1937–1940	Vols. 69–80
1940–1947	Vols. 81–109
1948–1954	Vols. 110–145
1954–1956	Vols. 146–160

Seanad Debates:

1922–1936	Vols. 1–20
1938–1948	Vols. 21–34

The indexes produced after 1954 are divided into sections which list alphabetically by subject and then by member's name both the general business of the House and questions. For the previous indexes, there is no division, so that general subjects, questions and members' names are all interfiled. The index gives the volume and column number of the reference.

Reports of Committees
Committees are appointed by either House, usually to consider technical or specialised Bills, which may then go to report stage before the House. Certain committees appointed regularly have produced a significant number of reports.

10–30   Tracing Official Publications
This is done by way of:

1. *Iris Oifigiúil*
   A weekly list of publications from the Stationery Office is listed in the Friday issue of this bi-weekly publication. Reprints are available from the Stationery Office on subscription.
2. *Catalogue of Government Publications*
   These are published by the Stationery Office
   (a) quarterly—published in typescript
   (b) annual catalogue of Government publications
   (c) consolidated catalogues for the years:

   1922–1925
   1926–1928
   1929–1931
   1932–1934
   1935–1937
   1938–1940
   1941–1950
   1951–1955
   1956–1960

Information given is as follows
   (a) order number
   (b) title
   (c) price and postage charge,
and is grouped into the following sections
   (a) Acts
   (b) Bills
   (c) Dáil Reports
   (d) Oireachtas Reports
   (e) Stationery Office publications—alphabetically by department
   (f) Statutory Instruments
   (g) General literature

3. Maltby and McKenna, *Irish Official Publications. A Guide*

to Republic of Ireland Papers with a Breviate of Reports 1922–1972. Here, the reports are grouped under broad subject headings and summarised. There are separate name and subject indexes at the end.

Periodicals

Periodicals and journals provide the main outlet for Irish legal   **10–31**
scholarship, and are also an important source of current developments in legislation.
   There are two major professional journals

1. The *Gazette of the Incorporated Law Society*
2. The *Irish Law Times* (I.L.T)

These provide articles and commentaries on legislation, relevant EEC and English legal developments, information on legal education and the role of the lawyer in Ireland, and reviews of recent publications. The I.L.T. also provides a useful update on the progress of legislation, both primary and secondary, and of recent superior court decisions.
   The other type of Irish periodical available tends toward the learned journal, providing a more scholarly dimension, or concentrating on a particular aspect of the law. The titles listed below fall into this category.

1. *Criminal Law Journal*
2. *Dublin University Law Journal* (D.U.L.J.)
3. *Garda Review*
4. *Irish Jurist* (I.J.)
5. *Irish Tax Review*
6. *Journal of the Irish Society for European Law* (J.I.S.E.L.)
7. *Journal of the Irish Society for Labour Law* (J.I.S.L.L.)

Citation
The citation of periodical articles follows the same format as that used in England. Abbreviations commonly used are given above.

Tracing Periodical Articles   **10–32**
Paul O'Higgins' *Bibliography of Periodical Literature Relating to Irish Law* (N.I.L.Q. 1966, supplements 1973 and 1983) provides excellent coverage of around 5,000 articles from over 130 periodicals. The titles are arranged within broad subject headings with cross references. Alphabetical subject and author indexes are provided along with a list of periodicals cited, and their abbreviations.

10–33   Textbooks and Bibliographies

When searching for textbooks on a given topic, your own library catalogue will probably provide the best starting point. However, bibliographies provide an important source, and can often be more effective in narrowing down a search strategy. Most textbooks will provide comprehensive bibliographies, and many give lists of possible further reading. An excellent subject guide to Irish legal textbooks can be found in R. G. Logan's *Information Sources in Law* (Butterworths, 1986) (para. 6–35) Bibliographic information relating to Ireland and Irish Law may also be found in:

> Twining and Uglow, *Law Publishing and Legal Information: Small Jurisdictions of the British Isles* (1981)
> Alan Eager, *Guide to Irish Bibliographic Material: Bibliography of Irish Bibliographies and Sources of Information* (2nd ed., 1980).
> A. G. Donaldson, *Some Comparative Aspects of Irish Law* (1957)
> *A Legal Bibliography of the British Commonwealth of Nations. Vol. 4: Irish Law to 1956* (2nd ed., 1957).

CHAPTER 11

European Community Law

INTRODUCTION

The study of European Community law is now an established **11–1** and important feature of higher education. Increasingly, lawyers are being confronted with legal problems arising out of the United Kingdom's membership of the various European Communities (EC) and today law students must have a working knowledge of the legal materials dealing with this subject. As you will discover it is not always easy to trace relevant material in the library. The complexity of the subject matter, poor standards of indexing and the sheer volume of material can combine to make research into EC law a difficult task.

This chapter will introduce you to the following materials which are published either commercially or by the EC:

the Community treaties;

secondary legislation made under the treaties;

case law of the Court of Justice of the European Communities;

introductory commentaries;

major bibliographical sources.

This chapter should be read as an introduction to these different types of material and their use. Many publications produce their own guides for users which you should also read. Even then you may need to ask a librarian for help in using publications on the EC The librarian knows of the difficulties and the common problems so do not be afraid to ask for assistance.

Most, if not all, of the materials described in this chapter will be available in your law library, particularly if it has been designated as a European Documentation Centre. This means that the EC has agreed to send one copy of all publicly available documents to the library. In return the library agrees to provide an information service on EC documentation. Currently, there are 44 centres based in academic libraries in the United Kingdom. The names and addresses can be obtained from your librarian or by contacting the London Information Office of the European Commission.

THE COMMUNITY TREATIES

11–2   The principal sources of Community law are the treaties which established the European Communities. There are three Communities:

   The European Coal and Steel Community, established by the ECSC Treaty (Treaty of Paris, 1951)
   The European Economic Community, established by the EEC Treaty (Treaty of Rome, 1957)
   The European Atomic Energy Community, established by the EURATOM Treaty (Treaty of Rome, 1957).

Each of these treaties performs two main tasks. The first is that they represent a system of substantive rules which are binding on the member states, and whose aim is the establishment of a Common Market. Second, and equally important, each treaty creates a set of institutions and a procedural framework through which these institutions can create secondary Community legislation and can take other measures which have legally binding effect.

In addition to these treaties there are two further general types of Community treaty, namely amending and accession treaties. The most significant amending treaties are:

   Convention on certain Institutions common to the European Communities (Rome, 1957).
   Treaty establishing a Single Council and a Single Commission of the European Communities (Brussels, 1965).
   Decision of April 21, 1970 on the replacement of financial contributions from Member States by the Communities' own resources.
   Act concerning the election of the representatives of the Assembly by direct universal suffrage annexed to the Council Decision of September 20, 1976.

Also classified as Community treaties are the treaties concerning the accession of new member states. There have been three changes to the Community's composition: in 1973 the

United Kingdom, Denmark and Ireland joined; in 1980 Greece joined and in 1986 Spain and Portugal entered the Community.

Together these Community treaties form the primary legislation of the European Communities. The text of the primary legislation is brought together in a single volume entitled *Treaties establishing the European Communities—Treaties amending these treaties—Documents concerning the accession* [E.C. 1978]. A supplement incorporating the Greek accession documents was published in 1982.

A convenient, pocket-sized, shortened version of the full text volume is the *Treaties establishing the European Communities— Abridged Edition* [EC 1983]. This includes the main text of the treaties and amended treaties. It excludes most of the associated annexes and protocols and includes texts up to 1978.

These works are useful because they bring together a number of the texts of the Community treaties. However, they are also printed in the *Official Journal* soon after their ratification. For example, the Greek accession documents are found in the *Official Journal* L291 1979; the *Official Journal* L302 1985 contains the Spanish and Portuguese accession documents. At the time of writing the Single European Act, signed February 1986, which is the most important amendment to the founding treaties, has yet to be ratified by all the member states. The text has been published by the Council of Ministers as the *Single European Act and Final Act* [EC, 1986]. This contains the provisions amending the founding treaties, the treaty provisions on European co-operation in the sphere of foreign policy (which introduces the forum called European Political Co-operation into the formal framework of the EC) and also various declarations. These texts are also published in the *Bulletin of the European Communities: Supplement 2/86*. After ratification by member states the text will be published in the *Official Journal: L Series*. A new consolidated edition of the text of the Community treaties, incorporating the developments of the 1980s, is expected in 1987.

In addition to these official sources you will find many of the important texts of primary materials have been published commercially. The two most popular student books are *Sweet & Maxwell's European Communities Treaties* (4th ed., 1980) and Rudden and Wyatt, *Basic Community Laws* (2nd ed., 1986). The first book is arranged in a chronological, unannotated sequence of texts, while the latter has some consolidation and rearrangement of the treaties to show how later amendments have affected earlier provisions. Rudden and Wyatt include some of the most important secondary legislation.

You can also find the text of the Community treaties in *Halsbury's Statutes of England* (3rd ed., 1975), Vol. 42A, and in the *Encyclopaedia of European Community Law* (1974), Vol. B. Both have provision for keeping the information up to date.

If you are looking for the text of the Community treaties in the *Encyclopaedia of European Community Law*, find the heading "Table of Community Treaties," at the beginning of Volume B1. This tells you the paragraph in the body of the volume where you will find the text you want. Both *Halsbury's Statutes* and the *Encyclopaedia* are extensively annotated.

SECONDARY LEGISLATION

11–3 Secondary legislation is that which is created by the institutions of the European Communities in implementing the powers granted to them in the Community treaties. It is important to note that there are a number of categories of legal measure which may be taken by the Community institutions, and that the designations of legal measures having their basis in the ECSC treaty differ from those of equivalent effect taken under the EEC and EURATOM treaties.

ECSC	EEC/EURATOM
Decisions (general)	Regulations
Recommendations	Directives
Decisions (individual)	Decisions
	Recommendations
Opinions	Opinions

The different types of legal measure which may be taken by the Community institutions under the EEC treaty are described in Article 189 of that treaty. The differences between some of these legislative acts may not be apparent to you. However when searching for them in the *Official Journal: Index* it is important to recognise the distinction, because in the methodological tables they are listed separately.

The Official Journal

11–4 The *Official Journal*, published by the EC, is the official and authoritative source of legislation. It carries the text of proposed and enacted legislation, and official announcements as well as information on the activities of Community institutions.

The *Official Journal* is published on most days and is made up of several sections:

1. *L Series* (meaning "legislation"). This consists of the texts of enacted legislation. This legislation is divided into two sequences:

   (a) Acts whose publication is obligatory (primarily Regulations or ECSC Decisions)

   (b) Acts whose publication is not obligatory (all other legislation).

   In effect this means that all legislative acts are published in the *Official Journal*; but note that they are listed in two sequences in the *Official Journal: Index*.

2. *C Series* (meaning "communications and information"). This contains a diverse range of information from the various Community institutions which include:

   (a) *Commission*. This covers such information as the rates for the European Currency Unit, and the text of proposed legislation.

   (b) *Court of Justice*. A list of new cases brought before the Court and judgments of the Court [only a summary is reported in this source.]

   (c) *European Parliament*. Minutes of the Plenary Sessions and written questions from the Members of the European Parliament (but see *Official Journal: Annex* below).

   (d) *Economic and Social Committee*. Opinions of the E.S.C.

   (e) Notices of invitation to tender for commercial and research contracts and staff vacancies.

3. *S Series* (meaning "supplement"). This publishes details of public supply contracts.

4. *Official Journal: Annex.*—*Debates of the European Parliament*. This contains the full text of the debates of the Plenary Sessions of the European Parliament and oral questions.

5. *Official Journal: Special Edition*. This gives an official English translation of the legislation enacted between 1952–1972 which was still in force in 1972.

The Official Journal Index

The key to any substantial source of legislative information is its index. Unfortunately, the index to the *Official Journal* is less helpful than you would wish. It is issued monthly with an annual cumulation. It is divided into two parts: **11–5**

a — Methodological Table
b — Alphabetical Index

The *Methodological Table* gives the *Official Journal* reference to all the legislative acts in numerical order. It also lists the cases brought before, and the judgments of, the Court of Justice for the period which is indexed. If, for example, you are given a reference to a legislative act, such as, Reg. (EEC) 123/86, or a case, 122/84, the methodological table will give you the reference in the *Official Journal* where you will find the text of the act or case.

The *alphabetical index* is used in a different way. If you have no reference, or it is incomplete or incorrect, but you know, for example, what subject you are dealing with then you use the alphabetical subject index to find the required references.

Citation of references to the Official Journal and to European Community legislative acts

11–6   The formal citation of an European Communities legislative act is made up of the following elements:

1. The institutional origin of the act (Commission or Council)
2. The form of the act (Regulation, Directive, Decision, etc.)
3. An act number
4. The year of the enactment
5. The institutional treaty basis (EEC, ECSC, EURATOM)
6. The date the act was passed.

The sequence of these elements can vary as is shown in the following examples:

Commission Regulation (EEC) No. 1139/86 of April 18, 1986 on the supply of common wheat flour to the International Committee of the Red Cross (I.C.R.C.) as food aid (this can be abbreviated to Reg. (EEC) 1139/86).

86/78/E.E.C. Commission Decision of February 21, 1986 amending Decision 83/402/EEC as regards the list of establishments in New Zealand approved for the purpose of importing fresh meat into the Community. (This can be abbreviated to Dec. 86/78/EEC).

The features to note are the order of the number and the year. A new sequence of numbers is started each calendar year. Between 1958 and 1967 this citation form varied. The variations are laid out in *Halsbury's Statutes* (3rd ed.), Vol. 42A, p. 12.

The citation of references to the *Official Journal* is not standardised but the usual form is: OJ L151 10.6.85 p. 15. This refers you to the *Official Journal*, L Series, Issue no. 151, dated June 10, 1985, page 15.

An EC legislative act is given a date of enactment but this does not indicate the date when the act is published in the *Official Journal*: publication there can be several months later.

Alternative Sources for EC Secondary Legislation

The most useful source is the *Encyclopaedia of European Community Law* (Sweet & Maxwell, 1974—Looseleaf Vol. C). Volume C is currently divided into seven large volumes and is destined to expand steadily. Some of these texts are annotated. A complete index to Volume C is found at the end of the last volume. Note that there may be a supplementary index at the back of the main index. This will contain references to the most recent developments. The references in the index are to the Parts *within* the binders or volumes *not* to the number on the spine of the binders. This index is much easier to use than that found in the *Official Journal*.   **11–7**

The *European Continuation volume* of *Halsbury's Statutes* (3rd ed., 1975), Vol. 42A contains a significant proportion of the secondary legislation made between 1952 and 1973. This volume is arranged according to the standard Halsbury subject headings. If you know the citation of the legislative act then you can use the tables at the beginning of the volume. If you do not know the citation then turn to the subject index at the back of the volume. The volume is kept up to date by an annual *Cumulative Supplement* and service binders (para. 6–19). The EC section is at the back of the *Cumulative Supplement*. *Halsbury's Statutes* is very helpful in providing references showing whether the United Kingdom has implemented EC secondary legislation.

References to EC secondary legislation still in force can be found in the *Directory of Community Legislation in Force*. A new edition is produced annually and lists legislation in two volumes. Volume I, called the *Analytical Register*, consists of 17 chapters with the acts arranged according to subject. Volume II contains both a chronological and alphabetical subject index. The alphabetical subject index should be used with caution as it is inadequate. An *Official Journal* reference is given for each legislative act listed.

A further source is the *Guide to EC Legislation* (North Holland, 1979, with Supplements and Telex up-dating service). This is an index to secondary legislation giving *Official Journal* references.

It also includes a short summary of each legislative act mentioned.

Europe Today (EC 1983) proved very popular with students but unfortunately the last edition was in 1983 and no more are planned. However, it is useful as an historical bibliographical source when looking for secondary legislation. It has a simple, easy to use subject arrangement which allows you to follow a proposal through the various legislative stages until its enactment. It also covers subsequent amendments.

As this chapter was being finalised Butterworths announced the publication of a major new index to the secondary legislation of the European Communities. This is called *European Communities Legislation: Current Status*. It will consist of an annual volume, kept up to date by three cumulative supplements published during the year. The comments made here are after only a brief inspection of some draft pages of the publication. *European Communities Legislation: Current Status* will list in chronological order references to all European Community secondary legislation published in the *Official Journal: Special Edition, 1952–1972*, and all subsequent secondary legislation. The advantages of this source over others mentioned in this section are significant. The use of supplements will make the work up to date. Any amendments to a legislative act, with the appropriate *Official Journal* reference, are clearly noted. Above all the alphabetical subject index is easier to use to that found elsewhere. This will make searching for the text of E.C. secondary legislation in the *Official Journal* much easier.

Finally we mention an important source for secondary legislation which is not yet widely available. This is CELEX, which is an EC inter-institutional, computerised documentation system for Community law. Legislation in force in 1979 and subsequent legislation is held in the computer's legislative file. Currently few law libraries have access to this computer database but the number is likely to expand, particularly if your library includes a European Documentation Centre.

How to Trace the Text of an E.C. Regulation/Directive

11–8   How do you find the text from this reference: 85/210/EEC Lead Content of Petrol Directive? "85" at the beginning of the reference tells you the year—1985. The text of all E.C. legislation is in the "L" series of the *Official Journal* (para. 11–4). Go to the *Official Journal: Annual Index* for 1985 and look in Volume 2: methodological table. In the contents look for the section "Acts whose publication is not obligatory" where you will see that the term, directive, is noted. Turn to the relevant pages and you will be able to find

85/210/EEC
Council Directive of March 20, 1985 on the approximation of the laws of the member states concerning the lead content of petrol.
No. 96 page 25   3.4.1985

This entry refers you to the *Official Journal* L series, no. 96, page 25 whose date of issue was April 3, 1985 where you will find the text of the directive.

If your reference is to the legislation made during the current year you will need to refer to the *Official Journal: Monthly Index* and then look to the methodological table in each monthly issue until you locate your reference.

How to Trace EC legislation on a Subject without a Reference

If you know there has been legislation on a topic such as "cosmetics" during a particular year but you do not have a reference to any specific legislation:

11–9

1. Look in the *Official Journal: Annex to the Index: Eurovoc Alphabetical Thesaurus* to check what words you should use when looking in the *Official Journal: Alphabetical Index*. The *Eurovac Thesaurus* directs you to the term "cosmetic products."
2. Look for "cosmetic products" in the *Official Journal: Alphabetical Index* for the appropriate year. For instance, in the 1984 Index you will find the following entry:

Keywords/expressions	Document number	OJ reference	Legal form
Corsica			
Community financing, regional development	84/71	L2/44/8	D/COM
cosmetic product			
action, CEC, restriction on imports, United Kingdom	193/84	C1/214/5	1/CJ
approximation of laws	84/415	L2/228/31	L/COM
	84/415	L2/255/28	Corr
commercial company, customs, preliminary reference, VAT	5/84	C1/26/6	1/CJ
cotton			
aid	1108/84	L1/113/18	R/CS
	1462/84	L1/142/1	R/CS

To find the directive on the approximation of laws you can ignore the "Document number" and "Legal form" column and just note the "OJ reference" which is L2/228/ 31 which means the *Official Journal* L228 for 1984 at page 31 (the 2 in the L2 need not be noted).

3. If you do not know the year of the directive you should refer to the index at the back of the last binder in the *Encyclopaedia of European Community Law*, Volume C, Community Secondary Legislation. Under the heading "Cosmetics, approximation of" is the reference C1 –952. This means paragraph 952 in Part C1 (note the C1 refers to *part* one volume C not the first *binder* of volume C). There you will find the text of the 1976 directive on cosmetic products plus references to subsequent amendments which includes the one in 1984. An *Official Journal* reference is also given. Alternatively use the alphabetical subject index in *European Communities Legislation: Current Status*

Let's look at alternative methods of finding what legislation exists on a subject. Suppose you want to find out what legislation there has been on company law. Because it is an important subject there are several textbooks written on it. A broad outline of the subject can be found in the *General Report on the Activities of the European Communities* or by looking in *Halsbury's Laws of England* (4th ed., Vols. 51–52).

In the *General Report on the Activities of the European Communities* turn to the contents pages and look for the heading that covers "company law." In the 1985 *Report* this heading comes under section 2 "Completing the internal market." However, this entry could be different in earlier *Reports*. You may have to go carefully through the contents pages to locate the particular subject you want. The section on "company law" is short but it gives you references to other sources where you can find further information. By reading a succession of *General Reports* you can build up a history of the subject.

Alternatively, you can use *Halsbury's Laws of England* (para. 6–3) to find out what the law is on a subject. At the back of Volume 52 of the 4th edition of *Halsbury's Laws of England* you will find an index to Volumes 51 and 52. Under the heading "company" there are various sub-headings including "EEC Law. See EC company law." Under that heading you will find a large number of sub-headings such as "draft directive—Fifth directive, 11.62." By turning to paragraph 11.62 in Volume 51 you will find the history of that directive.

Remember to bring the information up to date by referring to the *Cumulative Supplement* and looseleaf *Service* volumes of *Halsbury's Laws* (para. 6–4).

How to Trace if EC Legislation is still in Force

How do you discover if directive 79/7/EEC is still in force? You know it deals with equal treatment for men and women in matters concerning social security. The authoritative source to use is the *Directory of Community Legislation in Force*. Look in Volume II of the latest edition of the *Directory* and use the alphabetical index. Under the heading "social" you can see the sub-heading "social security." This refers you to a page in Volume I of the Directory. There you will find a list of all EC legislation on social security that is in force. It also gives you the reference to the *Official Journal* where you can see the full text. Amendments to the legislation are also listed.   **11–10**

This example illustrates the shortcomings of many indexes in EC publications. If your particular interest is "equal opportunities" or "women" rather than "social security" then you would find no entry for these terms in the index to the *Directory*.

In such a situation turn to another index such as in *Halsbury's Laws of England* (4th ed., Vol. 52). There the index uses terms such as "women," "social security: equal treatment of sexes" and "sex discrimination: social security." Similarly, if you go to the *Encyclopaedia of European Community Law* you would find that the index includes "equal treatment: men and women," "social security" and "social security schemes: equal treatment for men and women."

This problem does highlight the importance of being aware, when using EC indexes, of the context in which a particular piece of legislation was created and also the need to think of a number of alternative terms when using an index.

How to Know if a Proposal has become Law?

In the United Kingdom draft legislation is introduced into Parliament and becomes law during the same parliamentary session. This is not the case with EC legislation which may take years to become law or ultimately after a considerable time fail to become law. How, for example, would you know if the Commission's proposal for informing and consulting the employees of undertakings with complex structures has become law?   **11–11**

The Commission introduced a proposal on this subject in 1980, COM(80)423/final. An amended proposal was introduced in 1983, COM(83)292/final.

One way of tracing its progress is to look in the *General Report on the Activities of the European Communities*. If you do not know the date when the proposal was introduced go to the latest *General Report* and work backwards. If you know the date of the proposal then begin with the *General Report* for that year and work forwards. To bring your information up to date look at the most recent issues of the monthly *Bulletin of the European Communities*.

An alternative way to trace the progress of legislation is to consult a document issued by the EC entitled *Commission proposals on which the European Parliament has delivered an opinion, now pending before the Council*, more commonly referred to as the *List of pending proposals*. This is available in European Documentation Centres. All proposals which have passed through the various consultative stages in the legislative process and are awaiting the final sanction from the Council are listed under 19 broad subject headings. Using the 1986 edition of *List of pending proposals* (COM(86)412/final) and looking under the "Employment, Social Affairs and Education" heading you can trace the legislative history of the proposal. This shows that COM (83) 292/final was transmitted to Council on July 13, 1983. No further information was given which suggests that the proposal was facing considerable opposition. This was confirmed by the *Bulletin of the European Communities*, No. 7, 1986 which stated that the Council had decided to shelve this proposal until 1989.

European Access (University College, Cardiff 1982–) is also a good source for finding out about significant legislative proposals which are of interest to law students.

CASE LAW

11–12   The European Court of Justice interprets and enforces EC law. The case law of the court has assumed a position of great importance.

The C series of the *Official Journal* carries notices of cases pending before the Court. Brief details only of the nature of the proceedings and the judgment are provided.

The European Court Reports

11–13   The official source of Court of Justice judgments is *Reports of Cases before the Court*. These are more commonly known as the

European Court Reports (abbreviated to E.C.R.). In this series the opinion of the Advocate General is given alongside the judgment. An important stage in the proceedings before the European Court of Justice in all cases is the delivery of the report of the Advocate General. One of the six Advocates General is allocated to each case and it is the task of the Advocate General to deliver an opinion to the Court. This opinion is not binding on the Court but it is of great use to students of Community law in that it will include a thorough analysis of the facts and legal arguments in the case. There is an English language set of the *Reports* covering the judgments of the Court since 1954.

Although the E.C.R. is the official series it suffers from major delays in publication. Precise and accurate translation into the various Community languages results in delays of up to two years which makes it impossible to use it for recent cases. The indexing for this series is also poor and late. The index allows you to trace the case by the names of the parties, by subject and by case number. Cases are also indexed by reference to the specific provisions of Community law which were considered. For example, the 1982 index informs you that Article 190 of the EEC treaty was considered in six cases whose judgments were announced in that year.

Citation of a European Court of Justice case
The case citation is made up as follows: **11–14**

1. Case number
2. Year
3. Names of parties
4. Citation: indicating where the case can be found in the *European Court Reports* (E.C.R.).

e.g. Case 113/83 *Commission* v. *Italy* [1984] E.C.R. 4249.

Note that a case with a reference . . . /83, for example, means that the application or reference to the Court was made in 1983. The judgment was not necessarily given in that year. This means that you cannot automatically go to the E.C.R. for the year 1983 to find the judgment.

Other Sources of EC Case Law

Some libraries subscribe to *Judgments or Orders of the Court and*   **11–15**
Opinions of Advocates General. These are issued soon after the judgment is given and are printed in a cyclostyled format. They are not indexed and are not considered authoritative.

The *Proceedings of the Court of Justice* is a weekly bulletin giving a summary of the judgments and opinions of the Court during the week in question. It is not an authoritative source. It is primarily a current awareness service. It is useful because it provides synopses of judgments and proceedings. Students find this helpful and some libraries maintain an index of the *Proceedings*. At the end of 1985 the Court of Justice issued an index to the content of that year's issues. This arranged the judgments, but not the opinions, under 22 headings such as "approximation of laws," "social policy" and "free movement of persons." It is hoped that this will continue.

The *Times* and *The Financial Times* report the significant European Court judgments in their law reports section.

Common Market Law Reports

11–16   *Common Market Law Reports* (C.M.L.R.) is the main alternative source to the European Court Reports. It is published weekly by the European Law Centre and also covers cases with an EC dimension in national courts. It scores over the E.C.R. because it appears sooner with a full, if not official, report. Whilst it does not report all cases it does report all cases of significance. It has a similar range of indexes to the E.C.R.

Tracing Cases with an EC Dimension

11–17   As mentioned above, the *European Court Reports* and the *Common Market Law Reports* produce their own indexes. The *Current Law Case Citators* (para. 2–14) index some cases from both series. In addition, there are two cumulative indexes to European Community case law. The first is the *Gazetteer of European Law* (N.M. Hunnings, European Law Centre, 1983, with supplements). This is an index to the whole of the case law of the European Court of Justice, plus much national case law with an EC dimension. It covers the years 1953–1983. The *Gazetteer* allows you to trace cases through the names of the parties, the case number, the date of the case, or by subject.

The second cumulative index is the *Guide to EC Court Decisions* (North Holland, 1982, with supplements). This covers only the cases in the European Court of Justice and other EC institutions. It gives, in addition to the E.C.R. reference, a very short summary of the case plus some references to journal articles that discuss the case. Indexes are similar to those in the *Gazetteer* but it also has an index of EC legislative acts judicially considered.

Finally, the case law file of CELEX (para. 11–7) contains all the judgments and opinions delivered by the European Court of

Justice since 1970. These can be found through the numerous search techniques available in CELEX.

How to find a Court of Justice Judgment if you have the Reference

Let's put what you have read into practice. Suppose you have the following reference in your reading list: Case 139/79 *Maizena GmbH* v. *Council of European Communities*. How do you find it?

11–18

To trace the source of a full report of a case before 1984 you should use the *Gazetteer of European Law* (para. 11–17). This indexes all European Court of Justice cases from 1953 to 1983. When you have a case number, 139/79, go to Volume 1 of the *Gazetteer*, the Master List of Cases. There you will find a numerical list of cases. Under 139/79 is the date of the judgment, October 29, 1980 and a list of citations where you can find a report of the case. In the English language you will find the case reported in the *European Court Reports* and the *C.C.H. Common Market Reporter*.

If you do not have a full reference to your case but were given only the names of the parties, "Maizena" or "Council," look up these names in the alphabetical index in Volume II. This refers you to the Case Number, 139/79. You then look up this number in Volume 1 in order to find the full citation.

Alternatively, you may use the *Guide to EC Court Decisions* (para. 11–17). The main part of the volume is a list of case numbers. The main volume covers all cases until 1980 and there are annual supplements. Under the entry 139/79 you are told the *European Court Reports* reference, the EC legislation referred to in the case, a summary of the case, and four journal articles which deal with the case. At the back of the volume there is an index of parties.

If these reference works are not available, there are alphabetical and numerical indexes to the more important cases up to 1985 at the front of Volume 52 of *Halsbury's Laws of England* (4th ed.). More recent cases can be traced in the (separate) index contained in the table of cases in the *Current Service* binder, and in the *Cumulative Supplement* (para. 6–4), or in the table of cases in the *Encyclopaedia of European Community Law*. The *European Law Review* and other journals may enable you to trace full references to recent developments. The *European Law Review*, for example, has alphabetical and numerical indexes to cases.

How to Find a Judgment of the Court of Justice on a Subject

What can you do if you only have a reference such as *The Isoglucose Case*? This is neither the name of a party nor the number of the case.

11–19

Again you can use the *Gazetteer of European Law* and the *Guide to EC Court Decisions.* (para. 11–17) Both of these sources have subject indexes. In the *Guide* there is an alphabetical subject index at the back of both the main volume and the supplements. There you will find the term "Isoglucose" in the subject index with a list of cases including 139/79. The *Gazetteer* is more difficult for this particular case as the term "Isoglucose" is not used in the subject index. In fact, 139/79 is indexed under the heading "Constitutional law: institutions" because it concerns the relationship between the European Parliament and the Council of Ministers in the Community law making process. It is unlikely you would have found this case in this index. So, it may be necessary to use both sources at different times. *The Digest* (para. 6–11) summarises cases on European Community law under appropriate subject headings. Volume 21 contains the main collection of cases on EC law, with alphabetical and case number indexes.

How to Trace Cases which Refer to the Leading Case

11–20   Sometimes you will want to know if a European Court case has been referred to in a later judgment. You may wish to see whether the European Court of Justice has elaborated upon or qualified the judgment given in case 139/79 in any subsequent cases. Turn to the *Gazetteer of European Law.* The answer is in Volume II, in the section called Case Search, Part IV. This lists cases in numerical order. Under 139/79 there are nine cases listed. Those in thick black type are considered to be the most important.

How to Trace Cases on EC Primary or Secondary Legislation

11–21   What do you do if you want to find cases which are concerned with specific provisions of Community law? For example, how do you find out what cases have been heard in the European Court of Justice which were the result of references under Article 177 of the EEC Treaty? Turn to the *Guide to EC Court Decisions* (para. 11–17). Look in the contents for the section "Table of Legal Provisions—EEC".

Here you will find the Articles of the EEC Treaty listed in numerical order. Under Article 177 you will find a large number of cases listed. They are cases which have been referred under Article 177 by national courts for a preliminary ruling on the interpretation of a provision of the EEC Treaty or on the interpretation or validity of a provision of secondary EEC law. More recent cases can sometimes be found in the index to *European Law Review* (para. 11–18).

LEXIS (para. 7–1) will give not only a list of judgments of the European Court of Justice in such cases but also any United Kingdom cases where the national courts have had to decide whether to make a reference to the European Court of Justice under Article 177.

How to Trace Recent Judgments

Because of publication delays this can be a difficult task. Let's **11–22** look at case 13/83, *European Parliament* v. *Council of the European Communities*. The judgment in this case was announced on May 22, 1985. With an important case, such as this one, look for a report in the newspapers. Both *The Times* and the *Financial Times* carried substantial articles on the case on May 23, 1985. *The Times* carried the case in its "European Law Report" section on May 27, 1985. To find the newspaper references you can use the respective indexes to these newspapers but these are published about three months in arrears.

The essence of the judgment was published in the *Official Journal*, C144, 13.6.85, page 4 (use the alphabetical index to the *Official Journal*) and a substantial summary of the case was included at page 7, issue 13, 1985 of the *Proceedings of the Court of Justice of the European Communities* which was issued at the end of July 1985. (Use the Index to the *1985 Proceedings of the Court of Justice of the European Communities*). *Current Law Case Citator* (para. 2–14) gives a reference to *The Times* law report and also a digest of the case in the *Current Law Year Book* for 1985. (para. 6–10).

The first substantial report of Case 13/83 appeared in the *Common Market Law Reports* [1986] 1 C.M.L.R. 138. This was published in February 1986. The authoritative report in the *European Court Reports* appeared in 1987. *Current Law Case Citator* can be used to trace these references.

This pattern of publication is broadly similar for other cases. However, the less important ones will not appear in newspapers and *Current Law*. Check to see if your library maintains an index to recent European Court of Justice judgments. If the library is a European Documentation Centre it will take a current awareness bulletin called *European Access* (University College Cardiff, 1982–). This gives you sources of information for the significant Court of Justice judgments. Some libraries also take a series titled *Judgments or Orders of the Court and Opinions of Advocates General.* (para. 11–15). These are typescripts of the judgments rather than full law reports but they are available soon after the judgment.

SECONDARY SOURCES OF INFORMATION ON EC LAW

11–23   The EC publish a wealth of material which provides introductions, overviews and summaries of topics. A selection of the most useful includes the *General Report on the Activities of the European Communities* (para. 11–9) and the *Bulletin of the European Communities*. These are the annual and monthly reviews of the Commission. They cover, in a standard arrangement, the developments of the Community during the period in question. By reading through a succession of the *General Reports* you can trace the development of a policy over the years. The *Bulletin* brings you up to date with developments. These two sources have the advantage of providing references to the primary documentation.

A number of supplements are published to the *General Report*. The most useful for law students are a *Report on Competition Policy* and *Report on Social Developments*. The former is a particularly useful source of information on patterns of enforcement of Community competition law and explanations of Commission policy in this area. The latter is particularly useful for labour law developments.

Amongst series published by the EC which contain titles of legal interest are *European Perspectives*, *European Documentation* and *European File*.

The *European Perspectives* series is made up of substantial academic monographs on a range of subjects. Examples have included *Thirty Years of European Law* (1983); *The European Community, how it works* (1979); *The Community Legal Order* (1980); *The Rights of Working Women in the European Community* (1985); *The European Communities in the International Order* (1985); and *An Ever Closer Union; a critical analysis of the Draft Treaty establishing the European Union* (1985).

The *European Documentation* series is made up of 50–80 page booklets which look at aspects of Community policy. Three titles in particular should be noted: *The European Community Legal System* (No. 6, 1981); *The Court of Justice of the European Communities*, 4th ed. (No. 5, 1986); The *A.B.C. of Community Law*, 2nd ed. (No. 2, 1986).

The *European File* series is made up of 8–12 page booklets on a wide range of Community policies.

The Court of Justice issues an annual *Synopsis of the work of the Court of Justice of the European Communities* which is an account of the important cases of the year, plus a description of the organisation of the Court. This is a useful guide to the work of the European Court of Justice.

NON EC SECONDARY SOURCES OF THE EC LAW   11–24

Journals   11–25

Many legal journals cover EC topics in a selective manner. The major English language titles that specialise in the subject include the *European Law Review; Journal of European Integration; Journal of Common Market Studies; Common Market Law Review; Legal Issues of European Integration; European Industrial Relations Review*, and *The International and Comparative Law Quarterly*.

Legal Encyclopaedias   11–26

Halsbury's Laws of England (4th ed.), Vols. 51 and 52 cover the E.C. They are a comprehensive account of EC institutional and policy developments up to the middle of the 1980s. The information in these volumes is kept up to date by the *Cumulative Supplement* and looseleaf *Service* binders (para. 6–4). The *Current Service* contains EC developments at the back of each *Monthly Review*, including a separate index to EC matters. The *Annual Abridgement* to *Halsbury's Laws* also contains a substantial account of major EC developments during the year in question, including new secondary legislation and judgments.

Halsbury's Statutes (para. 6–19), (3rd ed., 1968) has designated volume 42A (published in 1975) as the European Continuation volume. This contains EC secondary legislation made between 1952 and 1973. This volume is kept up to date by the European supplement at the back of the *Cumulative Supplement*. The third edition is being replaced by a fourth edition which contains in Volume 17 (published 1986) an EC section which contains United Kingdom statutes that directly relate to the EC This is also kept up to date by the *Cumulative Supplement*. Volume 50 of the fourth edition will contain the text of EC treaties.

The Encyclopaedia of European Community Law (Sweet & Maxwell, 1973—looseleaf) is the only encyclopedia devoted exclusively to Community law. It is divided into three sections. Volume A consists of United Kingdom sources. This comprises the European Communities Act 1972 and United Kingdom legal measures implementing Community obligations (that is the statutes and statutory instruments which implement EC directives). Volume B contains the official English texts of all the European Community Treaties plus various additional agreements concluded between the member states and with non-member states. Volume C contains the EC secondary legislation. Each set of volumes has its own index at the back of the last binder in the volume.

11–27   Miscellaneous Sources

Newspapers are useful for topical information and social commentary. *The Guardian, The Times,* and in particular "The Financial Times" cover European Community cases and developments. These papers are comprehensively indexed. In the *Guardian Index* look for the headings "European Economic Community" and "European Court of Justice"; in *The Times Index* find "European Economic Community" and in the *Index to the Financial Times* find "EEC" Amongst the weekly journals the *New Law Journal* and the *Solicitors' Journal* cover major developments.

Finally, there are the Reports of the *House of Lords Select Committee on the European Communities.* These reports can often present a clear description of EC policy and may include a range of opinions from interested parties in the United Kingdom.

11–28   How to Find Books and Articles on EC Law

Let's look for recent articles and books on product liability. *European Access* (para. 11–22) is probably the best source of information. It lists books, journal articles and official publications under 19 broad subject headings. Under section 12 "Consumer" you will find "product liability" in section 12.2. As *European Access* is not cumulative you should look not only in the most recent issue but also in previous issues.

Alternatively you can look in the *Legal Journals Index* (para. 4–3) or in the *Index to Legal Periodicals* (para. 4–5) which are the major indexing services for legal literature. Entries are arranged by subject. At the back of the *Current Law Year Book* is found a subject index to articles written during that year (para. 4–4). The monthly issues of *Current Law* contain details of more recent articles (para. 4–4).

A major indexing service to the literature of EC law called ELLIS (*European Legal Literature Information Service*) is another choice if your library subscribes to it. Look in the subject index under "product liability" and you see many references to the subject. Some of these references are to materials in languages other than English.

Finally, you should check the newspaper indexes (para. 11–27) and social sciences indexes such as the *British Humanities Index* (para. 4–10) and the *Applied Social Science Index.*

CHAPTER 12

Public International Law

INTRODUCTION

Early definitions of international law described it as "a body of   **12–1**
rules governing the relations between states." In modern times,
this definition has been expanded so that the concept of international law includes regulation of the relationships not only
between states, but also between international organisations
and individuals.

This chapter helps you find the international law materials in
the library. Remember that public international law should be
distinguished from private international law, or conflict of laws,
which deals with the inter-relationship of the domestic municipal laws of different states, rather than regulating the international relations between different states.

International law has no legislature, and no system of binding precedent in its judicial forums. Its observance therefore
depends on the adherence by nations to its principles, which
are mainly embodied in international treaties and international
custom. The rules of international law only have binding effect
from their inclusion in a treaty or convention, or because they
have been recognised as an international custom. States which
do not ratify a particular treaty are not bound by its provisions.
With the growth of international organisations, another body of
international law is being created by them and it is therefore
necessary for you to know how to find the legal publications of
the major international organisations. You should also be aware
of the way in which international law is constantly developing

and expanding into new subject areas, such as the law of the sea, which means that there is a constant flow of new publications.

As a student of international law, you will need to look well beyond the confines of the traditional law library to locate the various materials you will need, as they will also be found in international relations and official publications collections. To help you in your researches, this chapter describes the various generally accepted sources of international law and tells you about the materials comprising each source. It then outlines how to use the most important works within each source.

SOURCES

12–2 The most frequently accepted definition of the sources of international law can be found in Article 38(1) of the Statute of the International Court of Justice which states that disputes submitted to it will be decided according to the principles of international conventions, international custom, general principles of law, judicial decisions and the writings of leading commentators.

TREATIES

12–3 As defined in the Vienna Convention on the Law of Treaties, a treaty is a written agreement concluded between two or more states or international organisations and governed by international law. Treaties come in many different disguises, such as protocols, conventions, charters, statutes, accords, etc. In this modern technological age, with its vastly improved communications, the huge growth in international trade and the growth of international inter-dependence, the volume of treaty publishing has become enormous and it is often difficult to trace particular treaties.

General Collections

12–4 The first major category of treaty publishing is the General Collection, of which there are three major series. The *Consolidated Treaty Series* (1969–) edited by Clive Parry, and published in 231 volumes by Oceana, covers the years to 1920. It attempts to reprint the original text and official translations of all treaties published during that period. The treaties are arranged chronologically, with French or English translations where available.

There is a multi-volume *Index-Guide* which contains a general chronological list of the treaties, plus a subject index.

How to use Consolidated Treaty Series
Start with the *Index-Guide* volumes, which can be distinguished   **12–5**
by the colour binding on the spine. They are divided into three sections. The *Party Index* is black (publication not yet complete). This lists countries alphabetically, and within each country gives a chronological list of the treaties concluded by that country, the names of the parties and the volume and page number within C.T.S. where the treaty is published. The *General Chronological List* is red. This lists all treaties from 1648–1920 by date. It is a useful listing of all the treaties traced by the editors of C.T.S. It not only gives the C.T.S. reference, but also references to the publication of treaties in other collections. The *Special Chronology* is green. This deals with colonial and other less important treaties and you will probably not need to use it.

Let's suppose that you are looking for a bilateral treaty between Great Britain and Belgium, settling the boundary between Uganda and Congo. You know the date of the Treaty was 1910; you can therefore go straight to the *Chronological List* and under 1910 you will find the following entry:

> 1910: 14 May Agreement between Belgium and Great Britain settling the boundary dispute between the Congo and Uganda, Signed at Brussels.
> 211 CTS 103
> CVII B.S.P. 348 (Eng)

You will therefore be able to find the Treaty in the *Consolidated Treaty Series* at Volume 211, page 103. The reference to B.S.P. is to *British and Foreign State Papers* (see para. 12–9).

If you do not know the date of the Treaty, go to the *Party Index* and in the entries under Belgium you will find:

> 1910   May 14
> Belgium   Great Britain
> 211 CTS 103

The *Consolidated Treaty Series* ends in 1920 because this is the first year covered by the *League of Nations Treaty Series*. This series continues until 1946 and contains over 4,000 treaties. There are subject and chronological index volumes interspersed between the texts.

How to Use United Nations Treaty Series   **12–6**
The third important series is the *United Nations Treaty Series* which started publication in 1946. The U.N. publishes the text

Treaties and international agreements registered or filed and recorded with the Secretariat of the United Nations

VOLUME 1087	1978	I. Nos. 16634-16656

TABLE OF CONTENTS

I

*Treaties and international agreements
registered on 27 April 1978*

1967 (*continued*)

14 Jul (*continued*)	Multil. (*continued*)	Berne Conv. for the protection . . . (*continued*) notif. under art.38(2) (*continued*)			
		Norway 1970,22 Jul		828	227
		Portugal 1970,25 Aug		828	227
		South Africa 1970,17 Sep		828	227
		Tunisia 1970,18 Sep		828	227
		Turkey 1970,17 Sep		828	227
		Yugoslavia 1970,20 Jul		828	227
		objections to access. by German Dem. Rep.:			
		Argentina, Belgium, Canada, Denmark, France, Gabon, Germany, Fed. Rep. of, Greece, Haiti, Holy See, Iceland, Iran, Ireland, Israel, Japan, Luxembourg, Madagascar, Niger, Portugal, South Africa, Spain, UK, USA		828	225
		sign.:			
		Austria, Belgium, Bulgaria (with decl. and reserv.), Cameroon, Congo, Denmark, Finland, France, Gabon, Germany, Fed. Rep. of, Greece, Holy See, Hungary, Iceland, India, Ireland, Israel, Italy, Ivory Coast, Japan, Liechtenstein, Luxembourg, Madagascar, Mexico, Monaco, Morocco, Niger, Norway, Philippines, Poland (with decl. and reserv.), Portugal, Romania, Senegal, South Africa, Spain, Sweden, Switzerland, Tunisia, Yugoslavia			
		See also: 1883,20 Mar v.LXXIV:289			
		1908,13 Nov v.1:217			
		1914,20 Mar v.1:243			
		1928,2 Jun v.CXXIII:233			
		1948,26 Jun v.331:217			
		1967,14 Jul v.828:3			
14 Jul Stockholm	Multil.	Paris Conv. for the protection of industrial property of Mar 20, 1883, as rev. at Brussels on Dec 14, 1900, at Washington on Jun 2, 1911, at The Hague on Nov 6, 1925, at London on Jun 2, 1934, at Lisbon on Oct 31, 1958, at Stockholm on Jul 14, 1967 access.(*a*), notif. of deposit of instrument of access.(*na*) and of ratif.(*nr*) and ratif.:	F I:11851	828	305
		Australia (with decl.) 1972,25 May(*na*)		828	309
		Bulgaria (with decl. and reserv.) 1970,27 Feb(*nr*)		828	309
		Canada (with decl.) 1970,7 Apr(*na*)		828	309
		Chad 1970,26 Jun(*nr*)		828	309
		Czechoslovakia (with decl.) 1970,29 Sep(*na*)		828	309
		Denmark (with notif. of applic. to Faeroe Islands) 1970,26 Jan		828	307
		Finland (with decl.) 1970,15 Jun(*nr*)		828	311
		German Dem. Rep. 1968,20 Jun(*a*)		828	307
		Germany, Fed. Rep. of (with decl. of applic. to *Land Berlin*) 1970,19 Jun(*nr*)		828	309
		Hungary (with decl. and reserv.) 1969,18 Dec		828	307
		Ireland 1968,27 Mar		828	307
		Israel 1969,30 Jul		828	307
		Jordan 1972,17 Apr(*na*)		828	311
		Kenya 1971,26 Jul(*nr*)		828	311
		Liechtenstein 1972,25 Feb(*nr*)		828	311
		Madagascar 1972,10 Jan(*nr*)		828	311
		Malawi 1970,25 Mar(*na*)		828	311
		Morocco 1971,6 May(*nr*)		828	311
		Romania (with decl.) 1969,28 Feb		828	307
		Senegal 1968,19 Sep		828	307
		Spain 1972,14 Jan(*nr*)		828	311

of every treaty entered into by any of its members, as all treaties have to be registered with the Secretariat. They are published in order of registration, and not by the date of conclusion, which can make them extremely difficult to locate. So far, over 1000 volumes have been published and they appear at the rate of over 40 a year. The series is very late in publication and is not useful for trying to obtain recent treaties. The figure on p.218 shows the title page of a typical volume from *United Nations Treaty Series*.

To locate a Treaty, start with the Index volumes, which are published for every 50 volumes of treaties. Each Index contains a *Chronological Index* listing treaties in order of the date on which they were signed, plus an *Alphabetical Index*. If you need to find the Convention of Paris on the protection of industrial property as revised in Stockholm in 1967, check in the *Chronological Index* for that period. The entry is shown in the figure on page 219.

The number in the first column is the volume number and that in the second column is the page in the *U.N. Treaty Series*. The index also tells you whether the treaty is bilateral or multi-lateral, and which states have acceded to it or ratified it.

If you are unsure of the date, check in the subject section of the *Alphabetical Index* under Industrial Property (see the figure on page 220.)

The symbol I denotes a treaty or international agreement *registered* with the U.N. Secretariat. Occasionally the symbol II appears, which means that the treaty is *filed and recorded* with the Secretariat. The other number following the I is the serial number of the treaty, and the other numbers are the volume and page numbers.

National Collections

The second method of publication of texts of treaties is by country and in recent years several countries have begun publi-cation of their own treaty series. The *United Kingdom Treaty Series* is the official series published by the Foreign Office. Trea-ties are published in this series only after ratification. They may have appeared earlier in the *Command Paper series* (para. 5–5) The *Treaty Series* forms a sub-series to the Command Paper series and every treaty has both a Command Paper number and a Treaty Series number followed by the year of issue.

The figure on page 222 shows the first publication of the Extradition Treaty with Italy which we have not ratified, in the Command Paper series.

12–7

$$\begin{bmatrix} \text{Royal Crest} \\ \text{omitted} \end{bmatrix}$$

Italy No. 1 (1986)

Extradition Treaty
between the
United Kingdom of Great Britain and Northern Ireland and the Italian Republic

Florence, 12 March 1986

[Instruments of ratification have not been exchanged]

Presented to Parliament
by the Secretary of State for Foreign and Commonwealth Affairs
by Command of Her Majesty
June 1986

LONDON
HER MAJESTY'S STATIONERY OFFICE
£1·90 net

Cmnd. 9807

The Agreement was
previously published as
China No. 1 (1984),
Cmnd. 9247

CHINA

[Royal Crest
  omitted]

Treaty Series No. 14 (1985)

Agreement

between the Government of the
United Kingdom of Great Britain and Northern Ireland
and the Government of the People's Republic of China

on the Establishment of a British Consulate-General at Shanghai and a Chinese Consulate-General at Manchester

Peking (Beijing), 17 April 1984

[The Agreement entered into force on 14 January 1985]

*Presented to Parliament
by the Secretary of State for Foreign and Commonwealth Affairs
by Command of Her Majesty
April 1985*

LONDON
HER MAJESTY'S STATIONERY OFFICE
£1·75 net

Cmnd. 9472

The figure on page 223 shows an agreement with China, published in the *Treaty Series*, which has been ratified. The heading on the top right hand corner gives the name of the country as it is a bilateral treaty (if it was a multilateral treaty, then the subject matter would be printed here). The number on the top left hand corner is the Command Paper series number, which is where this treaty was first published.

How to use United Kingdom Treaty Series

12–8   Start with the *Indexes to Treaty Series* which appear under three titles, *General Index to Treaty Series*, of which the latest issue to appear was for 1976–1979; the *Annual Index to Treaty Series* and the *Supplementary Lists of Ratifications, Accessions, Withdrawals etc.* which appears about four times a year. Each index is divided into numerical and subject sequences. The subject headings chosen are wide and slightly idiosyncratic, but once mastered are useful.

If you need to trace the Convention relating to a Uniform Law on the International Sale of Goods of 1964 and to find out if the United Kingdom is a signatory then it can be found in the *Index to Treaty Series* under Private International Law as illustrated on page 225. The entry gives details of the signatories to the Convention, its Treaty Series number and its Command Paper number.

British and Foreign State Papers

12–9   This series was produced by the Foreign Office Library between 1812 and 1968. It contains the texts of important treaties and conventions, not only between Great Britain and other countries, but also a selection of those made between other countries. Treaties are sometimes presented as part of a collection of all existing treaties on a particular topic, and the years indicated on the volume do not necessarily mean that the volume only contains material for those years. For example, Volume 1 has the years 1812–1814 on the spine but among its contents are "the treaties of alliance and commerce between Great Britain and Portugal subsisting in . . . 1814" The earliest of these treaties is dated 1373.

The best way of finding material in *British and Foreign State Papers* is by using the cumulative general *indexes* which are numbered volumes in the series. The index volumes are numbers 64, 93, 115, 138, 165 and 170. They contain both a chronological and an alphabetical subject index.

12–10   One other national series of note which you may be referred to is the *United States Treaties and Other International Agreements*

	Date	Treaty Series No.	Command No.
PRIVATE INTERNATIONAL LAW (continued)—			
Convention relating to a Uniform Law on the International Sale of Goods	The Hague, 1 July, 1964– 31 Dec., 1965	74/1972	Cmnd. 5029
Signatures—			
Belgium	6 Oct., 1965		
France	31 Dec., 1965		
Germany, Federal Republic of*	1 July, 1964		
Greece (*ad referendum*)	3 Aug., 1964		
Holy See*	2 Mar., 1965		
Hungary	31 Dec., 1965	} 74/1972	Cmnd. 5029
Israel*	28 Dec., 1965		
Italy	23 Dec., 1964		
Luxembourg	7 Dec., 1965		
Netherlands	12 Aug., 1964		
San Marino	24 Aug., 1964		
United Kingdom	21 Aug., 1964		
* With reservation in respect of ratification.			
Ratifications—			
Belgium (with reservations)	12 Dec., 1968	74/1972	Cmnd. 5029
Germany, Federal Republic of (also applies to Berlin (West)) (with declaration) ...	16 Oct., 1973	121/1973	Cmnd. 5586
Israel	3 Dec., 1971		
Italy (with declaration)	22 Feb., 1972		
Netherlands (for Kingdom in Europe) (with declaration)	17 Feb., 1972	} 74/1972	Cmnd. 5029
San Marino (with declarations)	24 May, 1968		
United Kingdom (with declarations) ...	31 Aug., 1967		
Convention relating to a Uniform Law on the Formation of Contracts for the International Sale of Goods	The Hague, 1 July, 1964– 31 Dec., 1965	75/1972	Cmnd. 5030
Signatures—			
Belgium	6 Oct., 1965		
France	31 Dec., 1965		
Germany, Federal Republic of*	1 July, 1964		
Greece (*ad referendum*)	3 Aug., 1964		
Holy See*	2 Mar., 1965		
Hungary	31 Dec., 1965	} 75/1972	Cmnd. 5030
Israel*	28 Dec., 1965		
Italy	23 Dec., 1964		
Luxembourg	7 Dec., 1965		
Netherlands	12 Aug., 1964		
San Marino	24 Aug., 1964		
United Kingdom	8 June, 1965		
* With reservation in respect of ratification.			
Ratifications—			
Belgium	1 Dec., 1970	... 75/1972	Cmnd. 5030
Germany, Federal Republic of (also applies to Berlin (West)) (with declaration) ...	16 Oct., 1973	121/1973	Cmnd. 5586
Italy	22 Feb., 1972		
Netherlands (for Kingdom in Europe) (with declaration)	17 Feb., 1972	} 75/1972	Cmnd. 5030
San Marino (with declaration)	24 May, 1968		
United Kingdom	31 Aug., 1967		
Convention on the Service Abroad of Judicial and Extrajudicial Documents in Civil or Commercial Matters	The Hague, 15 Nov., 1965	50/1969	Cmnd. 3986

(U.S.T.) published by the Department of State since 1950 and containing the texts of the many treaties signed by the United States.

12–11   The *European Treaty Series* contains the texts of treaties concluded between members of the Council of Europe. This series is produced as a number of separate booklets and each treaty is numbered according to the date of its signature. These treaties are also published in the *European Yearbook/Annuaire Europeén*.

Subject Collections

12–12   In recent years several collections of treaties covering particular subject areas have been published, frequently in looseleaf form. They can be a useful place to start a search when you know the subject matter of the treaty you are trying to track down. For example, the treaty establishing the Swiss Inter-Cantonal Arbitration Tribunal can be found in Clive Schmitthoff's *International Commercial Arbitration*. Tax treaties are amongst the easiest to find as there are several specialist publications devoted purely to them, most notably Diamond and Diamond's *International Tax Treaties of all Nations*.

Finding Treaties

12–13   If you cannot trace a treaty in the indexes to the various collections described above, then there are other indexes, both national and international, which can provide some extra help.

12–14   **National Indexes**

12–15   *United Kingdom*
For treaties concluded by the United Kingdom there are three more important sources. Parry and Hopkins' *Index of British Treaties* covers treaties concluded by this country between 1101 and 1968. Its usefulness is thus limited to that period and it cannot be of assistance when trying to trace recent treaties. It is published in three volumes, Volumes 2 and 3 being a chronological list of treaties giving details of the place and date of signature, entry into force and termination (where applicable). The references given in brackets at the end of the entry show where the treaty can be found. This index covers both bilateral and multilateral treaties to which the United Kingdom is a party. Volume 1 is the index volume, which is divided into separate indexes to bilateral and multilateral treaties; this is difficult to use due to its poor typographical layout.
The other United Kingdom publication is the *Index to Treaty*

Series which forms part of the Treaty Series and was described earlier. (para. 12–8)

United States   **12–16**
The best known American index is *Treaties in Force,* published annually by the Department of State. It lists all treaties and agreements which are in force in the United States on January 1 of each year. Part 1 lists bilateral treaties by country and by subject and Part 2 lists multilateral treaties by an alphabetical subject arrangement. In order to make use of this index easier, Kavass and Sprudzs have produced a *Guide to the United States Treaties in Force.* This enables you to find, for example, all bilateral United States treaties relating to copyright. To do this using *Treaties in Force* only would mean going through it country by country looking for any listings under that particular subject heading. In Kavass and Sprudzs you merely look in the subject index under the entry for copyright and all relevant treaties will be listed there.

International Indexes
A most useful new index is *Multilateral Treaties: index and cur-*   **12–17**
rent status, by Bowman and Harris, which is a product of the Treaty Research Centre at the University of Nottingham. It offers status information on over 800 major treaties. There are regular supplements which keep the work up to date.

How to use Bowman and Harris. A helpful feature of this index is   **12–18**
the word index within the subject index. If you need to find the Convention relating to a Uniform Law on the Formation of Contracts for the International Sale of Goods, check in the word index and under "Goods, Sale" you will find references by number to the relevant entries.

The figure on page 228 shows the entry for this treaty. The entry gives the full title, the date and place of conclusion, the date of entry into force, the duration, the language of the authentic text and a most useful "Notes" section which gives the purpose of the treaty and, in this instance, tells you that it is due to be replaced by a new U.N. Convention. This section also gives details of any periodical articles about the treaty.

To check whether the information in the original entry is still correct, look in the *Cumulative Supplement.*

If you need to find a bilateral or multilateral treaty agreed between two obscure parties, probably the best source is the *World Treaty Index* which has recently been published in a second edition. It is a massive computer-generated index covering the years from 1920–1984 and lists the treaties by subject

TREATY 462	CONVENTION RELATING TO A UNIFORM LAW ON THE FORMATION OF CONTRACTS FOR THE INTERNATIONAL SALE OF GOODS
CONCLUDED	**1 Jul 64,** The Hague
LOCATION	834 UNTS 169; UKTS 75(1972), Cmnd 5030; 45 Vert A 615; 3 ILM 864; 13 AJCL 453
ENTRY INTO FORCE	23 Aug 72. Later acceptances effective 6 months after deposit: Art 8
DURATION	Unspecified. Denunciation permitted on 1 year's notice: Art 10
RESERVATIONS	Certain declarations and derogations permitted under Arts 2-4. Withdrawal of same effective 3 months after notification: Art 5
AUTHENTIC TEXTS	E F
DEPOSITARY	Netherlands
OPEN TO	As for treaty 463: Arts 6, 7
PARTIES (9)	BELGIUM 1 Dec 70; GAMBIA 5 Mar 74; GFR* 16 Oct 73; ISRAEL 30 May 80; ITALY 22 Feb 72; LUXEMBOURG* 6 Feb 79; NETHERLANDS* 17 Feb 72; SAN MARINO* 24 May 68; UK 31 Aug 67
TERRITORIAL SCOPE	See Art 11. Declared applicable: GFR - Berlin (West); NETHERLANDS - Kingdom in Europe
SIGNATORIES	FRANCE 31 Dec 65; GREECE 3 Aug 64; HUNGARY 31 Dec 65; VATICAN CITY 2 Mar 65
NOTES	This Convention, to which the Uniform Law is annexed, will be replaced by the 1980 UN Convention on the Sale of Goods (treaty 775) for the parties to both.

and chronologically, but it is quite difficult to use and not very widely available as it is expensive.

An easier source, though not so up to date, is the *Harvard Law School Library Index to Multilateral Treaties,* which is a chronological listing of international treaties to which three or more countries were parties, from 1596–1963.

Other Sources of Treaty Information

12–19 Finding treaties can be difficult and there are some other helpful sources apart from the collections noted above.

International Legal Materials, published by the American Society for International Law, is very useful. It is a periodical which appears bi-monthly and provides up-to-date information on legal aspects of public and private international relations. It frequently reproduces the texts of treaties and other agreements before they are published elsewhere. Issues include items such as the texts of the documents showing the evolution of sanctions against Libya. It has an annual index and there is also a cumulative index to Volumes 1–18.

Government bulletins, press releases and circulars often contain the texts of treaties shortly after they are signed. The *U.S. Department of State Bulletin* is published weekly and has a special section entitled "Treaty Information."

National official gazettes also contain the texts of treaties concluded by that country and some gazettes have special sections devoted to the texts of international treaties. The British Library Official Publications Library in London has the best collection of such gazettes in the United Kingdom.

LAW REPORTS   12–20

Court Reports

As stated above, international law does not have a system of   12–21
binding precedent, although international tribunals are reluctant to change principles which they have laid down in earlier decisions. Because it is a permanent institution operating independently under its own statute, the International Court of Justice has developed a considerable body of case law and has thus been instrumental in the development of international law. The official reports of the Court are entitled *Reports of Judgments, Advisory Opinions and Orders*: this is published in parts, which are cumulated into an annual volume. Each volume has a subject index. A second series is entitled *Pleadings, Oral Arguments and Documents* and appears on an irregular basis. It contains the documents filed in each case heard by the Court. The I.C.J. publishes the *Yearbook of the International Court of Justice* which contains useful information on cases that the Court has heard during the year under review.

General Reports
Because it is difficult to isolate cases relating to international   12–22
law from the mass of domestic cases published each year, various series of specialised international law reports are published, the most important one being the *International Law Reports*. This covers reports from several countries, and includes the decisions of international tribunals as well as of international courts. Cases are published in full in their original form and where necessary translations of foreign judgments are provided. There are summaries following each report. The series is arranged according to a comprehensive classification scheme. Some volumes cover a particular topic, others cover several. Four volumes a year are published and a new consolidated table has recently been published. You will see that I.L.R. was originally published as the *Annual Digest of Public International Law Cases*, as it was originally just a digest (summary) of the cases. As the reports grew longer, this was reflected in 1950 in a change of title.

National Series
Some countries produce national series of international law   12–23
reports. In this country *British International Law Cases* covers

cases from 1607–1970. This series is designed to complement *I.L.R.* Cases are published in full, but no headnotes are added. Each volume gives a cumulative list of the cases published giving full references to the original reports. There is an index in each volume, plus a cumulative index for the last eight volumes. Unfortunately, it is doubtful whether any further volumes are ever likely to be published. Another useful source of information on law reports is the *British Yearbook of International Law* which every year contains a section entitled "Decisions of British Courts . . . involving questions of Public International Law." You should also remember that many of the leading textbooks contain comprehensive lists of cases.

In America the major series is the *American International Law Cases*, which contains full reprints of both federal and state cases involving international law.

Reports of Arbitrations

12–24   The awards of international arbitration tribunals have always been of importance as a source of international law. The most important series is the *Reports of International Arbitral Awards* published by the I.C.J. There are also various series of reports covering arbitrations before specific tribunals, for example the Iran-U.S. Claims tribunal. A. M. Stuyt's *Survey of International Arbitrations 1794–1970* (1970) is a useful source of information. The figure below shows a sample page.

Nr. 428

1. FRANCE — UNITED STATES OF AMERICA.

2. Interpretation of air transport services agreement of March 27, 1946.

3. Arbitral Tribunal: P. Reuter (F.), H. P. de Vries (USA), R. Ago (Pres.).

4. Compromis, Paris.
   a. **January 22, 1963.**
   b.
   c. RIAA XVI-7; UNTS 473-3; TIAS 5280.

5. I. Award, Geneva.
   a. December 22, 1963.
   b.
   c.
   d. RIAA XVI-11; ed. Geneva; AJIL 1964-1016; ILR 38 (1969)-182; RGDIP 1965-189.

   II. Decision interpreting the Award, Geneva.
   a. June 28, 1964.
   b.
   c.
   d. RIAA XVI-73; RGDIP 1965-259.
   e. AFDI 1964-352; Journal of air law and commerce 1964-231; RBDI 1966-1; RGDIP 1965-189; Revue française de droit aérien 1964-448.
      Text of Agreement March 27, 1946; UNTS 139-114.

The arbitrations are listed by parties and by subject matter. Details of the award are also given including the date, the party in whose favour the award was made, whether it was accepted and where the text may be found.

Digests of Case Law

During the early years of its existence, it was often difficult to obtain copies of the International Court's decisions and this prompted some commentators to produce digests of its reports. One of the most important of these is *Hambro's Case Law of the International Court* which appears in several volumes and which you may find useful if you cannot obtain full reports. It contains extracts from the decisions arranged by subject matter.

12–25

STATE PRACTICE/CUSTOMARY INTERNATIONAL LAW

Custom is regarded as the second source of international law. This term is generally defined as state practice. State practice comprises a wealth of sources of law and is the body of materials which together illustrate the type of action taken by a state in an international situation. These materials include national legislation, diplomatic correspondence, legal opinions, evidence given before courts and tribunals, parliamentary proceedings, etc.

12–26

Digests

Several states produce digests of these materials to make them more readily accessible. In the United Kingdom, the *British Digest of International Law* began publication in the 1960's but it is still incomplete and unlikely to be finished in the foreseeable future.

12–27

A new historical source of state practice has recently become available to scholars, with the publication of Clive Parry's *Law Officers Opinions to the Foreign Office 1793–1860* in 95 volumes. It is a collection of opinions, principally of the Advocate-General, on policy matters relating to the foreign and colonial affairs of this country during that period.

The *British Yearbook of International Law* contains a section entitled "U.K. materials on international law" which is an excellent survey of items published during the year under review relating to international law. It includes extracts from parliamentary debates, answers given to parliamentary questions, evidence given to committees, and speeches given by

United Kingdom representatives at international meetings. It also gives details of any United Kingdom legislation involving international law.

British and Foreign State Papers contain a wealth of international material. From 1812–1968, there are selections from diplomatic papers and circulars. These provide valuable background material to international events that is not easily obtainable elsewhere.

Collections of Documents

12–28 Other useful starting places for retrieving information relating to state practice are the commercially published multi-volume series on particular areas of international law. They are rather like vastly overgrown "cases and materials" books, but each series only covers one area of international law. They contain extracts from treaties, law reports, proceedings, background papers and international organisations' documents. Good examples are Durante and Rodino *Western Europe and the Law of the Sea*, Ruster and Bruno's *International Protection of the Environment; treaties and related documents*, and *New Directions in the Law of the Sea*. The advantages of these series are that you can find in one place extracts from all the different materials on a particular subject, plus information on where the original document can be found.

TREATISES

Textbooks

12–29 The writings of leading commentators, or jurists, are accepted as another source of international law. There is a very distinguished history of academic scholarship in international law. Famous writers include Grotius, Gentili, Puffendorf and Savigny. The Carnegie Endowment for International Peace has collected these works together and reprinted them in a series entitled *Classics of International Law*. Amongst later writers in this country, Oppenheim's *International Law* (1952) has been described as being "as nearly official as anything of the kind can be," though it is a little dated now. There are several other leading British and European commentators, including Schwarzenberger, Brownlie and Lauterpacht. A list of the major works can be found in D. P. O'Connell's *International Law* (2nd ed. 1970), which is itself a leading work.

Students' Textbooks

There are many good students' textbooks including Akehurst's *Modern Introduction to International Law* (5th ed., 1984), and D. W. Greig's *International Law* (2nd ed., 1976). The leading casebook is that by D. J. Harris, *Cases and Materials on International Law.* (3rd ed., 1983).

SECONDARY SOURCES   12–30

Journals

The first international law journal was the *Revue de Droit Inter-*   **12–31**
national et de Legislation Comparee which initially appeared in 1869, almost 50 years before the American Society of International Law started publication of the *American Journal of International Law* (1907). There are now large numbers of journals, both European and American, devoted to international law in general and to particular topics. Some of the better known titles, which may be available in your law library, include the *Virginia Journal of International Law*, the *Georgetown Journal of International Law*, and the *Harvard Journal of International Law*. Journals devoted to particular subject areas include the *Journal of International Law and Economics, Journal of World Trade Law* and the *International Business Lawyer*. Some of these journals occasionally contain extensive research guides and bibliographies, which can be a most useful source of information.

Newsletters and Bulletins

To trace very recent information on international law, newslet-   **12–32**
ters and bulletins can be useful. The *Bulletin of Legal Developments* is published fortnightly by the British Institute of International and Comparative Law and contains a wealth of useful information on legal developments and forthcoming legislation in both this country and abroad. There are other newsletters which cover particular subject areas including *Euromarket News* and *International Copyright Information Centre Bulletin*.

Yearbooks

Yearbooks, which normally contain a collection of articles and   **12–33**
documents relating to international law, are another useful

source of information and several countries publish their own versions. You will probably find several examples in your library. The Netherlands and Japanese Yearbooks are particularly well known. The *British Yearbook of International Law* is an excellent example of the genre. It contains not only the various items mentioned earlier in this chapter but also summaries of the decisions of leading international tribunals, such as the decisions of the European Convention on Human Rights, together with a comprehensive book review section, and digests of national cases relating to international law.

Yearbooks are also published in particular subject areas, for example, the *Yearbook of Commercial Arbitration*.

Proceedings

12–34   Other useful sources of articles on international law are proceedings of courses, conventions and other international meetings. The most notable of these are the *Hague Recueil des Cours* which contains the texts of lectures given at the Hague Academy each year by leading international law scholars from all over the world. There are regular indexes published to this series. The *Proceedings of the International Law Association* is another useful publication.

12–35   REFERENCE SOURCES

Bibliographic Sources

12–36   There are several bibliographies of international law on both general and specific subjects. John Merrill's *A Current Bibliography of International Law* and Ingrid Delupis's *Bibliography of International Law* are probably the most useful general guides. A major new publication is the *International Law Bibliography* (Oceana) which is a two-volume looseleaf collection of individual bibliographies on particular areas of international law.

There are several specialist institutes within universities devoted to research into particular areas of international law and they frequently produce excellent bibliographical tools. The Centre for the Study of the Law of the Sea at Dalhousie University in Halifax, Nova Scotia, produces a *Marine Affairs Bibliography*. The Centre for Air and Space Law at McGill has published Kuo Lee Li's *Worldwide Space Law Bibliography* (1978) and the Centre for the Study of Human Rights at Columbia has published *Human rights: a topical bibliography*.

Library Catalogues

The catalogues of the larger law libraries frequently contain   **12–37**
useful information about international law and some of them
are available in book form and may well be available in the
main reference section of your library. The Harvard Law School
Library *Catalog of International Law and Relations* (1965) and the
Law Catalogue of the Squire Law Library (1974) are the most
useful for international law.

Indexes to Periodical Articles

A most useful index is that published semi-annually by the Max   **12–38**
Planck Institute in Germany and devoted entirely to public
international law. It is entitled *Public International Law: a Current Bibliography of Articles*. It is a comprehensive bibliography
of articles on international law and should be the starting place
for research projects on international law. Many international
law journals are indexed in the general periodical indexes
including *Current Law Index* (U.S.A.), *Index to Legal Periodicals*
(U.S.A.) (para. 4–4) and the *Index to Foreign Legal Periodicals*
(U.S.A.) (para. 4–5). English journals covering international law
are indexed in *Legal Journals Index.* (para. 4–3).

Online Sources

There is not yet much international law available on databases,   **12–39**
in this country. LEXIS (para. 7–1) has little, if any, pure international law on-line. Other countries are a little more advanced.
In Belgium the ORBI database has been created. It consists of
the documentation system of the Belgian Ministry of Foreign
affairs and is available here through EURONET. There is some
international relations material available on DIALOG. Your
librarian can tell you whether it is possible to get access to these
databases.

INTERNATIONAL ORGANISATIONS

There is no agreed scientific classification of international   **12–40**
organisations. The term "international intergovernmental
organisation" is usually used to describe an organisation set up
by agreement between two or more states, as distinct from the
term "non-governmental" organisation which is used to describe an organisation set up by individuals.

There are currently over 4,000 international organisations in existence, of which one alone, the United Nations, produces over 180,000 items of documentation a year. The total number of publications produced by international organisations each year is therefore massive.

It is extremely difficult to trace the publications of international organisations, not only because there are so many of them, but also because the organisations themselves frequently do not produce comprehensive catalogues or lists of their publications. These publications can be most conveniently divided into two main groups: sales publications, and documents. You are most likely to need material in the first group, which includes all those publications issued in printed form and generally available. The second group comprises documents which are mainly produced for internal use by the organisation concerned and are not normally of wide outside interest. Obviously sales publications cover a vast subject area, and legal documents form only a small part of the total output of international organisations.

To take the United Nations as an example, it publishes its constitutional documents including its charter and other administrative rules and regulations. Valuable constitutional information is contained in its *Repertory of Practice of United Nations Organs*. It also publishes the official records of the meetings of its various organs and these in themselves are very extensive. It frequently convenes conferences on legal topics and then publishes the proceedings. The proceedings of the various conferences on the Law of the Sea are good examples of this type of publication. Such proceedings will frequently contain the texts of conventions or other agreements reached at the conference. The U.N. also produces a *Legislative Series* which contains materials on legal matters. These are normally compiled following a resolution from the General Assembly for further information on a particular topic. The U.N. also produces several Yearbooks, including the *Yearbook on Human Rights* and the *Juridical Yearbook*.

In order to find such publications, organisations like the U.N. do produce some bibliographies. The U.N. libraries in both Geneva and New York publish monthly bibliographies of books, articles and journals. *UNDOC: Current Index* is a product of the UNBIS computer-based on-line system. It is published in hard copy ten times a year and attempts to provide a key to recent U.N. documents, proceedings and publications. Each issue follows a standard arrangement and there is a subject index.

Your library may subscribe to the *International Bibliography:*

publications of intergovernmental organisations, which is a quarterly listing of publications of the major intergovernmental organisations received by UNIPUB, an American publishing house. Your library may have a separate United Nations or official publications collection, which will include material published by the major international organisations. The librarian in charge of this collection will be able to help you in your search for information. Most of the larger international organisations follow a similar pattern of publication to that of the U.N., though their materials may not be so widely available.

APPENDIX I

Abbreviations of Reports, Series and Periodicals

This alphabetical list contains a selection of the more commonly used abbreviations in the United Kingdom, EEC, and the Commonwealth. It is not exhaustive and further information can be found in D. Raistrick, *Index to Legal Citations and Abbreviations* and in the I.A.L.S. *Manual of Legal Citations* Vols. I and II. *Index to Legal Periodicals*, *Legal Journals Index The Digest* (Cumulative Supplement) and the *Current Law Citators* also contain lists of abbreviations, at the front.

A.C.—Law Reports Appeal Cases 1891–
A.J.—Acta Juridica
A.J.I.L.—American Journal of International Law
A.L.J.—Australian Law Journal
A.L.R.—American Law Reports Annotated
A.L.R.—Australian Law Reports, formerly Argus Law Reports
All E.R.—All England Law Reports 1936–
All E.R. Rep.—All England Law Reports Reprint 1558–1935
Am. J. Comp. L.—American Journal of Comparative Law
Anglo-Am. L.R.—Anglo-American Law Review
Ann. Dig.—Annual Digest of Public International Law Cases (1919–49). (From 1950 this series has been published as the International Law Reports—I.L.R.)
App. Cas.—Law Reports Appeal Cases 1875–1890
B.C.L.C.—Butterworths Company Law Cases
B.D.I.L.—British Digest of International Law
B.F.S.P.—British and Foreign State Papers

B.I.L.C.—British International Law Cases
B.J.A.L.—British Journal of Administrative Law
B.J. Crim.—British Journal of Criminology
B.J.L.S.—British Journal of Law and Society
B.L.R.—Building Law Reports
B.L.R.—Business Law Review
B.N.I.L.—Bulletin of Northern Ireland Law
B.T.R.—British Tax Review
B.Y.I.L.—British Yearbook of International Law
Bull. E.C.—Bulletin of the European Communities
Business L.R.—Business Law Review
C.A.R.—Criminal Appeal Reports
C.A.T.—Court of Appeal Transcript (unpublished)
C.B.R.—Canadian Bar Review
C.D.E.—Cahiers de Droit Européen
C.J.Q.—Civil Justice Quarterly
C.L.—Current Law
C.L.J.—Cambridge Law Journal
C.L.P.—Current Legal Problems
C.L.R.—Commonwealth Law Reports (Australia)
C.M.L.R.—Common Market Law Reports
C.M.L. Rev.—Common Market Law Review
C.P.D.—Law Reports Common Pleas Division 1875–1880
C.T.S.—Consolidated Treaty Series
Calif. L. Rev.—California Law Review
Camb. L.J.—Cambridge Law Journal
Can. B.R.—Canadian Bar Review
Ch.—Law Reports Chancery Division 1891–
Ch.D.—Law Reports Chancery Division 1875–1890
Co. Law.—Company Lawyer
Colum. L. Rev.—Columbia Law Review
Com. Cas.—Commercial Cases 1895–1941
Constr. L.J.—Construction Law Journal
Conv.; Conv.—N.S.—Conveyancer and Property Lawyer
Cox C.C.—Cox's Criminal Law Cases
Cr. App. R.; Cr. App. Rep.—Criminal Appeal Reports
Cr.App.R.(S.)—Criminal Appeal Reports (Sentencing)
Crim. L.R.—Criminal Law Review
D.L.R.—Dominion Law Reports (Canada)
D.U.L.J.—Dublin University Law Journal
E.C.R.—European Court Reports
E.G.—Estates Gazette
E.G.L.R.—Estates Gazette Law Reports
E.H.R.R.—European Human Rights Reports
E.I.P.R.—European Intellectual Property Review

E.L. Rev.—European Law Review
E.R.—English Reports
Eng. Rep.—English Reports
Eur. Comm. H.R. D.R.—European Commission of Human
  Rights Decisions and Reports
Eur. Court H.R. Series A Series B—European Court of Human
  Rights Series A & B
Ex.D.—Law Reports Exchequer Division 1875–1880
F.L.R.—Family Law Reports
F.L.R.—Federal Law Reports
F.S.R.—Fleet Street Reports
F.T.—Financial Times
Fam.—Law Reports Family Division 1972–
Fam. Law—Family Law
Grotius Trans.—Transactions of the Grotius Society
H.L.R.—Housing Law Reports
Harv. L. Rev.—Harvard Law Review
I.C.J. Rep.—International Court of Justice Reports
I.C.J.Y.B.—International Court of Justice Yearbook
I.C.L.Q.—International and Comparative Law Quarterly
I.C.R.—Industrial Cases Reports 1975–
I.C.R.—Industrial Court Reports 1972–1974
I.J.; Ir. Jur.—Irish Jurist
I.L.J.—Industrial Law Journal
I.L.M.—International Legal Materials
I.L.Q.—International Law Quarterly
I.L.R.—International Law Reports
I.L.R.M.—Irish Law Reports Monthly
I.L.T. or Ir.L.T.—Irish Law Times
I.R.—Irish Reports
I.R.L.R.—Industrial Relations Law Reports
I.R.R.R.—Industrial Relations Review & Reports
Imm.A.R.—Immigration Appeal Reports
Ir. Jur.—Irish Jurist
I.T.R.—Industrial Tribunal Reports
J.B.L.—Journal of Business Law
J.C.—Session Cases. Justiciary Cases (Scotland)
J.C.L.—Journal of Criminal Law
J.C.M.S.—Journal of Common Market Studies
J.I.S.E.L.—Journal of the Irish Society for European Law
J.I.S.L.L.—Journal of the Irish Society for Labour Law
J.L.S.—Journal of Law and Society
J.L.S.—Journal of the Law Society of Scotland
J. Legal Ed.—Journal of Legal Education
J.O.—Journal Officiel des Communautés Européennes

J.P.—Justice of the Peace Reports (*also* Justice of the Peace (journal))

J.P.L.—Journal of Planning and Environment Law

J.R.—Juridical Review

J.S.P.T.L.—Journal of the Society of Public Teachers of Law

J.S.W.L.—Journal of Social Welfare Law

K.B.—Law Reports: King's Bench Division 1901–1952

K.I.R.—Knight's Industrial Reports

L.A.G. Bul.—Legal Action Group Bulletin

L.G.C.—Local Government Chronicle

L.G.R.—Knight's Local Government Reports

L.J.—Law Journal 1866–1965 (newspaper)

L.J. Adm.—Law Journal Admiralty N.S. 1865–1875

L.J. Bcy.—Law Journal Bankruptcy N.S. 1832–1880

L.J.C.C.R.—Law Journal County Courts Reports 1912–1933

L.J.C.P.—Law Journal Common Pleas N.S. 1831–1875

L.J. Ch.—Law Journal Chancery N.S. 1831–1946

L.J. Eccl.—Law Journal Ecclesiastical Cases N.S. 1866–1875

L.J. Eq.—Law Journal, Chancery, N.S. 1831–1946

L.J. Ex.—Law Journal Exchquer N.S. 1831–1875

L.J. Ex. Eq.—Law Journal Exchequer in Equity 1835–1841

L.J.K.B. (or Q.B.)—Law Journal King's (or Queen's) Bench N.S. 1831–1946

L.J.M.C.—Law Journal Magistrates' Cases N.S. 1831–1896

L.J.N.C.—Law Journal Notes of Cases 1866–1892

L.J.N.C.C.R.—Law Journal Newspaper, County Court Reports 1934–1947

L.J.O.S.—Law Journal, Old Series 1822–1831

L.J.P.—Law Journal Probate Divorce and Admiralty N.S. 1875–1946

L.J.P.D. & A.—Law Journal Probate Divorce and Admiralty N.S. 1875–1946

L.J.P. & M.—Law Journal Probate and Matrimonial Cases N.S. 1858–1859, 1866–1875

L.J.P.C.—Law Journal Privy Council N.S. 1865–1946

L.J.P. M. & A.—Law Journal Probate, Matrimonial and Admiralty N.S. 1860–1865

L.J.R.—Law Journal Reports 1947–1949

L. Lib.J.—Law Library Journal

L.M.C.L.Q.—Lloyd's Maritime and Commercial Law Quarterly

L.N.T.S.—League of Nations Treaty Series

L.Q.R.—Law Quarterly Review

L.R.A. & E.—Law Reports: Admiralty and Ecclesiastical Cases 1865–1875

L.R.C.C.R.—Law Reports: Crown Cases Reserved 1865–1875

L.R. C.P.—Law Reports: Common Pleas Cases 1865–1875
L.R. Ch. App.—Law Reports: Chancery Appeal Cases 1865–1875
L.R. Eq.—Law Reports: Equity Cases 1866–1875
L.R. Ex.—Law Reports: Exchequer Cases 1865–1875
L.R.H.L.—Law Reports: English and Irish Appeals 1866–1875
L.R. P. & D.—Law Reports: Probate and Divorce Cases 1865–1875
L.R.P.C.—Law Reports: Privy Council Appeals 1865–1875
L.R.Q.B.—Law Reports: Queen's Bench 1865–1875
L.R.R.P.; L.R. R.P.C.—Restrictive Practices Cases 1957–1973
L.S.—Legal Studies
L.S. Gaz.—Law Society's Gazette
L.T.—Law Times
L.T.R.; L.T. Rep.—Law Times Reports (New Series) 1859–1947
L.T.Jo.—Law Times (newspaper) 1843–1965
L.T.O.S.—Law Times Reports, Old Series 1843–1860
L. Teach.—Law Teacher
Law & Contemp. Prob.—Law and Contemporary Problems
Lit.—Litigation
Liverpool L.R.—Liverpool Law Review
Ll. L.L.R.; Ll.L.R.; Ll.L. Rep.—Lloyd's List Law Reports *later* Lloyd's Law Reports
Lloyd L.R.; Lloyd's Rep.—Lloyd's List Law Reports *later* Lloyd's Law Reports
M.L.J.—Malayan Law Journal
M.L.R.—Modern Law Review
Man. Law—Managerial Law
Med. Sci. & Law—Medicine, Science & the Law
Mich. L. Rev.—Michigan Law Review
N.I.—Northern Ireland Law Reports
N.I.J.B.—Northern Ireland Law Reports Bulletin of Judgments
N.I.L.Q.—Northern Ireland Legal Quarterly
N.I.L.R.—Northern Ireland Law Reports
N.L.J.—New Law Journal
N.Y.U.L. Rev.—New York University Law Review
N.Z.L.R.—New Zealand Law Reports
New L.J.—New Law Journal
O.J.—Official Journal of the European Communities
O.J.C.—Official Journal of the European Communities: Information and Notices
O.J.L.—Official Journal of the European Communities: Legislation, *e.g.* 1972, L. 139/28
O.J.L.S.—Oxford Journal of Legal Studies
P.—Law Reports Probate, Divorce and Admiralty 1891–1971

P. & C.R.—Planning (Property from 1968) and Compensation Reports

P.C.I.J.—Permanent Court of International Justice Reports of Judgments

P.D.—Law Reports Probate Division 1875–1890

P.L.—Public Law

P.N.—Professional Negligence

Q.B.—Law Reports: Queen's Bench Division 1891–1901, 1952–

Q.B.D.—Law Reports Queen's Bench Division 1875–1890

R.D.E.—Rivista di Diritto Europeo

R.G.D.I.P.—Revue Générale de Droit International Public

R.M.C.—Revue du Marché Commun

R.P.C.—Reports of Patent, Design & Trade Mark Cases

R.R.—Revised Reports

R.R.C.—Ryde's Rating Cases

R.T.R.—Road Traffic Reports

R.V.R.—Rating & Valuation Reporter

Rec.—Recueil des Cours

Rec.—Recueil de la Jurisprudence de la Cour (Court of Justice of the European Communities)

S.A.—South African Law Reports

S.C.—Session Cases (Scotland)

S.C. (H.L.)—Session Cases (Scotland) House of Lords

S.C.(J.)—Session Cases Justiciary Cases (Scotland)

S.C.C.R.—Scottish Criminal Case Reports

S.I.—Statutory Instruments

S.J.—Solicitors' Journal

S.L.R.—Law Reporter/Scottish Law Review

S.L.T.—Scots Law Times

S.R.—Statutory Rules (Northern Ireland)

S.R. & O.—Statutory Rules and Orders

S.T.C.—Simon's Tax Cases

Scolag.—Bulletin of the Scottish Legal Action Group

Sol. Jo.—Solicitors' Journal

St. Tr.; State Tr.—State Trials 1163–1820

Stat.L.R.—Statute Law Review

State Tr. N.S.—State Trials, New Series 1820–1858

T.C.—Reports of Tax Cases

T.L.R.—Times Law Reports

Tax Cas.—Reports of Tax Cases

Tul. L. Rev.—Tulane Law Review

U. Chi. L. Rev.—University of Chicago Law Review

U.K.T.S.—United Kingdom Treaty Series

U.N.T.S.—United Nations Treaty Series

U.N.J.Y.—United Nations Juridical Yearbook

U.N.Y.B.—Yearbook of the United Nations
U. Pa. L. Rev.—University of Pennsylvania Law Review
U.S.—United States Supreme Court Reports
U.S.T.S.—United States Treaty Series
V.A.T.T.R.—Value Added Tax Tribunal Reports
V.L.R.—Victorian Law Reports (Australia)
W.I.R.—West Indian Reports
W.L.R.—Weekly Law Reports
W.N.—Weekly Notes
W.W.R.—Western Weekly Reporter
Y.B.—Yearbook (old law report), *e.g.* (1466) Y.B. Mich. (the term)
   6 Edw. 4, pl. 18, fol.7. (plea, folio)
Y.B.W.A.—Yearbook of World Affairs
Yale L.J.—Yale Law Journal
Yearbook E.C.H.R.—Yearbook of the European Convention on
   Human Rights

APPENDIX II

Words and Abbreviations in English and Latin

This alphabetical list contains some of the more commonly used words and abbreviations (in English and Latin) which you may encounter in textbooks and law reports. There is a separate list of abbreviations for the names of law reports in Appendix I.

A.G. or Att. Gen.—Attorney-General
A.G.—German incorporated company
Ab Initio—from the beginning
Abstracts—summary of periodical articles, books, etc. Usually arranged in subject order
Ad Valorem—according to the duty. A duty levied
Aliter—otherwise
Amicus Curiae—a friend of the court (a bystander who informs the judge on points of law or fact)
Annotations—notes
Anon.—anonymous
Applied (apld.)—the principle in a previous case has been applied to a new set of facts in another case
Approved—the case has been considered good law
Art.—Article (in an international Treaty or Convention)
Article—an essay published in a journal
Autrefois acquit—previously acquitted
Autrefois attaint—previously attained
Autrefois convict—previously convicted
B.—Baron (Exchequer)
B.C.—Borough Council

Bibliography—a list of books

Bills—draft versions of proposed legislation, laid before Parliament for its approval

Bl. Comm.—Blackstone, *Commentaries on the Laws of England*

Blue book—a government publication, issued with blue covers to protect it because of its length

c.—chapter (Act)

C.—Command Paper 1836–1899

C.A.—Court of Appeal

C.A.T.—Court of Appeal Transcript (unreported)

C.A.V.—*curia advisari vult*; the court deliberated before pronouncing judgment

C.B.—Chief Baron

C.C.—County Council

C.C.A.—Court of Criminal Appeal

C.C.R.—County Court Rules

c.i.f.—(Cost, insurance, freight) a contract for the sale of goods in which the price quoted includes everything up to delivery

C.J.—Chief Justice

cap.—chapter (Act)

Cd.—Command Papers 1900–1918

cf.—(confer) to compare or refer to

Chronological—arranged in order of date

Cie.—French abbreviation for company

Citation—(1) a reference to where a case or statute is to be found (2) the quotation of decided cases in legal arguments

Citator—a volume containing a list of cases or statutes with sufficient details to enable them to be traced in the volumes of law reports or statutes

Cl.—clause (in Bills)

Classification number—a system of numbers, or letters and numbers, used to indicate the subject matter of the book. In many libraries the books are arranged on the shelves in the order indicated by this number

Cm.—Command Papers 1986–

Cmd.—Command Papers 1919–1956

Cmnd.—Command Papers 1956–1986

Co. Litt.—Coke on Littleton

Command Paper—a form of Parliamentary paper, issued "by Command of Her Majesty." Every Command Paper has its own individual number

Comrs.—Commissioners

Considered—the case was considered but no comment was made

Cumulative; Cumulation—combining the information in a number of previous publications into one sequence

Cur. adv. vult.—Court deliberated before pronouncing judgment

D.C.—Divisional Court

D.P.P.—Director of Public Prosecutions (whose name appears in criminal appeals to the House of Lords, and certain other circumstances)

De facto—in fact

De jure—by right

De novo—anew

Deb.—Debates

Dec.—decision (Common Market), *e.g.* Dec. 82/112/**EEC**

Decd.—deceased

Delegated legislation—rules created by subordinate bodies under specific powers delegated by Parliament

Digest—a summary

Digested—summarised

Dir.—Directive (Common Market), *e.g.* Dir. 82/262/**EEC**

Distinguished—some essential difference between past cases and the present case has been pointed out

Doe d.—(Doe on the demise of)

Doubted—court's remarks tend to show case was inaccurate

E.A.T.—Employment Appeal Tribunal

E.C.H.R.—European Convention on Human Rights

E.C.J.—Court of Justice of the European Community

EEC—European Economic Community

E.C.S.C.—European Coal & Steel Community

Et seq.—(*et sequentes*)—and those following

Ex cathedra (from the chair)—with official authority

Ex officio—by virtue of an office

Ex p.—*ex parte* the person on whose application the case is heard

Ex post facto—by a subsequent act—retrospectively

Ex rel.—*ex relatione*—report not at first hand

Explained—previous decision is not doubted, but the present decision is justified by calling attention to some fact not clear in the report

ff.—and what follows

f.o.b.—free on board—cost of shipping to be paid by vendor

Folio—technically this refers to the way in which a book is made up; usually used to denote a large book, often shelved in a separate sequence

Followed—same principle of law applied

GmbH.—German incorporated private company

Green Paper—a government publication setting out government proposals, so that public discussion may follow before a definite policy is formulated

H.C. Deb.—House of Commons Debate

H.L.—House of Lords

H.M.S.O.—Her Majesty's Stationery Office

Hale P.C.—Hale, *Historia Placitorum Coronae* (Pleas of the Crown)

Hansard—Parliamentary Debates

Headnote—a brief summary of a case found at the beginning of the law report

I.C.J.—International Court of Justice

I.R.C.—Inland Revenue Commissioners

Ibid.—ibidem—in the same place

Id.—idem—the same

In b.—in bonis—in the goods of

In camera—hearing in private

In curia—in open court

In re—in the matter of

Infra—below

Inter alia—amongst other things

Inter vivos—during life: between living persons

Ipso facto—by the mere fact

J. (plurall JJ.)—judge

J.P.—Justice of the Peace

K.C.—King's Counsel

L.C.—Lord Chancellor

L.C.B.—Lord Chief Baron

L.C.J.—Lord Chief Justice

L.J. (plural L.JJ.)—Lord Justice

L.V.App.Ct.—Lands Valuation Appeal Court (Scotland)

Legislation—the making of law: any set of statutes

Loc. cit.—loco citato—at the passage quoted

M.R.—Master of the Rolls

M.V.—motor vessel

Microfiche; Mircrofilm—a photographic reduction of an original onto a sheet of film (microfiche) or a reel of film (microfilm). A reading machine (which enlarges the image) is needed to consult microfilm or fiche

N.S.—new series

N.V.—Dutch incorporated company

Nisi prius—unless before

Nolle prosequi—unwilling to prosecute

Non-Parliamentary papers—Government publications which are not required to be laid before Parliament for their approval. They are usually entered in the library catalogue under the name of the government department which publishes them

O.H.—Outer House of the Court of Session (Scotland)

O.S.—old series

Obiter dictum—a judicial observation on a point not directly relevant to the case (not binding as precedent)

Op. cit.—the book or reference previously cited

Ord.—Order (Rules of the Supreme Court)

Orse—otherwise

Overruled—a higher court holds the decision to be wrong

P.C.—Privy Council

P.C.I.J.—Permanent Court of International Justice

Pace—by permission of

Pamphlet—a small booklet usually less than 50 pages in length. It may be shelved in a separate sequence

Parl. Deb.—Parliamentary Debates

Pari Passu—on equal footing, or proportionately

Parliamentary Papers—papers required by Parliament in the course of their work. These include: House of Lords and House of Commons Papers and Bills, Debates, Command Papers and Acts

Per—as stated by

Per curiam—a decision arrived at by the court

Per incuriam—through want of care (a mistaken court decision)

Periodical—a publication with a distinctive title which appears regularly

Periodicals index—(1) an index to the contents of a particular journal (2) a subject index to articles in a number of journals

Per pro—*per procurationem*—as an agent—on behalf of another

Per se—by itself—taken alone

Post—after (a later line or page)

Q.C.—Queen's Counsel

Q.S.—Quarter Sessions

q.v.—*quod vide*—which see

Quantum meruit—as much as he had earned/deserved

r.—rule

R ( )—Decision of administrative tribunal—letter in brackets indicates the appropriate tribunal, *e.g.* R(SB) 15/84

R v.—Rex, Regina (the King, Queen) against

R.S.C. Ord.—Rules of the Supreme Court, Order

Ratio decidendi—the ground of a decision

Re—in the matter of

Rec.—Recueil

Reg.—Regina (the Queen)

Reg.—Regulations (European Communities), *e.g.* Reg. 467/82/ **EEC**

Regnal year—the year of the monarch's reign

s. (plural ss.)—section of Act

S.A.—French company/South Africa

s.c.—same case

S.G.—Solicitor-General

S.I.—Statutory Instrument

S.R. & O.—Statutory Rules and Orders

SS.—steamship

Sched.—schedule (to an Act)

Scienter—knowingly

Semble—it appears

Sessional Papers—a collection of all Parliamentary Papers published during a particular session of Parliament

Sessional set—a collection of all Parliamentary papers issued during a particular session of Parliament, bound up into volumes

Statutes—Acts of Parliament

Sub judice—in course of trial

Sub nom.—sub nominee—under the name

Sub voce.—under the title

Supra—above

T.S.—Treaty series

Table of cases/statutes—a list of cases or statutes in alphabetical order

Treaty—(1) negotiations prior to an agreement (2) an agreement between nations

U.D.C.—Urban District Council

Ultra vires—beyond the powers granted

Union catalogue/union list—a catalogue of the contents of a number of libraries (*e.g.* all the libraries in a university)

v.—versus

V.C.—Vice-Chancellor

Venire de novo—motion for a new trial

Viz.—videlicet—namely: that is to say

White Book—a term sometimes used to refer to the Supreme Court Practice

White Paper—a Parliamentary paper, usually containing a statement of government policy

APPENDIX III

How Do I Find? A Summary of Sources for English Law

ABBREVIATIONS (1–8; 2–12)

D. Raistrick—*Index to legal citations and abbreviations.*
Sweet & Maxwell's Guide to Law Reports and Statutes.
University of London Institute of Advanced Legal Studies—
  Manual of Legal Citations.
The front pages of: *Current Law Case Citator; The Digest,* Vol. 1,
  and the Cumulative Supplement; *Index to Legal Periodicals;*
  Halsbury's Laws of England, Vol. 1; *Legal Journals Index.*
Price and Bitner, *Effective Legal Research* (for American abbre-
  viations).
List in Appendix I.

BOOKS

Tracing Books on a Subject
Consult the Subject Index to the library catalogue, then look in
  the Subject (or Classified) Catalogue under the numbers, or
  letters and numbers, given in the Subject Index. (6–32)
Consult Bibliographies (see below).

Tracing Books by an Author
Consult the library's Author (or Name) Catalogue (1–4)
Consult Bibliographies (see below).

Tracing Books if you know the Title
If your library's catalogue does not contain entries under titles,

consult Bibliographies (see below) to find the author's name, then consult the Author Catalogue.

BIBLIOGRAPHIES

Raistrick, *Lawyers' Law Books* (entries under subjects). (6–34)
Law Books in Print (entries under authors, titles and subjects). (6–37)
Law Books Published (entries under authors, titles, subjects). (6–36)
Current Publications in Legal and Related Fields (authors, titles, subjects). *(6–39)*
Current Law and *Current Law Year Books* (entries under subjects). (6–9, 6–10, 6–38)
Legal Bibliography of the British Commonwealth (useful for older books). (6–42)
Bibliography on Foreign and Comparative Law. (6–42)
British National Bibliography (British books, on all subjects, published since 1950. Entries under authors, titles, subjects). (6–44)
British Books in Print (entries under authors, titles). (6–44)
Books in Print (American books in print—authors, titles, and separate *Subject Guide to Books in Print*). (6–44)
R.G. Logan (ed.)—*Information Sources in Law.* (6–35)
Bibliographical guide to the law (useful for foreign language books). (6–41)
Law Books 1876–1981. (6–40)
Specialist legal bibliographies (6–42)—Ask the library staff for advice.
The Catalogues of large specialist and national libraries, *e.g.* British Library's *General Catalogue of Printed Books; Library of Congress Catalog*, etc. (6–42, 6–44)

CASES

If You Know the Name of the Case (summary: 2–17)
Current Law Case Citators (2–14)
The Digest (for English, Scottish, Irish and Commonwealth cases of any date). Consult the Consolidated Table of Cases and the Cumulative Supplement (for more recent cases) (2–15)
Law Reports: Consolidated Index. (2–16)
English Reports, Vols. 177–178 (for English cases *before* 1865). (2–10)
All England Law Reports Consolidated Tables and Index 1936–, and *All English Law Reports Reprint Index*, 1558–1935. (2–16, 2–11)

For Very Recent Cases
Latest month's issue of *Current Law*—the cumulative Case citator. (2–17, 6–9)
Latest "pink" index to The Law Reports *and* the list of cases *inside* the latest issue of the *Weekly Law Reports*. (2–17)
Current Cumulative Tables and Index to the All England Law Reports. (2–17)
Cases in recent copies of *The Times.*
Summaries of cases in weekly journals, *e.g. Solicitors Journal; New Law Journal.* (2–17)

Scottish Cases
Scots Digest (8–4)
Faculty Digest (8–4)
Scottish Current Law Case Citators. (2–14)
The Digest. (2–15)

Irish Cases
Greer and Childs—*Index to cases decided in the Courts of Northern Ireland* 1921–1970 and supplement. (9–9)
Irish Digests. (10–23)
The Digest. (2–15)
Index to Supreme and High Court written judgments ("pink lists"). (10–24)
Index to Irish Superior Court written judgments 1976–1982. (10–25)

Commonwealth Cases
The Digest. (2–15)

Tracing Cases On A Subject (6–8)
The Digest. (6–12)
Current Law Year Book 1976, latest *Current Law Year Book,* and latest monthly issue of *Current Law.* (use subject indexes). (6–9, 6–10)
Halsbury's Laws of England. (6–3)
Law Reports: Consolidated Indexes. (6–13)

Tracing the Subsequent Judicial History of A Case (6–14)
Current Law Case Citators and latest monthly issue of *Current Law* (for cases judicially considered after 1947). (6–14)
The Digest. (6–13)
Law Reports: Consolidated Indexes (table of cases judicially considered). (6–14)
All England Law Reports: Consolidated Tables and Index (cases reported and considered). (6–14)

Are there any Periodical Articles on this Case? (2–18)
Legal Journals Index. (2–18, 4–3)
Current Law Case Citators (entries enclosed in square brackets
   are periodical articles). (2–14, 2–18)
Latest issue of *Current Law* (entries in lower case in the cumu-
   lative table of cases indicate cases judicially considered where
   the case appears in the title of the article. (2–18)
Index to Legal Periodicals (table of cases commented upon, at the
   back of the volume). (2–18)
Indexes to individual periodicals, *e.g. Modern Law Review; Law
   Quarterly Review.*

DIRECTORIES (1–13)

Solicitors and Barristers' Directory and Diary. (1–13)
Butterworths Law Directory and Diary. (1–13)
Hazell's Guide to the Judiciary and the Courts. (1–13)
Legal Aid Handbook. (1–13)

GENERAL STATEMENTS OF THE LAW

Textbooks. Consult the library catalogues and Bibliographies
   (see entry under Books) to trace relevant publications.
Halsbury's Laws of England. (6–3)
Specialised legal encyclopedias. (6–6)

GOVERNMENT PUBLICATIONS

Tracing Publications on a Subject (5–22)
Consult the subject index to the library's government publi-
   cations collection, if one exists.
Consult HMSO's daily, monthly, annual and five-yearly cata-
   logues of government publications. (5–18)
Sectional Lists of government publications. (5–22)
Subject Catalogue of the House of Commons Papers 1801–1900.
   (5–22)
General Alphabetical Index, 1900–1949, 1950–1959, etc. (5–18)
Catalogue of British Official Publications Not Published by HMSO
   (5–22)
*Keyword Index to British Official Publications Not Published by
   HMSO* (5–22)
Current Law and *Current Law Year Books.* (6–9, 6–10)
Lawyers' Law Books includes the main government reports on
   each subject. (6–34)

Indexes to Government Publications
Daily List of Government Publications. (5–18)
HMSO Monthly and *Annual Catalogues.* (5–18)
General Index . . . 1900–1949. (5–18)
Keyword Index to British Official Publications not Published by HMSO (5–22)
Catalogue of British Official Publications Not Published by HMSO (5–22)
HMSO in print (on microfiche) (5–18)

If you know the Name of the Chairman of a Report
Richard, British Government Publications; an Index to Chairmen and Authors (several volumes, covering 1800 onwards). (5–20)
Committee Reports Published by H.M.S.O. Indexed by Chairman. (5–20)
Monthly, annual and five-yearly Catalogues of Government Publications. (5–18)

Law Commission Reports And Working Papers (5–24)
The Law Commission's annual reports (issued as House of Commons Papers) include a complete list of all the Law Commission reports and working papers, showing whether the recommendations of each report have been implemented. (5–24)
Daily List, and the monthly and annual catalogues of government publications include new Law Commission reports as they are published. (5–18)

PERIODICAL ARTICLES

Articles on a Subject
Legal Journals Index (4–3)
Index to Legal Periodicals. (4–5)
Index to Foreign Legal Periodicals. (4–6)
Current Law (under appropriate subject heading) (6–4) and *Current Law Year Books* (at the back of the volumes). (4–4, 6–10)
Annual Abridgment to Halsbury's Laws of England (under appropriate subject heading) and the *Monthly Reviews* (in the looseleaf Service Volume) (4–7, 6–5)
Index to Periodical Articles Relating to Law. (4–9)
British Humanities Index. (4–10)
Other non-legal periodical indexes. (4–11 *et seq.*)

Articles on a Case
Legal Journals Index (4–3)

Current Law Case Citators (entries enclosed in square brackets are periodical articles). (2–14, 2–18)

Latest monthly issue of *Current Law* (entries in lower case type in the cumulative table of cases). (2–18)

Index to Legal Periodicals (table of cases commented upon). (2–18)

For recent cases, look through the editorial comments in weekly journals, *e.g. Solicitors Journal, New Law Journal, Justice of the Peace*, and specialist periodicals, *e.g. Criminal Law Review*.

Articles on an Act

Legal Journals Index (4–3)

Current Law Statute Citator 1947–1971 and the *Current Law Legislation Citator*

Indexes to periodicals (under the appropriate subject heading).

Tracing Periodicals

Consult the library's Periodicals Catalogue, if there is one. (1–9)

If the periodical is not available in your library, consult the *Union List of Legal Periodicals* (4–19) to find out where a copy is available.

Union lists of the periodicals available in your own area or region may be available—ask the library staff for advice.

STATUTES

Collections of the Statutes

Older Statutes

Statutes of the Realm. (3–21)

Statutes at Large (various editions). (3–22)

Firth and Rait, *Acts and Ordinances of the Interregnum.* (3–23)

Statutes in Force (3–8)

Modern Statutes

Public General Acts and Measures. (3–7)

Law Reports: Statutes. (3–10)

Current Law Statutes Annotated. (3–12)

Statutes in Force. (3–8, 6–16)

Butterworth's Annotated Legislation Service. (3–13)

Halsbury's Statutes. (3–14, 6–19)

Collections of Acts by subject

Statutes in Force. (6–16)

Halsbury's Statutes. (6–19)

Annotated editions of the Statutes
Current Law Statutes. (3–12)
Butterworth's Annotated Legislation Service. (3–13)
Halsbury's Statutes. (3–14, 6–19)

Statutes in Force
Statutes in Force. (3–8, 6–17)
Index to the Statutes. (6–18)
Halsbury's Statutes. (3–14, 6–19)
Chronological Table of the Statutes. (6–24)
Current Law Statute Citator and *Current Law Legislation Citator.* (6–25)
Is it in force? (6–23)

Tracing Statutes on a Subject
Statutes in Force. (6–17)
Halsbury's Statutes. (6–19)
Index to the Statutes. (6–18)
Halsbury's Laws. (6–3)
Current Law and *Current Law Year Books.* (6–9, 6–10)

Indexes to the Statutes
Chronological Table of the Statutes (shows whether Acts of any date are still in force). (6–24)
Is it in force? (6–23)
Index to the Statutes (alphabetically arranged by subject, and lists all the Acts dealing with that subject). (6–18)
Halsbury's Statutes (alphabetically arranged by subject. Consult alphabetical List of Statutes, then look in the Cumulative Supplement, and Noter-up Service to check if an Act is still in force). (6–19)
Public General Acts: Tables and Index (annual—brings the information in the *Chronological Table of Statutes* up to date). (6–24)

Local and Personal Acts—Indexes
Index to Local and Personal Acts 1801–1947. (3–29)
Supplementary Index to the Local and Personal Acts 1948–1966. (3–29)
Local and Personal Acts; Tables and Index (annually). (3–29)

Is this Act Still in Force? Has it been Amended?
Is it in force? (shows whether Acts passed since 1961 are still in force). (6–23)
Chronological Table of the Statutes (indicates if an Act of any date is in force). (6–24)

Current Law legislation citator and *Current Law Statute citator.* (6–25)

Looseleaf *Current Law Statutes,* Service -heading "Legislation not yet in force." (6–25)

Public General Acts: Tables and Index (annually—brings the information in the Chronological Table up to date—see the table "Effects of Legislation"). (6–24)

Halsbury's Statutes (consult the main volumes, the Cumulative Supplement *and* the looseleaf Service. (6–21)

What Cases have there been on the Interpretation of this Act?

Current Law Statute Citator and Current Law Legislation Citator. (6–25)

Halsbury's Statutes. (6–19)

What Statutory Instruments have been made Under this Act?

Current Law Statute Citator and *Current Law Legislation Citator* and *Current Law Statutes* looseleaf volume. (6–25)

Index to Government Orders. (6–28)

Halsbury's Statutes. (6–19)

Have Any Periodical Articles Been Written About This Act?

Current Law Statute Citator and *Current Law Legislation Citator.* (6–25)

Indexes to periodical articles (see PERIODICAL ARTICLES, above) under appropriate subject heading.

Has this Act been Brought into Force by a Statutory Instrument?

Halsbury's Statutes (Current Statutes Service). (6–23)

Current Law Statute Citator, Current Law Legislation Citator and Current Law Statutes (current looseleaf volume—heading "Legislation not yet in force.") (6–25)

STATUTORY INSTRUMENTS

Collections of Statutory Instruments

Statutory Rules and Orders and Statutory Instruments Revised (all statutory instruments in force in 1948). (3–33)

Statutory Instruments (annual volumes—subject index in last volume of each year). (3–27)

Halsbury's Statutory Instruments (selective—arranged by subject). (6–27)

Is this Statutory Instrument in Force? Has it been Amended?
Statutory Rules and Orders and Statutory Instruments Revised (a
collection of statutory instruments in force in 1948, arranged
by subject). 3–33)
Table of Government Orders (indicates for every statutory instru-
ment whether it is still in force). (6–31)
Halsbury's Statutory Instruments (6–27)
List of Statutory Instruments (monthly and annually). (3–33)

What Statutory Instruments Have Been Made Under This Act?
(6–30)
Current Law Statute Citator and *Current Law Legislation Citator.*
(6–25)
Index to Government Orders. (6–28)
Halsbury's Statutes. (6–19)

Is this Statutory Instrument still in Force?
Current Law Legislation Citator. (6–29)
Halsbury's Statutory Instruments. (6–31)
Table of government orders. (6–31)

Has this Act been Brought into Force by a Statutory
Instrument?
Halsbury's Statutes (Current Statutes Service). (6–23)
Current Law Statute Citator, Current Law Legislation Citator and
Current Law Statutes (looseleaf current volume).(6–25)

Indexes to Statutory Instruments
Table of Government Orders (chronological, showing whether
each Instrument is still in force). (6–31)
Index to Government Orders (arranged by subject). (6–28)
Halsbury's Statutory Instruments (by subject). (6–27)
Lists of Statutory Instruments (monthly and annually—entries by
subject, and under the numbers of the Instruments). (6–29)
Daily List of Government Publications (includes all new Instru-
ments as they are published). (6–20)

THESES

University of London Institute of Advanced Legal Studies—
Legal Research in the United Kingdom 1905–1984. (6–45)
University of London Institute of Advanced Legal Studies—*List
of Current Legal Research Topics.* (6–45)
Index to Theses (6–45)
Dissertation Abstracts. (6–45)

WORDS AND PHRASES

For the meaning of words and phrases use legal dictionaries.
  (1–12)
For Latin phrases use legal dictionaries and Broom's *Legal
  Maxims.* (1–12)

Judicial and Statutory Definitions of Words and Phrases
Words and Phrases Legally Defined. (6–15)
Stroud's Judicial Dictionary. (6–15)
The entry "words and phrases" in: *Law Reports: Consolidated
  Indexes; Current Law* and *Current Law Year Books;* and indexes
  to the *All England Law Reports, Halsbury's Laws,* and *The
  Digest.*

INDEX OF AUTHORS, TITLES AND POPULAR NAMES

A selective index to the works mentioned, including some popular names, *e.g.* the White Book. References are to paragraph numbers. Where there are a number of entries for the same work, the main entry appears in bold type.

SUBJECT INDEX

References are to paragraph numbers.